ROMAN BUILDERS
A STUDY IN ARCHITECTURAL PROCESS

How were the architectural ideas behind great Roman building projects carried out in practice? *Roman Builders* is the first general-interest book to address this question. Using the Baths of Caracalla, the Pantheon, the Colosseum, and the great temples at Baalbek as physical documents for their own building histories, this book traces the thought processes and logistical considerations – the risks, reversals, compromises, and refinements – that led to ultimate success. Each major phase of the building process is considered: design, groundwork, support structures, complex armatures (such as the superstructures of amphitheaters), vaults, and decorations. New hypotheses are advanced on the raising of monolithic columns, the construction sequence of the Colosseum, and the vaulting of the Pantheon. The illustrations include archival and original photographs, as well as numerous explanatory drawings.

Rabun Taylor is Assistant Professor of History of Art and Architecture at Harvard University. The author of *Public Needs and Private Pleasures: Water Distribution, the Tiber River, and the Urban Development of Ancient Rome,* he has excavated in Italy and the United States and has contributed articles to many journals, including the *Journal of Roman Archaeology,* the *American Journal of Archaeology,* and the *Journal of the Society of Architectural Historians.*

ROMAN BUILDERS
A STUDY IN ARCHITECTURAL PROCESS

RABUN TAYLOR
Harvard University

PUBLISHED BY THE PRESS SYNDICATE OF THE UNIVERSITY OF CAMBRIDGE
The Pitt Building, Trumpington Street, Cambridge, United Kingdom

CAMBRIDGE UNIVERSITY PRESS
The Edinburgh Building, Cambridge CB2 2RU, UK
40 West 20th Street, New York, NY 10011–4211, USA
477 Williamstown Road, Port Melbourne, VIC 3207, Australia
Ruiz de Alarcón 13, 28014 Madrid, Spain
Dock House, The Waterfront, Cape Town 8001, South Africa

http://www.cambridge.org

© Cambridge University Press 2003

First published 2003

Printed in the United Kingdom at the University Press, Cambridge

Typefaces Sabon 10.5/14 pt. and Trajan   *System* Quark XPress™   [MG]

A catalog record for this book is available from the British Library

Library of Congress Cataloging-in-Publication Data
Taylor, Rabun M.
Roman builders: a study in architectural process / Rabun M. Taylor.
p. cm.
Includes bibliographical references and index.
ISBN 0-521-80334-9 (HB) – ISBN 0-521-00583-3 (pbk.)
1. Building – Rome – History. 2. Architecture, Roman. 3. Rome – Antiquities. I. Title.
TH16.T38 2003
690´.0937 – dc21

2002073306

ISBN 0 521 80334 9 hardback
ISBN 0 521 00583 3 paperback

To my parents

CONTENTS

ILLUSTRATIONS

ACKNOWLEDGMENTS

This book was written initially over the course of the summer of 2000. I am grateful to Harvard University for the opportunity to refine my thoughts and their expression over the first half of a sabbatical in the year 2001. I extend special gratitude to James Ackerman and Bettina Bergmann, each of whom offered encouragement and criticism on various parts of the manuscript; to Kathleen Coleman, for her moral support after reading an early draft; to Natalie Taback, who in addition to undertaking the arduous role of a production assistant, offered invaluable advice on the text; and to my summer assistant, Alison Syme, who pitched flawless relief in the late innings. Numerous friends and colleagues offered encouragement at various phases of this project's development. Of these I feel especially indebted to Lynne Lancaster. She and I maintained a lively and revelatory e-mail dialogue on numerous issues covered in the book, and thanks to her careful attention and genuine engagement this book is a much better effort than it would have been otherwise. Robert Ousterhout's timely sojourn at Harvard's Graduate School of Design in 2000 gave us both an opportunity to become acquainted with the other's work. His course on building methods in antiquity and the Middle Ages sowed the seeds of many thoughts in this book. Thomas Howe of Southwestern University and Donald Hammer of the Minnesota Society of the Archaeological Institute of

America generously offered me the opportunity to try out some of my central ideas on audiences in March of 2001. The alpha and omega of this book is its senior editor, Beatrice Rehl. She initially suggested the topic to me during a fortuitous convergence in Istanbul in June 1999. Our host to the city's architectural wonders was Ahmet Çakmak, a humanist who also happens to be a distinguished man of science. To him I owe the awakenings of my interest in structural design; and while my interest is that of an engaged amateur, he gave me reason to believe, when others would not, that the two cultures of science and humanities can be assimilated in interesting and refreshing ways.

My thanks to a number of scholars and institutions for allowing permission to reproduce photos and illustrations: Kathleen Coleman, Janet DeLaine, Katherine Dunbabin, Federico Guidobaldi, Lothar Haselberger, David Jacobson, Lynne Lancaster, Elaine Lancha, Claudio Mocchegiani Carpano, James Packer, Friedrich Rakob, Jürgen Rasch, Eugenia Salza Prina Ricotti, Frank Sear, Fikret Yegül, Cambridge University Press, Centre Jean Bérard, Chrysalis Books, the Deutsches Archäologisches Institut, the Duke University Museum of Art, the École Française de Rome, Edizioni Quasar, Fototeca Unione, the *Journal of Roman Archaeology,* the Metropolitan Museum of Art, the Musei Capitolini, the National Gallery of Art, the Société Nouvelle Librairie Orientaliste Paul Geuthner, the Soprintendenze Archeologiche of Naples, Ostia, and Rome, the University of Chicago Press, and Yale University Press.

INTRODUCTION

I am the tomb of Harpalos. Which Harpalos? Why, Harpalos most skillful in the Daedalian craft. This I know, o Fates: his all-inventive art has perished with him. What other man alive was his peer? He who laid out beetling temple walls, who raised columns for high-ceiled porticoes – he would often move the very mountaintops, servants to his puny ropes, as easily as boys gather twigs. So Amphion, so Orpheus once charmed the rocks with song and led them effortlessly away.[1]
– Greek inscription from Hermoupolis Magna

Rabirius modell tooke from heav'n to build
Our wondrous pallace sure; hee is so skill'd.
For Phidian Jove a worthy fane to reare,
Pisa must begg him of our Thunderer.[2]
– Anonymous translation of Martial 7.56

In 1586 Domenico Fontana oversaw one of the greatest spectacles in the history of building, the moving of a monolithic Egyptian obelisk from its nearby site in the Vatican, where it had been placed by the Roman emperor Caligula, to its modern position in the Piazza San Pietro. This undertaking involved a towering wooden derrick, miles of rope, hundreds of men and horses, the moral support (or otherwise!) of a huge throng of onlookers, and – most important of all – the oversize personalities of Fontana himself and his patron, Pope Sixtus V. It has thrust itself into the annals of ingenuity, even if the achievement itself pales in comparison to the building for which it serves as a frontispiece. The original transport and erection of the obelisk must have generated excitement on a similar scale. Pliny the Elder remarks on the specially built ship for its transport, complete with its ballast of eight hundred tonnes of lentils![3] Yet the Vatican Obelisk was only one of many extravagant projects punctuating an almost continuous program of urban monumentalization in the late Julio-Claudian period. Many other great building campaigns were to follow. One scholar has recently brought to life a comparably ostentatious project in the early second century, the raising of the Column of Trajan – another monument of calculated difficulty contributing to a stupendous building program. Another has estimated that the largest blocks and column shafts of the Baths of Caracalla would have required carts drawn by three hundred pairs of oxen apiece.[4] The great temple complex at Baalbek in Lebanon included the famous Trilithon blocks in the podium of the Temple of Jupiter, the largest weighing perhaps a thousand tonnes.[5] The fine limestone of the superstructure was cut with laser precision into interlocking shapes of remarkable complexity and worked into a glistening lather of carved decoration (Fig. 1).

Great building projects have always been glamorous. Even today, in an age of high-tolerance materials and low-risk methods, construction sites present an irresistible spectacle. How much greater the interest and excitement in antiquity, among a people notorious for their love of a good show. The stonecutting in the workyards, the thickets of timber scaffolding, the processions of carts and sledges carrying stone quarried a thousand miles away, the creaking capstans and chanting gangs, and (of course) the occasional spectacular, homicidal failure must all have seemed as profoundly Roman as the blood sports to which so much architectural ostentation was devoted. But they also gave material proof of the rigid Roman system of social control. The imperial granite quarries in Egypt were so notorious for their expenditure of labor and lives that they became the setting for a martyrology, the *Passio sanctorum quattuor coronatorum,* in which the four saintly protagonists (still patron saints of stoneworkers today) quarried a single column shaft in twenty-six days while their wretched colleagues labored at the same task for three months.[6] These events putatively happened in the time

1. Baalbek: Temple of Dionysus before excavation. David Roberts, *The Holy Land* (1843). By permission of Duke University Museum of Art.

of the emperor Diocletian: Perhaps the story evolved not only from traditional mythopoeic processes, but from firsthand knowledge of the great persecutor's imperial baths in Rome, their hulking Egyptian granite columns visible to all. And so they remain today, standing intact in the old frigidarium, which serves the new dispensation as the transept of the church of Santa Maria degli Angeli (Fig. 2).[7]

From our clouded vantage point, we have trouble looking beyond the forms that loom in front of us or lie broken on the ground

to inquire into the narrative behind them. Rarely have we attend-
ed to the *facture* of buildings, instead beginning our inquiries with
the *fact* of their existence. This is puzzling. Architectural process is,
after all, supreme theater, captivating onlookers and participants
alike in ways that the completed building does not. Moreover, the
phases of a building's potentiality – the evolution of its design and
construction – can contribute much to our understanding of it.
Scholars have relied too heavily for their understanding of Roman
architectural process on Vitruvius' *Ten Books on Architecture (De
architectura)*, written probably in the 20s B.C.[8] Grateful as we are
for this treatise from a professional Roman practitioner, we must
also recognize its limitations. It was intended not as a manual for
working architects but rather as a "work expounding the virtues of
architecture to patrons and other non-specialists . . . who were yet
concerned with putting buildings up."[9] It is more didactic than practical, as much a product of reading and research as of experience;
indeed the scope of Vitruvius' book exceeded the breadth of his own
experience. And for all their historical value, his descriptions of the
design and building process exclude many essentials. He does not
acknowledge the inevitable compromises when design evolves into
execution.[10] Even as he prescribes numerous size options for buildings of various kinds, he seems indifferent to the structural or logistical problems of scale (a most odd omission for a man with a background in military engineering). He is even silent on his method for
erecting the fifty-foot columns for his basilica at Fano.[11] Apart from
large engines, he says little about tools, and nothing at all of wood-
en scaffolding, of the centering for arches and vaults, of formwork
for concrete. His style is often elliptical, even scattershot. For example, even though he describes the *chorobates*, or leveling instrument, he never even hints at what one does with it after it has been
set up (8.5). Vitruvius shows minimal interest in the sequential logic
of design and construction, such as the allocation of labor or the
overlapping of tasks to ensure timely convergences. Like most modern studies of Roman materials and techniques, his book is a series
of descriptive or prescriptive snapshots organized topically without
much attention to the binding matter of architecture as a process,
the generation of design and the logistics of building.

Vitruvius would probably have agreed that the building process
itself was a principal concern of architectural patronage and a leading component of design. The potency and effect of a building re-

2. Rome: Baths of Diocletian, frigidarium. Now the transept of Church of S. Maria degli Angeli. Photo: R. Taylor.

sided as much in its conception and construction as in its finished state. The Latin word *magnificentia*, a term favored by Vitruvius and tailor-made for such display, evokes not the immanent greatness of a thing but the "making much" of it – the appearance and emergence of greatness. In a similar mold, the companion term *auctoritas* evokes the author of the enterprise (i.e., the patron, not the architect) and his or her investment of intellect, energy, money, and generosity in monumental buildings.[12] The imprint of monumental architecture came as much from its staggering difficulty, great expense, and organizational intricacy as from its finished form. The intended effect, heightened by the theatricality of process, was amazement tempered by unease. These natural reactions are largely processual. They highlight ingenuity and craftsmanship. They invite the questions, How is it done? and Is it being done soundly? Cataclysmic failure would not have been a mere abstraction in the mind of the average Roman. Suetonius writes of a panic attack in the Theater of Marcellus shortly after its completion under

Augustus, brought on by the crowd's fear for the building's structural integrity. And the collapse of an amphitheater at Fidenae, which killed perhaps twenty thousand people (fifty thousand dead and wounded are reported independently), was considered such a grievous calamity that it drew the reclusive emperor Tiberius off his island retreat of Capri.[13] A frisson of fear no doubt informed the awe and pride that many Romans felt in the event of a great building project.

This is a study of the realization of architecture. I wish to evoke, if only hypothetically, the cultural and cognitive processes involved in the act of creating buildings. My method exploits the case study, progressing in a roughly logical sequence from the planning stage to final decoration. No effort is made to follow a single narrative; rather, I try to find the essence of each distinct procedure wherever it presents itself. I will bypass the "typical" Roman project in favor of the especially creative, the remarkable, the monumental. Somewhat unfairly, I adduce only a handful of famous buildings, each chosen not because it is a paradigm of architectural process but because it is sufficiently complex, well preserved, and well published to merit extensive treatment. While I cannot hope to restore any such project in its vast but now obscure complexity, or resurrect the pragmatic wizardry of the master builders, I do hope that this study of architectural process will animate those old stone and concrete bodies afresh, projecting a kind of mind into the matter.

This book deals mostly with Roman architecture in its maturity, between the first and fourth centuries. It therefore encompasses the famous central-Italian vaulted concrete style, associated with an economy of means and speed of execution. But even the purest concrete forms of this so-called Architectural Revolution were married to the more traditional and measured style of columnar orders, sometimes on a colossal scale, rendered in solid stone. In conjunction, these styles generated dialectical tensions that have drawn commentary ever since the Renaissance. Quite apart from their aesthetic astringencies, they also unsettle presumptions about the Romans as quintessential pragmatists. Dressed stone, the preferred monumental building material in most pre-Roman Mediterranean societies and in many building traditions within the Roman Empire as well, embodies prolonged effort, diligence, high craftsmanship, and expense. Concrete is a vehicle of speed, efficiency, and expressiveness mediated only by its modes of containment during construction. Roman patronage never settled on one style or the other, choosing instead to mix them; I will say more about their two economies below. Munificence required a level of ostentation and *auctoritas* – old-fashioned monumental grandeur – that could not be achieved in haste or indifference. At the same time, however, the sheer volume of building from Augustus onward, the demand for skilled artisans, and the nearly miraculous properties of pozzolanic concrete driving these changes must have shaken up the old ways of building on a scale that Vitruvius, writing at the beginning of the boom, could barely imagine.

ROMAN ARCHITECTURE IN TIME

The architecture that accompanied Roman conquest emerged from a repertory of symbols, forms, and types mostly emanating from Italy. Whether or not they had originated there (and many had not), their Romanness stems from the fact that they flowed into the provinces through the city of Rome and its environs, a region extending from the Bay of Naples to Tuscany. Central Italy was a laboratory where architectural ideas, mostly native or Greek, were tested and tempered before being distributed abroad. A visual and spatial language emerged around the empire. The arch, the vault, the Greek or Tuscan columnar order, the pediment, the bathing suite, the garden courtyard, the ornamental fountain, the aqueduct, and many other architectural features all became part of the pan-Mediterranean koine.

During the mid-Republic, Roman architecture began to reveal qualities that distinguished it from earlier traditions. Alongside the usual criteria driving architectural decisions, such as patronage, form, and function, two other considerations gained predominance in a building's creation: speed and accountability. The ancient Greek practice of engaging an architect for most of his career in a single grand building project without comprehensive budget projections[14] became virtually unthinkable in the context of the Roman imperial bureaucracy. Roman building contracts were not normally open-ended. Vitruvius deems allocation of time and resources one of the basic components of the architect's profession, and he particularly notes how the Romans' "passion for quick results" influenced their technical approaches to building.[15] The habit of speed emerged directly from the political system. During the Republic, magistrates

were expected to produce physical results within the short span of
their offices – in the case of the censors, a year and a half. And it
was the censors who drove many advances in Roman architecture,
including the widespread use of concrete in vaulted structures.[16] At
least some Roman building contracts included a promise to complete the project within a given span of time; a sample *stipulatio*
contract specifies two years for the completion of an apartment
building.[17] Under Augustus building activity reached a furious pace,
and for the next two centuries it continued at a volume that would
have been unimaginable in earlier societies. By the second century
of our era, a vast and reasonably efficient bureaucracy controlled
the movement of fine building stones all around the Mediterranean
basin.[18]

The result was not what we might expect: simplification, pattern-
book building strategies, a degradation of the process and the product. Instead, architects and builders made practical innovations.
Among these were the widespread use of working drawings and the
development of concrete. Made with volcanic sand first quarried
near Pozzuoli (hence, pozzolana), Italian concrete proved so strong
and durable that it revolutionized building design. Structurally comparable to stone while enjoying the advantages of malleability,
cheapness, and speedy application, it is an artistic medium for expression in large forms of an architecture "more modeled than assembled," in William L. MacDonald's phrase.[19] Fueled in part by
concrete, the ferment of architectural styles, types, and forms was
so intensive, the permutations so numerous, that the idea of pure
and "classical" architectural paradigms, even if Vitruvius promoted
them at the very beginning of the imperial period, seems misplaced
at the height of Roman power and productivity.

Roman buildings always carried meaning; indeed they could not
be called Roman without it. In one way or another, they expressed
the unifying principles of dominion lying at the heart of the empire's
diversity. They spoke of strength, control, and stability. The intent
was to induce participatory pride and willing submission and alle-
giance to the emperor. Sometimes meaning was straightforward:
Public imagery exhibited a taste for triumphalism heavy with war
narratives and sculptural allegories of pacified nations. At other
times the message came by a subtler, more sensory way: by a mythological vignette on a wall, the chatter of a fountain, the lure of a
verdant courtyard through darkened bowers of imported columns.

Roman buildings always had an imagined center: the idea of Rome, the source of power and prosperity. Architecture was rarely, if ever, revolutionary in a political sense. Innovation, far from signaling a rude reversal of tradition, always seems to have been turned to the advantage of continuity and familiar Roman values such as religion, militarism, and patronage.

ARCHITECT AND PATRON

In English the word "architecture" can mean either a process – the thoughts and acts of designing and erecting a large artifact – or its product – a building, a bridge, a defensive wall, a ship. Viewing buildings from a distance over time, we tend naturally to focus our attention on the finished product. We try to "read" it much as we do works of art, music, and literature. We ask what a building has to say, or how it resonated among its contemporaries and later generations. We trace the influence of styles and ideas. While this approach yields rewards, we must not presume that architectural achievement in Roman society (or any other, for that matter) was regarded in the same light as other intellectual or artistic achievements. In some respects the differences are obvious. Buildings have a functional importance in life quite apart from aesthetics. They do not carry a "subject matter," such as a mythological narrative or a moral message, in the same straightforward way as other artistic genres. Yet it was understood that architecture was full of meaning, and every effort was made to exploit its expressive and communicative potential, often through ornamentation. Almost uniquely among the creative arts, credit for architectural achievement redounded to the patron; the architect or builder was reduced to a facilitator.[20]

Like other artists, architects strove to be recognized for their accomplishments. The finest gained widespread respect among their fellow practitioners and the educated patron class. The extent to which they achieved recognition in society at large, however, has never been fully appreciated. A recent compilation of architects' inscriptions in the Roman period suggests that as artists they were held in high esteem indeed.[21] Nevertheless, an architect's social stature could never be allowed to match that of his patron. A few prominent architects are associated in Roman literature with individual building programs but never with personal styles that transcended their sponsors' wishes. It was the lot of every architect, from the humblest jobber to a great imperial architect such as Rabirius or Apollodorus of Damascus, to subordinate himself to his patrons. Roman architects might commemorate themselves in inscriptions on or near their buildings, but characteristically their names ceded the marquee position to the patrons, dedicatees, or presiding officials.[22] In the rare event when an architect made an independent claim to fame, he did so indirectly, as by inscribing his name and deeds on a secondary monument appended to the principal building or becoming a sponsor of the enterprise.[23] The celebrated Trajanic bridge of Alcántara in Spain listed the sponsors, a group of Lusitanian towns, on the central commemorative arch spanning its deck (Fig. 3).[24] But on an arch at one bridgehead was the following grandiose proclamation:

A consecration to Imperator Nerva Trajan Caesar Augustus Germanicus Dacicus: a temple on the rocky shore of Tagus, filled with images of the gods above and of Caesar, where art succumbs to its own building material. Who gave it, and with what vow, might the curious traveler ask, and whom does its newfound glory delight? The one who completed this mighty bridge in all its bulk – Lacer – made that sacred place with well-omened sacrifices – noble Lacer, who with divine skill made a bridge that will endure for all earthly eternity. Lacer, who made this bridge, dedicated the new temple as well; of course even a single benefaction pleases the gods. He founded the temple for the gods and Caesar: Happy are both objects of the consecration. Gaius Iulius Lacer with his own money made and dedicated it with his friend Curius Laco of the Igaeditani.[25]

Lacer, evidently the architect but not a sponsor of this magnificent bridge, was almost as skillful at self-promotion as at his craft. Through his cosponsorhip of an unrelated project, a riverside temple to the gods and the imperial cult, he found a way (perhaps after the fact) to attach his name to the bridge. But not too directly: The patrons of the bridge held the privileged position at its center.

At most Roman sites there are no artists' signatures on the buildings at all – though they do sporadically appear on their discrete parts, an extension of independent artistic traditions.[26] The foremost claimants to the act of making are the patrons, those with the initial generative urge and the resources to realize the project. The patron's privilege of attribution in architecture is so obvious, and so universal across many societies, that we rarely pause to reflect on

it. A fairly recent historical study of public construction in Roman Italy and Africa, for example, barely acknowledges the existence of the mostly anonymous architects and builders, instead crowding its five hundred pages with data and analysis on those it calls the *constructeurs* – the private sponsors and public magistrates so commonly encountered in inscriptions.[27] And yet nobody would have claimed that Augustus wrote the *Aeneid*, even though he was Virgil's patron. Why, then, do we allow that he was the *constructeur* of the Forum of Augustus in Rome when we know that it was the creation of anonymous professional artisans?

Buildings were the most expensive and laborious of commissions, and depended most heavily on patronage and thus the will of the patron.[28] Sculptures, paintings, poems might be created purely for art's sake; but buildings, almost never. Because of their incomparable usefulness in ideology as in daily life, buildings were seen as entities embedded in real time and space. Their formal integrity was violable, and subject to personal manipulation, in a way that timeless artistic masterpieces were not. Whereas a single building could host a long and ever-evolving sequence of styles and rearrangements

3. Alcántara: Roman bridge of the Trajanic period. Fototeca Unione c/o American Academy in Rome, neg. 15184L.

of space, most other arts were realized as autonomous typological or stylistic units. Other arts were reducible to forms and ideas, and could be propagated mechanically in any medium that would reify them. Canonized literary texts demanded exact scribal replication. Sculptors and painters, though free to transgress the stark mandate of iteration, nevertheless had their own canon of masterworks. Wealthy Romans commissioned copies or adaptations of famous sculptures by the thousand. Their marble furniture and many household accent pieces were often mass-produced from a repertory of types. Roman fresco and stucco artists used pattern books or their own memories to reproduce well-known images, many of them doubtless adapted from venerable prototypes.[29] With these acts of replication the original generative process of an artwork lost much of its signification. The sculpted, recited, or painted artifact was distanced from the paradigm(s) from which it was copied or adapted, and the means by which it was reproduced receded in importance as the viewer shifted attention from the thing in itself to the idea informing it. But with architecture too much of the text, or idea, resided in the fabric of the building.

In a way, then, Lacer's inept conceit "art succumbs to its own building material" should be granted a certain force. Architecture is the only one of the major arts that necessarily mediates in its own creation. Buildings cannot be built from the top down but must emerge from and upon themselves. Perhaps because of this powerful sense of bound-in contingency, the built environment was never commodified in Roman society to the same extent as art and literature. Within the Roman sphere we rarely find buildings perfectly replicated. Almost never, as far as I know, does wholesale architectural copying extend outside a single, unified project of buildings constructed in serial.[30] A large part of a Roman building's importance and signification resided in the process of its creation or reinvention, and this was always a unique act.

ROMAN ARCHITECTS AND BUILDERS

Almost without exception, Roman architectural achievements are poorly documented in literary sources. And while we may learn something from inscriptions commemorating a given building, these too tend to discount the generative process. Even when we consider the Roman building profession as a whole, we know too little about the human dynamics of design and construction. Apart from Vitruvius, who downplays this aspect of the building profession, we have occasional references in literature to the interactions of patrons and architects; hints at building procedures in the texts of surviving laws and edicts; a substantial body of information on contract law; and about 180 inscriptions memorializing architects and hundreds more for various members of the building trade. What we lack are the kinds of detailed records that turn up in Greek public inscriptions in the classical period, or Troyes in the Gothic age, or Rome and Florence in the Renaissance.[31] The Roman sources have no real equivalent of the famous Greek contract describing in detail the procurement of materials for and construction of the arsenal of Piraeus, or the inscriptions of Athens, Epidauros, and other cities providing accounts or inventories for work on local temples.[32] However, two surviving general contracts are partly preserved in Italian inscriptions. The most complete is the *lex Puteolana* of 105 B.C., a meticulous document outlining the city's expectations of contract labor and material for a tiny construction project at Pozzuoli.[33]

One certainty is that the organization of Roman building projects varied considerably over time and distance. As the emperor gained more control over public building in large urban centers, the historical documentation of construction and organization dwindled. It is therefore unprofitable to try to delineate the roles of the architect, master builder, and contractor in any single building project; the scattered evidence is variable enough to suggest that no single pattern existed anyhow. Sometimes the same man assumed all of these roles, as Vitruvius did, sometimes not. Vitruvius himself recognized more than one arrangement, for he insists that good architects "should exercise a legislator's care in their dealings both with contractor and with client."[34] The general contractor is a particularly elusive character in the high imperial age. Although he remained a central figure in Roman private law, it is not clear whether general, all-inclusive building contracts were let for public or imperial projects in Rome itself after the rise of the emperor's department of public works in the first century. Instead contracting, along with the building trades in general, seems to have become more specialized.[35] The same may be said of other cities around the empire, which seem to have acquired their own bureaus of public works.[36]

Certainly the principal job of an *architectus* was always to design buildings. But even in Vitruvius' time the architect's precise function during construction varied widely according to his own training, the wishes of the patron, and the nature of the project.[37] Vitruvius includes allocation among his basic components of architecture, which first and foremost is the architect's responsibility for managing costs.[38] Large public or imperial projects must have involved several tiers of authority. At or near the top would have been the chief architect; below him, builders of various attainments (*fabri, structores*), some of them perhaps accomplished designers or master builders in their own right.[39] If they did not have extensive engineering experience, then they would have employed engineers, most likely drawn from the army. In Rome the ranking professionals would have had regular dealings with officials of the department of public works or other imperial bureaus, which probably held the purse strings for the project and oversaw the drafting of contracts and requisitioning of materials.[40] In an increasingly centralized bureaucracy that controlled the production and procurement of building materials drawn from around the empire, as well as the engagement of hundreds or even thousands of workers at one time, it would have been almost impossible for a single man to control the entire project. With Janet DeLaine's monograph on the Baths of Caracalla, and now Elizabeth Shirley's detailed study of the construction of a legionary fortress, we are able for the first time to comprehend the impressive scope and complexity of such enterprises.[41] But we remain ignorant of the organizational structure that made them possible. A few inscriptions, especially from the Greek East, offer the merest hint of the complexity of large projects.[42] Since there is no way to recover the precise division of labor in any Roman project, I will use the term *architect* when treating issues of design and *builder* when discussing construction, contractual matters, and logistics, without meaning to imply that two and only two individuals or groups were necessarily at work. In truth, there were probably many people in constant communication.

PLANNING

The word "plan" is an ambiguous term in architecture. It can mean specifically a diagrammatic map of a building floor by floor, or in the plural, diagrams in general. Or it can designate the overall strategy of the project. We Anglophones further complicate the matter by our tendency to use its gerund, "planning," to mean something distinct from design in the architectural process. If design encompasses everything from vaporous creative impulses to the unforgiving science of infrastructure, it remains a creative process throughout. Planning is concerned less with creation than with production; it is the engine by which ideas become realities. It encompasses everything from the procurement of money, labor, and materials to emergency management, feeding the labor force, guarding the site, and stroking the patron's ego. If the designer is the project's director, the planner is its producer.

Planning of buildings is intimately related to design, and for one reason more than any other: site logistics. Buildings intervene in their own manufacture, as I have said already: If materials, men, and machines cannot be gotten to where they are needed in the right sequence, or if the wrong technique of construction is chosen, the whole process will founder. There are only so many ways to design a form that can be built in reality, and some are better than others. Good designs tend to take full account of planning and technique.[43] Robert Mark narrates the nearly disastrous decision taken by the architects of the Sydney Opera House in the late 1950s to realize their daring new design with questionable principles of structural "honesty" rather than the most stable techniques available to them.

And so tens of millions of dollars were spent for years of engineering and computing time to produce a design for a vastly intricate, self-supporting, prestressed-concrete roof system.

Still more money went into reconstructing the terraced platform on which the [roofing] shells were to rest after the designers found that the one originally constructed, in an attempt to make up for lost time and to schedule an even flow of work, would not hold up the roof.[44]

It is a cautionary tale for every architect with a glamorous commission. Here planning and design ran afoul of each other. Designs were produced without a full appreciation of the planning problems they would produce, while the planning strategy demanded the optimal exploitation of the labor force without adequate consideration of a compatible structural design. Logistics are a delicate balancing act between potential and fulfillment. Too much attention to one or the other tends to lead to costly error. In antiquity too it benefited the architect, planner, and builder to be intimately aware of one another's responsibilities and thought processes.

The simplest building contract type in Roman law, *stipulatio*, was inadequate to address the complex issues of accountability surrounding most large public projects. The elder Cato, when outlining the contents of a generic contract for a villa, indicates that the project's price is calculated not by labor, or even by materials, but simply by counting the number of roof tiles used on the building at one *sestertius* per tile.[45] This contract appears to be open-ended. There is no deadline; a season of work presumably sufficed.[46] No price is fixed, only the formula for calculating it. The tile count and calculation were undertaken after completion by disinterested assessors (*mensores*), described by the agricultural writer Columella as "those who measure structures after they have been built and reckon up the cost of the finished work by applying a method of calculation."[47] The *stipulatio* remained a popular form of private contract, but its weaknesses – especially with regard to timely completion – are well documented in the legal sources.[48]

At the other extreme, a contract could specify almost everything. The *lex Puteolana* of the late second century B.C. is so exacting that it hardly leaves any discretion to the contractor at all. A characteristic passage reads as follows:

In the building across the road, let the contractor open a gap in the middle of the wall which is near the street; let him make it 6 feet wide and 7 feet high. From that wall he shall project towards the sea two antae that are 2 feet long and 1 foot and 0.25 thick. Above the gap let him place a lintel of hard oak, 8 feet long, 1 foot and 0.25 wide, 0.75 foot high. Above that and the antae let him project out from the wall on either side for 4 feet, hard oak topping-beams, 2.67 feet thick and 1 foot high.[49]

We cannot expect such specificity in the individual contracts of large projects; the sheer complexity of the building process would not have allowed it. However, in many respects the Puteoli contract reflects general Roman practice of the standard type of public-building contract, the *locatio conductio*.[50] It gives a deadline for the conclusion of work.[51] It calls for surety from the contractor against failure to complete the project properly, and it specifies terms of payment – in this case, half the total sum when the estates of the sureties were registered, the other half upon completion. The sum itself is also specified in this document.

Many public contracts were established by a bidding process. Plutarch notes that cities, "when they give public notice of intent to let contracts for the building of temples or colossal statues, listen to the proposals of artists competing for the commission and bringing in their estimates and models, and then choose the man who will do the same work with the least expense and better than the others and more quickly."[52] Evidently both a time and a cost estimate were included in bids along with detailed visual aids. If overall time was to be calculated, then it is likely that an overall price, rather than just a rate, was established as well, especially if the bidders went to the trouble of making models.[53] In some form these obligations would have made their way into the contract.

Reasonably accurate estimates of labor and material, then, were desirable if not always forthcoming. Imperial projects often required the importation of expensive materials and craftsmen from considerable distances, and they had a contractual deadline. Principles of geometry were applied to materials estimates in the Byzantine period,[54] and there can be little doubt that they were used in Roman times as well. While mathematicians such as Pythagoras and Hero of Alexandria developed rigorous formulas for determining the surface area of polygons, it is likely that most architects and builders resorted to more approximate formulas. The need to measure irregular or geometrically complex land allotments led to the development of various provisional methods of calculating area, such as those offered up by Columella.[55] For example, he calculated the area of a circle by multiplying the diameter by itself, multiplying the total by 11, and dividing that total by 14. The resulting approximation of the actual area would have sufficed for material estimates, say, of the amount of lime needed for the floor of a circular sweat bath. Three-dimensional forms, especially vaults with varying thicknesses, presented a greater challenge. Vaults, often made of inexpensive concrete, could have been estimated by rough formulas or tables with the help of simple variables such as area covered and vault type. Labor costs were much less predictable, especially in projects of great complexity. In some cases, they may have been figured in direct proportion to materials. But in highly specialized and exacting genres such as stone carving, mosaic, painting, and stuccowork, cost estimates most likely were established only after discussions among the architect, patron, and master craftsmen.

A time estimate was hardest of all. Materials and labor, presuming they are in adequate supply, are relatively inelastic resources. With a few variables, one can estimate output by units and satisfy the patron. But as far as time management is concerned, there is always room for doubt and for improvement. Even so complicated a project as the Colosseum could be completed in the miraculous interval of five years if the labor and materials were exploited efficiently. But efficiency is a relative term. Ideally every worker available should be at his task continuously until the end of the project, which will thereby be completed in the shortest possible time span. In reality most tasks were contingent upon other tasks. Thus the real-world efficiency model tested a building planner's ability to mesh the parallel with the sequential.

Not surprisingly, cost overruns were common. A group of inscriptions from Africa studied by Richard Duncan-Jones records the initial sums promised for statues or buildings. In many cases the inscriptions record that additional expenses were incurred, presumably by inclusion of riders (*leges locationis*) in the contract.[56] The initial sums are almost always round numbers – for instance, 400,000 *sestertii* for the theater at Calama. We should conjecture not a low level of precision in the contracts, or a tendency to pledge a round sum to a public project, but rather an epigraphic convention of rounding off large numbers. Duncan-Jones's attempt to match the size of known theaters to their recorded cost is futile, for it ignores the potentially vast and variable expense of decorating a building. His own evidence of the high cost of individual statues cautions against this modular approach to estimation. Most statues are in the range of 3,000–8,000 *sestertii* apiece, but some are several times higher. At Benevento in Italy a silvered statue of Hadrian with his triumphal quadriga cost a million *sestertii,* a sum that alone exceeds any of the recorded building outlays in Africa, and all but three in Italy![57] It is misleading, then, to follow the prescriptions of Cato and Columella in calculating the price of a building by a unit of horizontal surface area. Their formulas are strictly for construction and do not consider the amenities that characterized so many buildings sponsored by the Roman elite.[58]

THE TWO ECONOMIES OF CONCRETE AND STONE

Although Rome seems to have developed an unparalleled model of efficiency in building projects, we should not exaggerate its extent or pretend that it superseded traditional materials and methods. Most Roman buildings of substance paid homage to Greek architecture with the inclusion of columnar orders. Columns and entablatures, usually of the Corinthian, composite, or Tuscan orders, were applied to all manner of public and private structures – often, admittedly, in a most un-Greek fashion. These were traditionally made of stone, although modeled brickwork was a common alternative in central Italy. As colored marble, porphyry, and granite became available from quarries around the empire, Roman builders suppressed the Greek tradition of creating columns from stacked cylindrical drums of white marble and adopted new column styles with solid monolithic shafts in exotic imported stone. (Capitals and bases, for the most part, continued to be made of light-colored imported marbles.)

Core building materials – local stone, brick and mortar, concrete – had no symbolic significance, and were hidden behind surface decoration. But columnar orders were inherently ideological, and demanded to be seen. The incorporation of these styles and materials had absolutely nothing to do with efficiency: Whatever labor was saved by the elimination of column drums was expended with interest in the tasks of producing, transporting, and installing monolithic shafts. The sheer investment, both in cost and in labor, of working these stones contributed directly to their evocative power. Intentionally ponderous and labor-intensive, they ensured that different, and hardly compatible, construction models would often be operating concurrently within a single building project.

The supply of marble and granite "appears to have been governed by a . . . rationale . . . which has nothing to do with economics but was designed as a display of imperial power."[59] In the strict sense of finance, DeLaine's observation is absolutely right. Stonework required a larger pool of skilled labor and costlier materials than faced concrete. But in the broader economy of patronage and public obligation, the most powerful Romans considered the dichotomy justifiable and, indeed, economical. Elite Roman architects thus operated in two parallel and conflicting economies. One was localized and market-driven, the engine of Vitruvius' "allocation"; the other was artificially sustained for ideological purposes. One model saw unnecessary expenditure of resources as an economic evil; the other embraced it as a political virtue.

The clash of these two economies doubtless took its toll both on architectural vision and on efficiency. Hadrian's Pantheon stands today as a product of this uneasy partnership and as a metaphor of its limitations. The incompatibility of the columnar facade to the brick-and-concrete rotunda nearly wrecked the whole project, and left the building permanently compromised.[60] The intended fifty-foot column shafts proved a logistical impossibility. Their failure to materialize forced a change of plan in midcourse to accommodate a lesser colonnade. By then the great brick-and-concrete drum was too far advanced to be adapted to the new scheme, and the intermediate block, though modified, preserves the scar of the original pediment like a thunderbolt across its brow (see Fig. 67).

Compromise is a natural, even desirable component of architectural design and planning, for no great project is accomplished exactly as conceived. Let us then turn to the process itself and try to envision some of its difficulties and triumphs. First we examine the act of designing, then we characterize the practical realization of Roman design, progressing in a loosely chronological and logistical sequence from foundations to vaults, and finally to decoration.

1

PLANNING AND DESIGN

Let no one suppose that I selected an insignificant accomplishment, proposing to adorn it with my rhetoric. For I think it is a sign of no small intelligence to conceive of new patterns of beauty for common things; such is the accomplishment the marvellous Hippias provided for us. It has all the virtues of a bath: utility, convenience, good illumination, proportion, harmony with the site, provision for safe enjoyment; and furthermore, it is adorned with the other marks of careful planning: two lavatories, numerous exits, and two devices for telling time, one a water clock with a chime like a bellowing bull, the other a sundial.[1]

– Lucian, *Hippias* or *The Bath*

All these works should be executed so that they exhibit the principles of soundness, utility, and attractiveness. The principle of soundness will be observed if the foundations have been laid firmly, and if, whatever the building materials may be, they have been chosen with care but not with excessive frugality. The principle of utility will be observed if the design allows faultless, unimpeded use through the disposition of the spaces and the allocation of each type of space is properly oriented, appropriate, and comfortable. That of attractiveness will be upheld when the appearance of the work is pleasing and elegant, and the proportions of its elements have properly developed principles of symmetry.

– Vitruvius 1.3.2

Vitruvius' principles of good design continue to resonate. Even today his triad *firmitas, utilitas, venustas* adorns the emblem of the Society of Architectural Historians. In themselves they are strong and enduring principles (despite attempted repudiations of the third); but they are not immune to the vicissitudes of taste and cultural change. To varying degrees, all three are subject to semantic drift. Suitably, soundness is the least culturally encoded of the principles. We all obey the law of gravity and design our buildings accordingly. But although every building benefits from a good foundation and high-quality materials well applied, these alone do not complete the idea of soundness. As I suggest below, structure has a psychological as well as a physical dimension. It must withstand the test not only of time and travail but of human reception. Attractiveness is of course the criterion most likely to change its rules over time and distance. Little has been written on aesthetics of the Roman period, perhaps because our own culture tends to view Roman architecture (and to a lesser extent Roman art) with an approving and sympathetic eye. The reaction of a Roman like Lucian to a kind of architecture that we like rather well – even if it is sadly fragmentary today – would seem to approximate our own. Roman architecture, which for all its bursts of genius and ferment was never a vessel of social revolt, was firmly embedded in mainstream culture. Moralists like Cicero and Seneca might rail at the built *luxuria* of the idle rich, but when it comes right down to it, an archaeologist would be hard pressed to distinguish the villas of one breed from those of the other.

UTILITY AND SOCIAL FUNCTION

Let us briefly discuss Vitruvius' second criterion of successful architecture, utility. For the architect this was the primary concern in the early phases of design. What use would a projected building have, and how would the building maximize its usefulness? Buildings of importance were never useful in just one way. Beauty was itself utility; an ugly building was likely to be avoided, especially if it was eclipsed by competing structures. Martial's epigrams are full of plaudits and indictments of one bath or another according to appearance, clientele, or water quality. As I have already suggested, signification was another form of utility. Whether or not an architect was aware of the fact, every building's form, function, and decorative scheme were steeped in cultural meaning. Some structures, such as honorary arches and triumphal monuments, functioned *principally* as signifiers; their function was to engage one's attention and convey an ideological message. Another way in which architecture made itself useful in Roman cities was to articulate a larger urbanistic scheme. Thus the built environment could serve as a catalyst of movement through the fabric of the city.[2]

Vitruvius is concerned primarily with utility as it is commonly understood, the ability of a building to meet its preassigned role as a place for enabling, sheltering, and organizing human or divine activity. Certainly function is one of the most important determinants of form. A structure must be envisioned in terms of the ways people will use it. Will it be a multifunction facility, like a basilica? Or will it serve a narrow range of functions, like a theater or odeum, or a single function, like a latrine? What special uses has the building's sponsor stipulated? The architect, then, will start with a known plot of land, a designated building type (temple, amphitheater, villa, bath, etc.), the patron's stated wishes, and probably a variety of other factors that will condition his design (building codes, geological and hydrological conditions, availability of labor and materials, etc.).

In his studies of the divisions of private architectural space in Pompeii and Herculaneum, Andrew Wallace-Hadrill has developed a simple but practical matrix for evaluating the social uses of the Roman house.[3] His two scales of social functionality – public–private and grand–humble – operate independently to form the axes of a sort of Cartesian plane. This model can be adapted to Roman architecture outside the private sphere, but with different axes of differentiation. The grand–humble scale is still applicable, especially in contrasting discrete parts of a building; however, depending on the circumstances, one might choose instead a scale of social integration (segregated–integrated). Roman class-consciousness, which was extreme, was not always manifested by absolute physical separation. Seating at spectacles was rigidly segregated according to class or sex, but people of all classes (and occasionally both sexes) bathed together, and the systems of slavery and patronage ensured regular interaction between the grand and the humble in the same space. The public–private scale is less useful outside of houses and villas, and could profitably be replaced by a scale of specificity of purpose (dedicated–multipurpose). Roman building types generate a scatter in at least three quadrants of the new Cartesian plane: dedicated + segregated (amphitheaters, theaters, etc.); dedicated + integrated (baths, markets, etc.); and multipurpose + integrated (basilicas). The social reasons for this variability are too complex to pursue here, but it is obvious that the architect had to be aware of them and of the special wishes of his patron. In segregated buildings he would be responsible for establishing not only physical barriers but also psychological ones, such as a change in decoration, ceiling height, or corridor width to suit the social status of those in spaces of especial privilege or ignominy.[4] And he must account for the positioning and distribution of human beings within his building, both visitors and those who controlled them. In the Colosseum, one of the most segregated of all buildings, one can see the diminution of grandeur in decoration as one passes from the grand stuccoed senatorial entrance at ground level to the upper corridors, though the architectural armature remains impressive throughout. A network of gates, grilles, and guards would have helped to reduce ambiguity for the spectator entering at a numbered gate and climbing to his seating section. In equal measure a skilled Roman architect would have been expected to create *integrated* spaces that were psychologically inclusive by emphasizing their public nature. Roman baths are famously "democratic" in this respect; even emperors were known to share an occasional bath with their subjects in the great thermae of Rome. We must not forget, however, that these establishments were operated by a huge service staff, which remained largely unseen by the bathers.

VITRUVIUS AND DESIGN

Vitruvius identifies six components of architecture: ordering (*ordinatio*), design (*dispositio*), shapeliness (*eurythmia*), symmetry (*symmetria*), correctness (*decor*), and allocation (*distributio*).[5] These terms have been the subject of endless debate.[6] Whether they merit such scrutiny is itself a point of contention. One thing is relatively certain: Vitruvius is not interested in characterizing Roman architecture as we have defined it. Except in domestic architecture, his most important models were Greek; on the most "Roman" of all building types, such as amphitheaters and triumphal arches, he is silent, while he expounds at length about some of the great temples of the Greek world. His adherence to Greek traditions carries over to his intellectual system as well, which borrows terms and ideas from Greek rhetorical and aesthetic theory.

Not that his six "components" are systematic. Shapeliness, symmetry, and correctness seem to be *properties* of structures; design and allocation are *processes* involved in building them. Ordering (*ordinatio*), depending on how it is interpreted, could fall into either category. It pertains to the common use of a *module*, usually a unit of measurement used for some iterative purpose such as the spacing of columns. In the Vitruvian scheme this became the standard unit by which many other features were determined: width and height of columns, height of capitals, and so on.[7] As a principle by which to design a whole building it was rarely used outside of temples. Whatever the precise meaning of *ordinatio*, one must remain skeptical of attempts to marshal Vitruvius' ragged sextet into two symmetrical triads in which each property is the imagined result of a congruent process in the other.[8]

Vitruvian *symmetria* is not symmetry in the modern sense but a carefully proportioned relationship among elements. Since each element has its own inherent proportions (e.g., a column's height-to-width ratio), symmetry can be understood, at least in some passages, as the proportioning of proportions.[9] A pediment must not be too large, too small, nor too steeply or shallowly pitched for the columns on which it stands; thus the correct symmetry of a temple facade is a function of both variables (columns and pediment), among others. Shapeliness (*eurythmia*), probably a notion borrowed from Plato,[10] seems to refer to the simple, inherent proportions of each element, such as the aforementioned height-to-width ratio of a column. It has recently been argued that these Vitruvian qualities do not inhere in buildings but are rather processes involved in their creation. They are physically evident in a number of Roman buildings as refinements made upon established plans or rules.[11]

It is unclear how symmetry and shapeliness should be distinguished from ordering, or sometimes even from each other. Vitruvius himself, who often seems to be talking over his head, may have been unequipped to explain himself.[12] But plainly all three terms presuppose an unmediated aesthetic process governed by psychological principles. Correctness (*decor*) is something again, having more to do with cultural convention or received common sense than to first principles of cognition. It is the component of reception drawn from outside the object itself. In Vitruvius' opinion, a correct design must not mix Doric elements with Ionic, or match masculine gods like Mars or Hercules to a "feminine" order like the Corinthian: Such mismatches would offend the sensibilities of a culturally conditioned Roman.[13] And common sense or functionalism would dictate "natural" correctness: The orientations of various rooms should suit their functions. Winter quarters should face west to gain the benefits of the afternoon sun in the winter, bedrooms should face east to make full use of the morning sun, and so on.

There is nothing mysterious about allocation (*distributio*). It is, in Vitruvius' words, "the efficient management of resources and site and the frugal, principled supervision of working expenses." Like Plato's *architektôn*,[14] Vitruvius' architect oversees all aspects of the job from start to finish. Such was common practice in the Roman world, but not necessarily the norm.[15] While keeping within a budget may seem an obvious necessity today, it was not always obvious in antiquity. Large building projects of earlier and later times were often open-ended, either enjoying unlimited royal sponsorship or occupying generations of master builders and patrons who could each vouch for only a fraction of the overall budget. Many of the grandest Greek temples were never completed at all.[16] In the Roman period it became possible as never before (and rarely thereafter until the Renaissance) to complete a large project on time and on budget. And for this, one needed a fairly comprehensive plan.

For our purposes, the most important of Vitruvius' six elements is design (*dispositio*). In a sense, it encompasses most of the others, for one cannot envision the act of laying out a building without constant attention to aesthetic principles. And it is only through design that one can make meaningful projections of time, labor, and materials. Vitruvius tells us that design is manifested in three ways: *ichnographia* (floor plan), *orthographia* (elevation), and *scaenographia* (perspective drawing). These are still essential tools of the architect today. A *plan* shows the disposition of walls and floors as seen from directly above. It is the natural first step for an architect who is dealing, after all, with a relatively horizontal plot of land enclosed within definite boundaries. An *elevation* is a drawing of the upright structure without perspectival distortion. It may take a frontal view, as Vitruvius says, or in more complex projects, a view of another exterior surface or of a section cutting through the proposed building on a flat plane. An elevation usually is derived from the plan;

yet its proportions may cause one to rethink the plan, for a building's vertical substance is as fundamental to good design as the treatment of the horizontal plane. *Perspective* drawings have a more analytical purpose; they strive to give the viewer a "feel" for a building in space. They are uniquely valuable for the representation of interiors, which are so important in Roman architecture.

I am not suggesting that Vitruvian drawings were the lingua franca of all Roman architects. Romans probably designed a wider repertory of buildings than any society before the nineteenth century.[17] Quotidian structures could have been planned on site from experience and rules of thumb with the help of simple surveying and leveling tools and perhaps a scale drawing of the ground plan. Even some large-scale imperial structures show evidence of on-site planning in the form of optical or structural corrections.[18] A certain amount of improvisation was to be expected in every project; but occasionally a builder's failure to use drawings effectively got him into serious trouble. The Sanctuary of the Deified Trajan at Pergamon, it would seem, was surrounded on three sides by colonnades, the two lateral examples of which were adjusted in height after construction had begun in order to harmonize them with the back colonnade.[19] Lapses of this kind, while not exactly rare at the sites of imperially sponsored building projects, are not common either. Most changes that leave traces in the remains – and there are many – have other causes, such as shifts in resources or ideology.

DRAWINGS AND MODELS IN ROMAN DESIGN

According to a well-known story, the famous imperial architect Apollodorus of Damascus, annoyed at the architectural pretensions of the future emperor Hadrian, told him, "Be off, and draw your pumpkins."[20] The reference is to the pumpkin-shaped domes of the sort that Hadrian later employed in his villa at Tivoli. Whether or not the story is true, its implications are clear: Hadrian and the architects in his circle saw the value of thorough designs, not just of floor plans but of elevations and vaulting structures too.

In recent years much attention has been given to the mechanics of ancient architectural design in general, and specifically to the techniques applied to architectural drawings and models. We now have a much better understanding of the ways in which ancient architects and builders communicated spatial ideas nonlinguistically.

Drawings, used at least as early as the Egyptian and Mesopotamian periods, appear also in the Roman era. They survive in various scales and with varying degrees of care, etched in stone or drawn on papyrus, even in one instance appearing on a mosaic.[21] Relatively crude area maps, showing buildings without wall thicknesses, are known from Rome and other sites. A much finer effort appears on a funerary plaque from Rome, now in Perugia (Fig. 4). Plans had varying purposes and functions. Some were used in building contracts.[22] Some were maps; that is, they represented an actual, not a planned, state. The Perugia inscription, however, may be a direct transcription of architectural plans, for the three buildings represented on it are all on different scales and show many of the wall measurements. There seems to be no good explanation for this unless the inscriber was copying three separate plans directly. This plaque and the fragment from Rome, showing the floor plan of the Temple of Castor and Pollux near the Tiber River, reveal that even in the cumbersome medium of stone plans could be rendered with apparent accuracy.[23]

It has been suggested that Roman elevations were drawn on a larger scale and in greater numbers than plans, just as they are today, to account for the many more details of vertical surfaces – column capitals, moldings, friezes, and so on.[24] Certainly elevation drawings with some degree of detail were used in ancient Egypt; a beautiful, and rather meticulous, elevation of two faces of a shrine has come down to us on carefully gridded papyrus from the eighteenth dynasty.[25] On the other hand, matters of detail in stonework may have been left to the master craftsmen, just like the later phases of decoration such as mosaics and plasterwork. Greek craftsmen seem to have relied on templates (*anagraphês*) or full-scale models (*paradeigmata*) for detailed stone carving, not on drawings.[26] At both Greek and Roman sites full-scale drawings of architectural features in elevation have been found etched onto stone or plaster surfaces, where they served as templates for preassembly of building features.[27] It is much more likely that elevations, rather than plans, were resolved in medias res by means of such templates or drawings. But in certain situations, such as the hillside construction of the Esquiline Wing of the Golden House (Domus Aurea) of Nero, which was built on the ruins left by the great fire of 64 A.D., even some of the plan may have been improvised on site.[28] We have no evidence that drawings in antiquity were ever granted the kind of

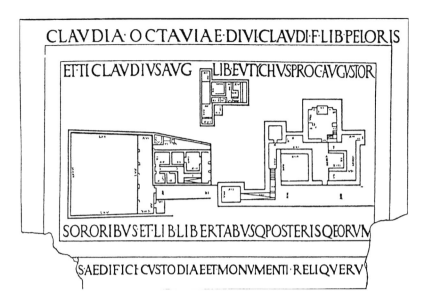

CLAVDIA·OCTAVIAE·DIVI·CLAVDI·F·LIB·PELORIS

ET·TI·CLAVDIVS·AVG LIB·EVTYCHVS·PRO·CAVGVSTOR

SORORIBVS·ET·LIBL·IB·ERTABVSQ·POSTERIS·QEORVM

S·AEDIFICI·CVSTODIA·EET·MONVMENTI·RELIQVERV

4. Perugia: funerary plaque found near Rome. *Corpus Inscriptionum Latinarum.*

autonomy they acquired in the Italian and Spanish Renaissance and still hold today.[29] The tyranny of design at Sydney would have held feeble court in Sardis or Syracuse. The Roman way was not to generate a design of perfect refinement and supreme authority but to establish a finite set of objectives pictorially. The means to accomplish the ends, sometimes utterly unpredictable, were a matter of daily dialogue and improvisation on the site; it is these means that occupy most of this study. Drawings alone can never plot a path to completion; they can only set the destination.

It is possible to envision how great stone temples, stoas, arsenals, and other rectilinear structures were built in antiquity without plans. One may even conceive of a Gothic cathedral or a middle-Byzantine church being raised without them, bay by bay, overseen by a master builder of great skill and experience.[30] But grand bath buildings, theaters, and amphitheaters of the Roman period exceed these in volumetric complexity, and the sheer speed of their realization would not have allowed the careful cross-checking or methodical pace of some Greek or Western medieval construction. It is inconceivable that such complex buildings as freestanding theaters or amphitheaters – veritable warrens of tubular voids wending through the building's swooping fabric, wrapped about one another, carefully penetrating or bypassing their neighbors – were given form without detailed plans and elevations (Fig. 5). While published handbooks may have existed to aid in design and planning, ulti-

mately every project was unique. Any structure with so many rising diagonals or conic surfaces – seating banks, ramps, stairways –
presents a supreme challenge to the draftsman. A few sections in
elevation may suffice, but planimetric (horizontal) sections must be
made in quantity, for none resembles the next. Each drawing must
to some extent have generated a logistical plan for construction;
many issues of building material, method, and sequence would only
have occurred to the architect during this expository phase of the
creative process.

   Exposition – the elaboration and communication of ideas – comes
only after those ideas are in place. Plans, elevations, and sections

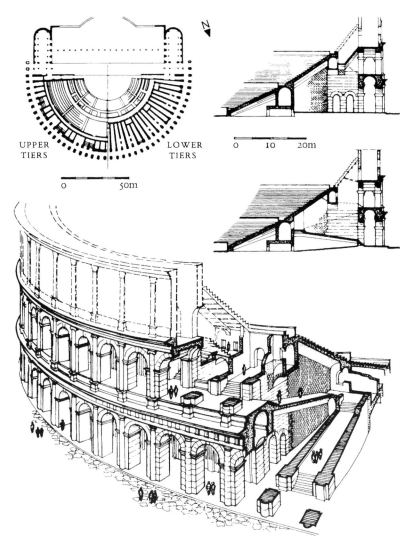

UPPER
TIERS

LOWER
TIERS

0   50m

0   10   20m

5. Rome: plan,
elevations, and recon-
structed cutaway
view of Theater of
Marcellus. Ward-
Perkins 1981. By
permission of Yale
University Press.

6. Oplontis: megalographic fresco. Deutsches Archäologisches Institut, neg. 74.2689. Photo: Sichtermann.

carrying the authority of blueprints tend to be generated toward the end of the design phase, when a fairly complete general concept is well in hand, even if logistical and constructional details are still uncertain. For the *development* of ideas and envisioning the whole one needs a more dynamic medium in which the creator can experience the emerging building as a living environment. Vitruvius' term *scaenographia*, often translated as perspective drawing, is generally thought to designate a technique that renders buildings as they would appear optically, replicating the entire cone of vision. Approximations of the latter technique appear in many Pompeian wall paintings (Fig. 6).[31] *Scaenographia* probably had two functions, as an aid in the design process and as a means of presenting a concept to the client. Drawings for clients are mentioned several times in the literary sources,[32] and Pierre Gros has made a good case for the use of *scaenographia* as a perceptual aid in the design process.[33] Roman architects were fond of establishing horizontal corridors of vision ("enfilades") through multiple spaces by the artful alignment of doorways, intercolumniations, and windows. Such effects, along with sensations of verticality, could have been tested and "experienced" with perspective drawings, even if the principles of perspective were not fully realized.

Scale models are the most direct, paradigmatic means of developing and conveying architectural ideas. Plutarch's bidders for public works may have used presentation models, though his term *paradeigmata* could simply refer to drawings.[34] It is only natural that the semieducated artisans who spent their lives working in three dimensions would have been able to read and comprehend models far more directly and completely than the comparatively schematic shorthand of drawings or diagrams. Michelangelo evidently built elaborate limewood (i.e., linden) and poplar models for the Medici Chapel for similar reasons.[35] Indeed Plato seems to suggest that a builder (*oikodomounta*) of his own time should be trained by playing with "toy houses" (*paideia oikodomêmata*).[36]

The preferred material for working architectural models has always been wood,[37] which rarely survives from antiquity. Fortunately we possess a number of partial scale models in stone which, even if simple in conception, probably served as design tools and perhaps as blueprints for the craftsmen as well.[38] The finest example, found adjacent to the building it represents, is a carefully carved 1:24 stone replica of the podium and stairs of a temple at Niha, Lebanon (Fig. 7). The superstructure, now lost, was probably made of wood. It would appear at first sight to be a presentation piece, but a closer look reveals otherwise. Several steps on the model are inscribed with dimensions in feet. These refer not to the model itself but to the actual building. Evidently the model was a conceptual aid onto which the builder inscribed his modifications for the final design. A polygonal design is inscribed on the model's cella floor, and this too was realized in the temple itself (after yet another phase of modification) as a sort of columned baldachin to shelter the cult statue. Another marble model, in the museum at Ostia, also represents a temple podium and stairs. It too was a working model: Two variant positions of the column bases are represented. Dowel holes in the preserved bases indicate that the superstructure was separate. Again, the latter was probably of wood, and most likely was detachable from the podium so that the builder or client could examine its ground plan and interior.

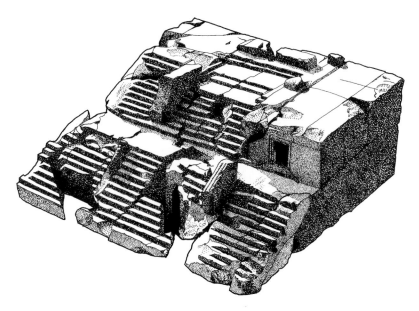

7. Niha: marble model of temple. Illustration: R. Taylor after Will 1985.

Perhaps the most precious and least remarked of all known Roman models is the 1:30 fragment of the elaborate Great Altar of Baalbek. It appears to be one of several stacked sections that could be dismantled to reveal the staircases inside (Fig. 8).[39] Its form is schematic but unmistakable. The two tower-altars opposite the Temple of Jupiter at Baalbek are themselves tours de force of stereotomy, each among the most complex organizations of space ever realized in solid stone (Fig. 9, 10).[40] Their components are not, like most building materials, small modular units assembled around a void. Within the structure solid and void compete as volumetric

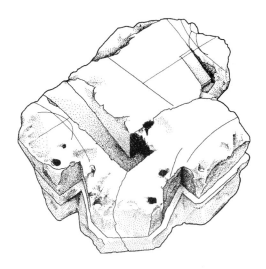

8. Baalbek: fragmentary stone model of Great Altar. Illustration: R. Taylor after Kalayan 1971.

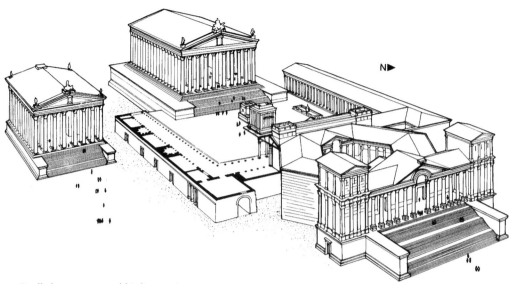

9. Baalbek: reconstructed bird's-eye view
of Sanctuary of Jupiter Heliopolitanus.
Great Altar shown in center of courtyard.
Ward-Perkins 1981. By permission of
Yale University Press.

10. Baalbek: cutaway
perspective recon-
struction of Great
Altar. Collart and
Coupel 1951. By
permission of Société
Nouvelle Librairie
Orientaliste Paul
Geuthner.

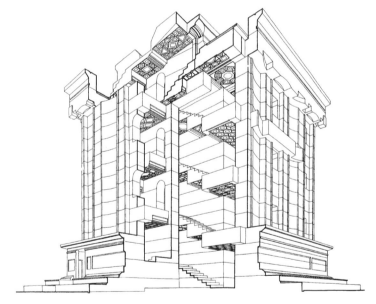

equals, each interlocking with the other. Joints and seams cease to
correspond consistently to edges; angles are incorporated into the
solids themselves. A component block of the altars might comprise
dozens of curved and planar surfaces defining both figures and voids
and cut to a perfectly conceived analytical plan, their multiplanar

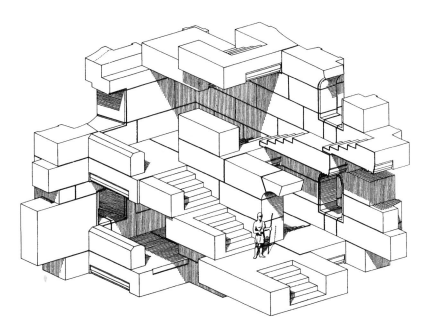

11. Baalbek: analytical view of interior components of Great Altar. Collart and Coupel 1951. By permission of Société Nouvelle Librairie Orientaliste Paul Geuthner.

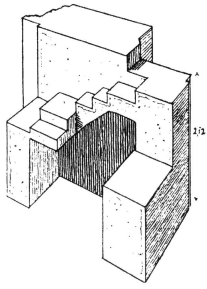

12. Baalbek: a single block from Great Altar. Wiegand 1921–5.

faces commingling as snugly as organs in an anatomical model (Figs. 11, 12). Taken separately, each part conveys a distinctive, identifiable fragment of the larger idea. Without models, indeed several generations of models, the Great Altar was unbuildable. The surviving model fragment reflects the principal formal ideas of the final product, but considerably simplified. It is a prototype, the first or second in a series that evolved from a medium of exploration into a tool of communication.

The obvious benefit of models should not obscure the likelihood that for Roman architects themselves, as opposed to the stonemasons and bricklayers, perspective drawings were the most important creative aids. Models are invaluable tools but they are expressively opaque, even misleading in the oblique bird's-eye perspective they force upon the beholder. Especially in such an interior-dominated architecture as the Roman, human perspective and scale, the interaction of body and building (even if both must be virtual) are paramount. You cannot get inside a model to experience it, to intervene in its volumes, to probe its voids. But you can read the script of a picture and imagine yourself in the action. No doubt this is why, in a well-known passage from Aulus Gellius, Fronto's builders presented rival plans and "specimens" for a proposed bath building in the form of paintings on parchment (*depictas in membranulis varias species balnearum*).[41]

GENERATING DESIGNS

A new building design emerges from such disparate concerns as site specifications, the patron's needs, traditional form, innovation, and available methods for building the mental construct. This final variable comprises a sort of visual phonetics of architectural language deeply embedded in Greco-Roman intellectual culture and tradition. The basic linear elements of planar design were the straight line, the simple curve, and the complex curve (such as a three-point oval or an ellipse), each with the capacity to project any of the others into the third dimension. The principles binding these elements together into coherent forms were the module (i.e., a relative measurement specific to a building), absolute measurements in standard units, and pure proportions derived from geometric and mathematical theory. All were used in Roman design, sometimes in combination.[42] Classic modules based on the distance of an intercolumniation, so essential to the Greeks and to Vitruvius, continued to govern many building designs, as did a host of other units and relationships in a process Mark Wilson-Jones calls aggregative composition.[43] Modules emerged in guises entirely apart from colonnades or arcades, such as a simple square or circle from which all other geometric designs of the ground plan emerged. Standard units of length based on the Roman foot (the *pes*, 0.296 m) were instrumental in beginning any design and were commonly used to

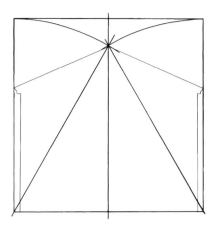

13. A common method of establishing an equilateral triangle in Greco-Roman architectural design. Illustration: R. Taylor.

round off lengths and distances that may have been established by proportional means.[44]

Let us then briefly examine proportions themselves, understood as the relative lengths of two separate elements or the relation of two dimensions of a single element. *Arithmetic* proportions, among which modules are counted, come in simple numeric relationships: 1 : 2, 2 : 3, 5 : 4, 9 : 1, and so on. Vitruvius works with arithmetic proportions, as when he prescribes the inner proportions of domestic atria or the sizes of subsidiary rooms in relation to them.[45] These continued to be important in columnar orders and in overall design; for example, the height of the colossal columnar order of the frigidarium at the Baths of Caracalla was equal to a third of its overall width.[46] *Geometric* proportions, usually manifested in the ratio of width and length of a room or building, or either of these measures in proportion to its height, were often based on popular irrational relationships in pure geometry – for example, the ratio of the side of a square to its diagonal, $1 : \sqrt{2}$. Many proportions were facilitated by the use of the compass, which could quickly transfer lengths of diagonals to the sides of rectangles, or turn side lengths inward to intersect with each other. A common proportion in Greek architecture is the length of a base of an equilateral triangle to its height ($1 : \sqrt{3}$).[47] The proportion could be easily drawn by turning the compass inward from one side of a square to the midline of the square (Fig. 13).

The extent to which such methods actually were used by the Greeks, especially in the design of the elevations of buildings, is still hotly debated.[48] There is no such disagreement about Roman architecture, even if there will always be uncertainty about the exact pro-

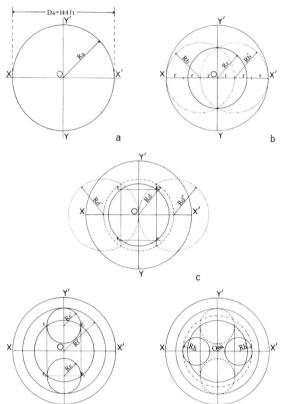

14. Tivoli: Hadrian's villa, hypothetical design sequence for Island Enclosure. Jacobson 1986. By permission of D. Jacobson.

cedures used in specific circumstances.[49] New architectural forms were devised on the basis of elaborate and even abstruse inner relationships comprising tangents and intersections of lines, circles, and polygons, as surely was the case with the fanciful buildings at Hadrian's villa (Fig. 14). Plans were drawn exclusively with a compass and a ruler[50] and were later transferred onto the ground, floor, or slope with larger versions of the same tools. Protractors seem to have been avoided; instead, angles were established by geometric tricks of the trade. Simple right angles could be produced with set squares forming a 3–4–5 triangle, a method that Vitruvius inverted for establishing the profiles of stairways.[51] A more precise method is to draw two intersecting circles centered on a baseline and then to connect their two points of intersection (Fig. 15, *a*).[52] If those two circles are made to share a radius along the baseline, then sixty-degree angles (and equilateral triangles) can be formed by running lines from the centers to the intersections (Fig. 15, *b*). Any angle can be bisected by swinging a cord of a uniform length from equal dis-

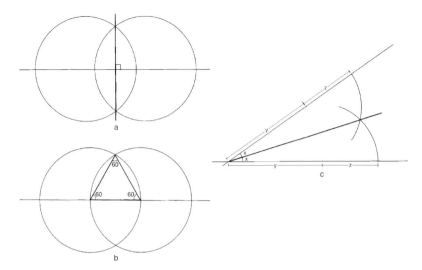

15. Simple geometric methods to establish angles in ancient planimetric design. Illustration: R. Taylor.

tances along its sides from the vertex and running a line from the vertex to the point where the two arcs intersect (Fig. 15, c). Many other similar procedures allowed architects to lay out buildings with very few actual measurements, either of angle or of distance. It has been proposed, for example, that the great bath block of the Baths of Caracalla was designed geometrically around a few initial linear measurements of a hundred-foot module.[53]

Although proportions are widely observed in Greek architecture, many temples of the Ionic order and some of the Doric seem to have been laid out in a sequential fashion, allowing them (at least in part) to be designed and modified as they went up.[54] Such may have also been the case for some conventional Roman stone temples. But concrete, and the operational problems and opportunities it created, fundamentally changed the old ways. First, its malleable nature and stonelike integrity enabled buildings to be increased in complexity. Second, the speed with which it was laid demanded efficiency. Concrete and worked stone, both of which continued to be used together in buildings of many types, took shape at different speeds in a nonlinear process. Stone entablature A had to be fully envisioned and its surfaces of contact dressed before its place in concrete wall B was realized. Otherwise it would not be ready to be positioned at the critical moment, in turn delaying concrete vault C, which would rest upon the entablature, and so on. Concrete demanded speed, and it inspired complexity. The corollary of speed and complexity is high design.

By high design I mean a reasonably comprehensive process in which numerous visual approaches to the building are played out at the drawing board, and by which multiple drawings are produced to be used as blueprints on site. The procedure is far from spontaneous: "designing is a process that proceeds from the simple to the more complex, in which an initial scheme may inevitably become compromised."[55] To the extent that complexity could be minimized up front, it was. Roman architects were fond of simple internal proportions and round numbers. But Vitruvius allows that a judicious designer will know how to compromise on principles of proportion for visual effect. The use of principles other than pure geometry was widespread. As buildings grew more complicated, merging straight lines and flat planes with curved surfaces, perfect inner logic retreated out of reach. A classic example of this is the mensural tension of circular and oval buildings such as rotundas, theaters, and amphitheaters. It is impossible to design a circular building with both diameter and circumference in round numbers of feet, for example. Usually one of the two core generative processes – geometry and arithmetic – will yield to the other.[56] As a general rule Roman plans seem to use a minimum of calculation, perhaps because a profusion of numbers invites error. If a circular colonnade has an irrational circumference, the intercolumniations can be determined either by division or simply by bisecting angles from the circle's center. The second method requires no units of measurement at all, and is far less prone to error.

Recent studies on amphitheaters have investigated how Roman designers tried to reconcile regularity of measurement and practicality with the elegance of pure geometry.[57] As so often happened, the very first design decision was a geometric one. How to generate the shape? Though amphitheaters look like ellipses in plan, very few of them – and none of importance – are true ellipses, because of the difficulty of producing a continuous grandstand with a perfectly uniform width around an elliptical arena. Almost all amphitheater plans comprise segments of circles with different radii, joined at carefully predetermined points where they share tangents. Typically there are four segments, two with longer radii forming the long sides and two with shorter radii forming the "ends." One of the most straightforward schemes is used for the amphitheater at Verona (Fig. 16). The basic units are two equilateral triangles sharing a side on the main axis. The four corners of these joined triangles are the centers of the four circles whose segments merge to form the oval. All

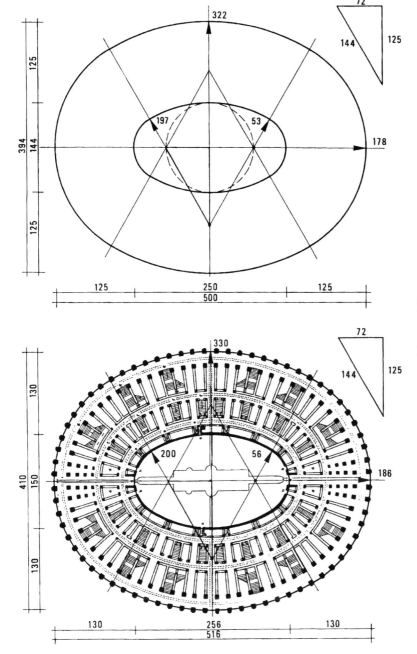

16. Verona: design
scheme of amphi-
theater. Wilson-Jones
2000. By permission
of Yale University
Press.

the rings, whatever the size, are formed by the compass from these
four points.

Wilson-Jones proposes the following sequence of design.[58] Once
the geometry has been decided, then a scale is determined. It so hap-

pens that the amphitheater of Verona is 512 Roman feet long, twice the length of its inner arena. This suggests that its original, unrefined form had called for an outer length of 500 feet around a 250-foot arena. But it was realized that the circumference of a 500-foot oval of this shape, at 1,405 feet, was not divisible into round, even numbers. A modest expansion of the structure's actual dimensions creates a circumference of 1,454 feet, which allows seventy-two arched bays around the periphery, each twenty Roman feet wide, with a few additional feet for the two broader bays at each end of the long axis. The twenty-foot unit around the exterior, a common one in amphitheater exteriors, achieved primacy over linear dimensions. It is suggested that the new dimensions were derived by means of a simple formula, but actually no mathematical calculation was necessary. Reasonably quick experiments could be made at the drawing board simply by "walking" a small compass, set precisely to scale for an interval of twenty feet, around the circumferences of ovals of slightly different size until a satisfactory size was achieved by trial and error.

STRUCTURAL AESTHETICS

Structure has two important applications to design, physical and psychological.[59] The architect-builder must determine how each will play out in his or her building, and how each will relate to the other. A building must be strong and stable, and to achieve this one must apply whatever physical knowledge suits the situation. While mathematics was a tool of formal design in Roman antiquity, it was not used to calculate structural action. The best that could be done in the pre-Galilean scientific environment was to establish rules of thumb founded on observations in proportion and scale. At the Baths of Caracalla, for example, wall thicknesses were typically calculated at one-tenth the span of the vault they carried.[60] But if a single wall supported vaults of roughly equal span and height on both sides, it was allowed to be thinner, since the two vaults would counteract each other's outward thrusts.

Proportion – the favored relationships in size, number, and position among architectural elements – is a psychology of structure. As such it is immensely important to Vitruvius, whose celebrated optical corrections are all based on perceptions of structure such as the strength of supports and the verticality of standing elements.

The larger the space between the columns, the greater the diameters of the shafts must be. For if an araeostyle temple had columns whose diameters were equal to one-ninth or one-tenth the height of the column, the building would seem flimsy and inconsequential, because all along the intercolumnal spaces the air itself seems to diminish the apparent thickness of the shafts. . . . Thus the proportional system for each type of work should be fully observed. The corner columns, moreover, must be made thicker than the others by one-fiftieth of their diameter, because they are cut into by air on all sides and therefore seem more slender to the viewer.[61]

All the elements to be placed above the capitals of the columns . . . should have a front surface that inclines outward to one twelfth its own height. This is why: When we stand opposite any facade, and two lines might be extended from our eye so that one would touch the lower margin of any part of the building, and the other touch the very top, that line which reaches the upper margin will be the longer of the two. Inasmuch as a longer line of sight extends to the upper part of the building, it will make it seem to tilt backward. But if, as we have stated earlier, the elements of the facade are made to incline, they will seem perfectly vertical to the viewer.[62]

The mind welcomes certain proportions more than others, Vitruvius suggests, because they satisfy one's innate sense of stability. Actually the phenomenon is much more widespread than even he acknowledges. Columns, cornices, and entablatures may have no structural function at all, but they often create the illusion of support and stability. Ground-level colonnades never support colonnades of larger size or wider spacing because such a thing would be an affront to perceived stability. The upward taper of columns, exaggerated by entasis, follows the natural logic of the firmly rooted tree. Distinguishing the support from the supported is another Roman trick of structural aesthetics. An unmediated wall or pier rising up to an arch or vault shades imperceptibly from one to the other. Such smooth transitions were thought to be disorienting.[63] Many (but not all) Roman designs emphasize the transition from support to ceiling by horizontal dividers such as cornices or by abrupt shifts in decoration (Fig. 17). The intuited demarcation drawn by this horizon is perfectly correct, for a vault and a wall, even if they are all part of a solid mass of concrete, function in different ways structurally. A vault always wants to flatten and expand horizontally, that is, become more like a straight line. This in turn causes the upper parts of the walls or piers to bow outward, bending what by all rights

17. Rome: main vault and decoration of Arch of Septimius Severus. Photo: R. Taylor.

should be straight. The process of distinguishing one from the other has a certain logic, for the formal continuity of the two elements by no means implies that they are structurally homogeneous.

STRUCTURAL INNOVATION IN DESIGN

To say that Roman architects and builders had a scientific method is an unsupportable indulgence. There is no evidence that they, or the engineers responsible for many architectural innovations, ever resorted to repeated experiments under controlled circumstances in order to advance their profession. Yet imperial projects often involved some kind of innovation, and innovation is not mere guesswork. Many ad hoc experiments could have been performed on the ground before a new vaulting method was applied to a building, for example. It has been argued that buildings in antiquity, because their structural behavior was not an observable or measurable continuum, could not be subjected to the kind of objec-

18. Istanbul: interior
of Hagia Sophia.
G. Fossati, *Aya Sofia,
Constantinople*
(1852).

tive testing and calibration that was applied to machines. "Structures either stand or fall, and if they stand then by how much is neither obvious nor measurable."[64] Such statements are too extreme;
in fact, gradations of stress can be observed in the form of cracks
and deformations in standing buildings. Careful observation of existing structures did allow architects to gain some understanding of
structural nuances and to apply a heuristic method to design.

Let us consider the central dome of Justinian's Hagia Sophia (Fig.
18), built in a later period but nonetheless steeped in Greco-Roman

traditions and methods. The initial experiment toppled in an earth-quake twenty years after completion of the building, but the more conservative replacement, still essentially in place today, shares many of its properties.[65] Why would the architect of the second dome have retained the forty windows from the previous structure? Here the actions of other large domes in the city would have been instructive. By observing that meridional cracks form toward the bottom, but not the top, of hemispherical domes, he seems to have understood – as had his Roman predecessors – that ordinary domes are compressive in their upper parts and tensile near the base. In almost all unreinforced masonry domes with a deep profile, hoop stresses around the base pull the dome apart in segments, causing vertical cracks.[66] The structural action is easy enough to deduce from the evidence, and one can envision various ways to counteract the forces. But, far more important, he recognized that such cracks *were not usually symptoms of a fatal weakness*. Once the cracks formed through the entire thickness of a dome, there was nothing binding the two sides of each crack together – yet the dome survived anyway, unless it fell in an earthquake. This observation seems to have led to the brilliant epiphany that a dome could retain most of its fundamental strength without carrying a solid, continuous band of masonry in its lower zone. One could eliminate unsightly cracks simply by introducing window voids where the cracks would have formed anyway![67] The remaining ribs, if properly buttressed, could absorb some deformation without fracturing the dome's fabric.

The sheer pride of innovation in structural design may not find a voice in the conservative Vitruvius, but it does appear in another Roman text, Caesar's *Gallic Wars*. Challenged to build a timber bridge across the Rhine, Caesar's military engineers devised a design whose originality and elegance must have impressed their general enough to prompt him (characteristically) to take full credit for it himself. The description of its construction is probably the longest and most informative exposition of a single architectural process in all of Roman literature outside Vitruvius (Fig. 19).

Even though he was confronted by the greatest difficulty for making a bridge because of the river's width, swiftness, and depth, nevertheless he decided that he had to make the effort or else not lead his army across. He used the following method for the bridge. At intervals of 2 feet, he joined pairs of timbers that were 1.5 feet thick, sharpened a bit at their bases, and measured for the depth of the river. Having low-

ered these into the river with machines, he fixed and rammed them down using pile drivers, not quite perpendicular in the manner of piles, but leaning forward and sloping so that they inclined with the natural flow of the river. In addition, he planted two piles opposite these at an interval of 40 feet downstream, fastened together in the same manner but turned into the force and flow of the river. These two rows were kept firmly apart by inserting into their tops beams 2 feet thick, which were the same length as the distance between the piles, and that were supported with pairs of braces at the outer side of each pile. As a result of this combination of holding apart and clamping together, so great was the stability of the work and its character that the greater the force of the water rushing against it, the more tightly its parts held fastened together. These beams were interconnected by timbers laid at right angles, and then these were floored over with long poles and wickerwork. In addition, piles were driven at an angle into the water on the downstream side, which were thrust out underneath like a buttress and joined with the entire structure to take the force of the river. Similarly others were emplaced a little bit above the bridge so that if tree trunks or vessels were sent by the barbarians to knock down the structure, the force of those objects might be diminished by these defenses and prevent the bridge from suffering harm.

Ten days after the timber began to be collected the bridge was completed and the army was led across.[68]

Rarely does this famous episode appear in architectural histories, for it is absurdly presumed to represent something "less" than architecture. (Even historians of technology, it seems, have never taken such

19. Hypothetical reconstruction of Caesar's wooden bridge over the Rhine. O'Connor 1993. By permission of Cambridge University Press.

an interest as to envision the whole procedure.) In fact, it carries the essence of architectural method, including the characteristic Roman chutzpah of emphasizing the process in equal measure with the product. Caesar (i.e., his engineers) built the bridge not because it was militarily necessary but because he thought it would overawe the enemy with Roman might and ingenuity. This was more than engineering, which has purely pragmatic ends; it was an act of signification. As if to emphasize the fact, he burned his work of art eighteen days later after an aimless foray into Germany.[69] Apart from ideology, the bridge was a product of almost pure structural design in which formidable natural forces were used to the structure's advantage. There can be little doubt that its realization followed upon a period of deliberation, even experimentation; the use of heavy pile drivers angled off vertical must have been particularly difficult from floating rafts fighting a current.[70]

While Roman architects and builders had no sophisticated mathematical method to determine the physical laws of structure, they were capable of very intelligent extrapolation. Simple solid geometry, together with an intuitive recognition of weight, ensured that they understood one of the most fundamental rules of structural design: that gravitational loadings increase with the cube, and cross sections with the square, of a structure's linear scale. For example, a pillar consisting of ten perfectly uniform stacked one-meter cubes (1 m^3), weighing one tonne per cubic meter, weighs a total of ten tonnes. It is understood that the cross section of that pillar at its base (the one square meter of bearing surface between the bottom cube and its foundation) must bear the entire load. If we double the *linear* dimensions of each cube to 2 m^3, we now have ten cubes each weighing eight tonnes, or eighty tonnes overall. The cross section of the base, however, has only been squared to 4 m^2. Each square meter of that area is now carrying twenty tonnes, twice as much weight as the same area carried before. In simplest terms, the new pillar is twice the height, four times the cross section, and eight times the weight as before. Builders easily understood such economies of scale, since the amount of building material (presuming it is uniform) is directly proportional to the weight. Eight times as much material would be quarried for the second pillar as for the first, and four times as much area had to be prepared in order to bear its weight. The corollary to this rule was that the gravitationally induced stresses inherent in a given form and material (we call

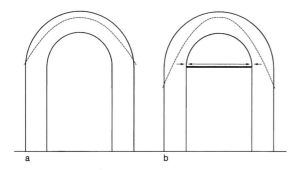

a   b

20. Structural actions
of an arch with and
without a tie-rod.
Illustration: R. Taylor.

them tension, compression, bending, shear, etc.) would become
more critical – and at an exponential rate – as it got bigger.[71]

Roman builders also intuited, on some level, the principle of
structural redundancy, or *statical indeterminacy*.[72] All standing
buildings are in equilibrium; that is, they bear their loads by means
of a complex and invisible mesh of stress lines. A structure with the
minimum number of elements to accommodate those stresses is said
to be statically determinate: It is completely efficient under static
(unmoving) conditions, but if any element should fail, the whole
structure would collapse. Ancient architects were unable to create
such superefficient systems, nor would they have wanted to: Their
buildings had to withstand dynamic (moving) loadings such as
wind, earthquakes, human and animal weight and movement, and
the partial failure of their own materials over time, not to mention
the building process itself. After all, incomplete buildings are not
stable in the same way as when they are completed. Thus statical
indeterminacy was a necessity for all architecture, even the most
daring. Buildings were designed with structural margins of error creating more than one path for each loading action.

A typical Roman arch, made of stone voussoirs, can serve as an
illustration. The line of pressure of an arch is not semicircular but
parabolic in shape (Fig. 20, *a*).[73] At each springing of the arch, the
tangents to this line are never vertical: They project downward and
outward. All arches, then, have an outward thrust as well as a
downward thrust. The weight and stiffness of the piers supporting
the arch must be adequate to counteract the outward component;
otherwise the arch will flatten and spread, eventually collapsing.
Most arches with reasonably large voussoirs and solid supports are
already statically indeterminate and can accommodate loads of different magnitudes translating into parabolas of different shapes. If
we add an iron tie-rod (Fig. 20, *b*), then we are compounding the

21. Rome: Basilica of Maxentius. Fototeca Unione c/o American Academy in Rome, neg. 14459F.

arch's statical indeterminacy.[74] Firmly embedded in the haunches of the arch, it is subjected to tension – that is, a pulling in opposite directions – because of the arch's outward thrusts on the masonry elements in which it is anchored. But how much tension? And to what degree does it relieve the piers of their duty to counteract the outward thrusts? No Roman engineer could have answered these questions precisely. Different configurations of forces may have no visible effect on the structure. For example, the tie-rod could be loose at either end, having no structural effect whatsoever, without any *visible* change in form; but the structure would be changed nevertheless – a reminder that form and structure are not perfectly correlated.

Probably only the most advanced Roman architects actually used this principle, for they were most inclined to take form and material to structural extremes. By wishing to minimize the *degree* of indeterminacy within a given design scheme they would have respected the *principle* of indeterminacy all the more. A good architect could manipulate the psychology of the viewer by visual means, sometimes emphasizing structural stability and sometimes undermining it. But

he was required to answer all of a building's physical demands from his knowledge of the actions of its components while minimizing unnecessary and disruptive elements. The trick was to apply, wherever one could, rules of thumb gathered from experience; and where those fell short of the circumstances, to temper one's sense of daring with intuition, common sense, and careful observation.

22. Rome: reconstructed view of interior of Basilica of Maxentius. Fototeca Unione c/o American Academy in Rome, neg. 12240F. Illustration: Trabacchi, 1907.

By experiment and observation, architects diminished the statical indeterminacy of characteristic Roman forms over time. Successful forms, as their structural properties became better understood, were isolated from redundant "supporting" elements. Perhaps the most straightforward example of this phenomenon is the Basilica of Maxentius in Rome (Figs. 21, 22). This was a huge, freestanding brick-and-concrete hall derived directly from bath architecture. Almost identical forms had been used for the frigidaria of imperial bath structures for at least two centuries previously. All had four great piers rising on either side of an oblong hall to a three-part cross vault above. The frigidaria, however, were smaller and had been partly embedded within a cluster of barrel-vaulted satellite structures that served in part as buttresses to counteract the large out-

23. Rome: recon-
structed cutaway
view of Baths of
Diocletian. E. Paulin,
*Restaurations des
monuments antiques*
(1890).

ward thrusts of the cross vaults upon the piers (Fig. 23). As a result,
the main sources of direct light in these halls were from the lunette
windows around the upper register, which rose above the rooftops
of the surrounding vaults. The designer of the Basilica of Maxentius, who would have carefully examined the visible cracks and distortions in the great frigidaria in Roman imperial baths, conceived
a radical and dangerous idea: Isolate this powerful and simple form
from its cluttered surroundings, add windows to the lower levels,
and present it on a larger scale than anything that had been tried
before. The result seems to have succeeded, although the central and
western parts eventually collapsed, probably in an earthquake.

Architectural refinement did not always lead to a decrease in statical indeterminacy over time. Sometimes the result was an increase,
especially when architects combined old forms in new ways. We
may take as an example the annular vaulted colonnade. In simplest
terms, this is a barrel vault that has been bent horizontally into a
circle. The vault is supported by a circle of columns on the interior
and by a solid wall on the exterior. Only one example of this form
is preserved in isolation before late antiquity; it is the Teatro Marit-
timo, or Island Enclosure, at Hadrian's villa near Tivoli, Italy (Fig.
24).[75] Mere colonnades supporting one or both sides of a barrel
vault are a risky proposition, for columns do not have the bulk to

24. Tivoli: Hadrian's villa, view of Island Enclosure. Photo: R. Taylor.

counteract significant outward thrusts from vaults above them. But the Island Enclosure overcomes this problem by creating, in effect, a compression ring: This is the continuous circular entablature resting upon the columns. A very thin horizontal ring can provide remarkably strong resistance to thrusts applied to its exterior surface, provided that the thrusts are uniform all around the circumference and are directed toward the center of the ring. Such were the conditions in this light colonnaded structure, whose form did not resurface until about two centuries later in tombs, churches, and baptisteries, and then only in a much different guise. In the tomb-church of S. Costanza outside Rome the annular vaulted colonnade no longer stands in isolation but girdles a high central covered space (Fig. 25). What had simply been a low attic above the entablature at Hadrian's villa was extended up into a cylindrical drum supporting a dome or a conical timber roof. The dead weight and (in the likely case of a dome) outward thrusts of this structural elaboration compounded the statical indeterminacy of the vaulted colonnade. The two principal elements, central space and surrounding corridor,

now acted in counterpoint. But uniquely, only one of these vaulted
forms, the domed drum, required the buttressing effect of the other.

The *oculus* – a circular hole in the crown of a dome – is a splendid example of the Roman capacity to marshal structural knowledge to aesthetic ends. Whether or not the architects of Hadrian's
villa fully appreciated the statical possibilities of the Island Enclosure (and this seems unlikely, since they also constructed a similar
barrel-vaulted colonnade around a rectangle, which offers none of
the same advantages), the widespread use of the oculus is proof that
Roman builders understood the principle of the compression ring.
Early domes seem to have been built in this fashion: Those in the
Stabian and Forum baths of Pompeii, dating perhaps to the early
first century B.C., have oculi and follow a roughly conical shape; the
"Temple of Mercury" at Baiae, of the Augustan period (27 B.C.–14
A.D.), is built in radial rings of concrete (Fig. 26).[76] Although wood-
en centering was certainly necessary for its construction because of
the irregularity of the stones and the liquidity of the mortar matrix,

26. Baiae: engraving of interior of "Temple of Mercury," by G.-B. Natali. P. A. Paoli, *Antichità di Pozzuoli* (1768).

it was understood that when the concrete had set each horizontal zone of the dome would hold itself in place and further consolidate those below it. The process could be halted at any stage.

Domes are often described as a group of arches conjoined radially around a vertical axis. Just as arches exert outward thrusts in the plane of their curvature, a dome exerts outward thrusts all around its periphery – as if it were a series of arches sharing a common keystone. But the reality of an oculus – the complete *lack* of a keystone – indicates that something is radically different in a dome. No arch, or group of isolated arches sharing a single crown, could stand without the crown.[77] The dome's advantage consists in circumferential or hoop stresses. Toward the crown these act in compression. The imaginary "arches" constituting the dome crowd into a single con-

verging mass, clamping one another in place so that their crown can
be excluded without incident. A rugby scrum, in which many play-
ers lean inward shoulder-to-shoulder in a tight huddle, provides similar equilibrium. Indeed, actions of human bodies in opposition (as
in gymnastics and wrestling) may have inspired some of the earliest
arch and vaulting techniques.

Baiae's dome must have been large for its time. But it was structurally conservative, being anchored close to the ground. Architects
took note of its success (it lies in an active seismic zone), or in the
success of others like it, and within a few decades were constructing
oculus-lit domes of comparable size raised high above the ground.
The oculus proved ideal for daytime lighting of heated bath halls
(if not for energy efficiency) and eventually became a highly desirable aesthetic element in its own right, achieving pride of place in
such spaces as the octagon room of the Golden House of Nero and
the great dome of the Pantheon (Fig. 27).

When the principle of the compression ring was recognized, it
must have come as a stunning validation of a distinctly Roman architectural intuition: that a void, simply by virtue of its shape and
the continuity of its outer limit, could emulate a powerful buttress.
This *structural* reality conformed to a longstanding Roman *formal*
tendency to express power by subtracting from or displacing solid
matter, balancing the void against the enclosing mass. The dome as
compression ring is an intuitive internalizing: Space shoulders the
load. Roman architecture is primarily concerned with shaping spaces
rather than filling them, addressing form first and foremost as an
interior concern. This tendency is deeply implicated in design and
process: It accompanied the drive for ever greater spans of vaulted
spaces, the sweeping aside of interior supports, the sequencing of
interior spaces without any special attention to their intelligibility
from outside.

Of course we cannot reconstruct the exact process by which any
Roman building was designed; an architect's ideas are ultimately
personal. Whatever the means by which they emerged, these ideas
were shaped by tradition and expectations, on the one hand, and
inventiveness on the other. They found ready expression in a variety
of preparatory media, from blueprintlike drawings to scale models
and perspective sketches. Professional knowledge, rules of thumb,
and careful observation of existing structures governed structural

27. Rome: interior of the Pantheon. G. P.
Panini, ca. 1734. Samuel H. Kress Collec-
tion, photograph © Board of Trustees,
National Gallery of Art, Washington, D.C.

design decisions. It is likely that these decisions were sometimes refined further by experimentation or improvisation during construction. The design process spilled over into the phase of actualization,
as was only natural. But we should not exaggerate the tendency to
defer important decisions. In the next chapter we appraise the extent to which buildings on the imperial scale were shaped early by
carefully laid plans.

2

LAYING THE GROUNDWORK

> He had set his heart upon building upon the Palatine a paved
> portico three hundred feet long with apartments opening from
> it and commanding a magnificent view, possessing a spacious
> colonnade and other such accessories, with the intent to sur-
> pass all other men's houses in roominess and imposing appear-
> ance.
>
> – Cicero, *De domo sua* 116

THE SITE

According to the modern truism only three things matter in the real-estate hunt: location, location, location. Ancient Roman buildings, though they were not subject to stringent zoning ordinances, certainly were not immune to the location mantra. Sites that we would deem the best today – those with a good view, with good drainage and air quality, with ready access to urban amenities or good acreage – were seen in a similar light in antiquity and belonged either to the wealthy, to the public trust, or to religious concerns. A building's *context* is a different thing, more enmeshed in the urban fabric – streets, open spaces, other buildings – than to the practical and aesthetic concerns of its direct beneficiaries. Put simply, location is how a building's physical situation plays to its residents or regular users; context is how it plays to everyone else. Roman architecture was alternately sensitive and indifferent to context. Indifference is evident in towns and cities, where many buildings were so compromised by the density of their surroundings that they had little or no outward presence whatever. Boxed in by urban clutter, city houses and public or semipublic buildings such as neighborhood baths turned their radiance inward to colonnaded courtyards and halls sheathed in mosaic, frescoes, or marble.

Still, the artful contextualization of buildings in their environment is also abundantly evident. One has only to read Pliny the Younger's or Statius' descriptions of villas, or Cicero's *De domo sua*, to understand the importance of surroundings to the value and meaning of elite private architecture.[1] Building sites not only could be exploited for maximum visual and practical effect but could have symbolic or ideological importance.[2] The site of a victory in war or in politics was likely to acquire an aggressively propagandistic architecture. Cicero's archenemy Clodius, after succeeding in confiscating the orator's property on the Palatine Hill in Rome, destroyed the house and built a monument on the site dedicated to the goddess Liberty, a symbolic rebuke of Cicero's perceived tyranny. Building sites with military significance are more numerous. Perhaps the best known of these is at Adamklissi in Romania, where Trajan raised a monumental trophy to his victory in the Dacian Wars encrusted with sculptural propaganda.[3]

Site choice was usually the patron's decision, of course. Cicero sought the perfect garden villa site for his daughter's tomb and his own retirement with a single-mindedness bordering on obsession: It must not be a mere plot (*area*) but must have public accessibility (*celebritas*) and be "worthy of a paterfamilias" (*oikodespotika*).[4] If a site was found, the architect could exploit its potential in any number of ways. Orientation was one way to achieve practical ends. Pliny the Younger is preoccupied with the effect of climate on his private pavilions, dining halls, and corridors, and Vitruvius shows a similar attention to the elements. One could exploit nature's power or mitigate its effect by orienting buildings or rooms in particular directions. Mitigation is evident in Vitruvius' prescription that summer dining rooms and picture galleries should face north, away from the punishing sun; exploitation, in his recommendation to direct winter dining rooms and the hot rooms of baths toward the setting winter sun (southwest) to harness the radiant heat.[5]

Orientation could also have religious or ideological benefits. Vitruvius suggests that temples should face west, though the widespread violation of this principle in practice indicates there was no force of doctrine behind it. In general temples follow his more flexible rule that they should face the direction from which they can be most appreciated or command a view reflecting the god's power and scope.[6] A Roman temple on a hillside always faced outward as if to take command of the god's greater realm outside the immediate sanctuary.[7] In the secular sphere, views offered opportunities to generate similar acts of signification. Pliny boasts of the multiple views from rooms at his Laurentine villa; Statius, those of his patrons' villas.[8] The direct visual alignment of the Pantheon in Rome with the Mausoleum of Augustus to the north was probably a conscious ideological decision by the emperor Hadrian, or maybe even Augustus' lieutenant Agrippa, who built the first version of the building, to offer tribute to Augustus and his dynasty.[9]

Architecture must conform to the law. The *Digest* of Justinian and the Theodosian Code are awash in points of law related to buildings.[10] Design was constrained by many things: the dimensions of the site, the rights of neighbors (as to an unobstructed view or to daylight), rights of passage across property, interdicts against building in various kinds of places, restrictions on water runoff, religious scruples, and so forth. Most important of all was the primacy of private property. Roman civil law appears to have prohibited expropriation even for public utilities such as aqueducts, let alone for buildings.[11] Consequently a perfect, unencumbered plot of land could not always be found even for a building project with the imperial imprimatur. Thousands of legal compromises and settlements, made either before or after the fact, leave traces in the fabric of Roman ruins today: irregular plots, diverted waterways, trimmed walls, blocked doors and windows, and so forth. Even the mighty Temple of Jupiter Optimus Maximus, it was said, was built with a hole in its eaves to accommodate the tiny shrine of a god worshiped in the open air.[12]

Legal limitations were just as real as physical ones. They had a tangible effect on the building's form and function. Height could be limited by building codes such as the one established by Nero after the fire of 64 A.D.[13] Infrastructure could be affected by the presence of a property that lay in the desired path of a storm drain or downwind from a projected chimney. Even condensation on a partition wall caused by a bath could instigate a lawsuit.

SURVEYING

Architects have always designed conceptual or hypothetical buildings, but ultimately their commissions must conform to the chosen site. Vitruvius has skewed modern perceptions of Roman design by relegating topographical considerations to a late phase of the design process: A building's principles of symmetry are established first, then modified to suit the site.[14] Yet the same author acknowledges the primacy of topography in the choice and layout of a site for founding a city and in finding water sources.[15] Few would doubt that the initial survey of a site is vitally important in isolated architectural projects as well. While some Roman buildings indicate that the ground plan was modified on account of the site, these cases can be explained as reactions to unanticipated subsurface conditions after ground was broken. In fact, one class of architectural design incorporated the inevitability of unanticipated conditions into its very process. Bridge designers habitually took advantage of the best sites for the pier footings; consequently Roman bridges, for all their beauty and clarity of conception, often do not have equally matching arch spans; sometimes they even follow a crooked plan.[16] Certain projects with a small footprint, such as modest tombs, could be designed without much consideration of the plot beyond its dimensions. But it can be safely surmised that for major projects the architect would visit the site at an early stage in the design process. With him he would probably bring an assistant or two and equipment for a rudimentary survey: a sighting instrument that could be leveled, a graduated stadia rod that could be placed vertically anywhere on the surface and sighted with the instrument to establish ground levels, and horizontal measures such as ropes or wooden rods marked in Roman feet.[17] Surveying was done in several phases. In this, the initial survey, the architect examined the plot of land, perhaps recording its visible hydrology, horizontal dimensions, and vertical features. He would need to ensure that the legal boundaries of the site were well marked and the building code and site-specific legal limitations well understood. He might take *soundings* (vertical shafts dug into the ground) to determine the geology of the site. Soil quality, level of groundwater, direction of watershed, and disposition of bedrock all contribute to structural decision making and can have profound effects on the cost of a project.

The next survey was done in coordination with the earth moving. This too was three-dimensional, and drew information from the initial survey to direct the land's transformation. By this time the general shapes, dimensions, and positions of the projected building(s) would have been established with some degree of certainty. As a terrace took shape, surveyors would periodically check its evenness with the sighting device and stadia rod. Calibrated cords or measuring rods were used to check the overall dimensions of the surface. The surface area may have exceeded the projected building's dimensions to allow for landscaping and the lateral dispersal of the dead weight through the soil. A third survey was necessary for the laying out of the buildings themselves; this is discussed momentarily.

EARTH MOVING

Lucian describes how Hippias began work on his baths: "The site was not level, but quite sloping and steep, and when he undertook it, excessively low on one side. But he made the one side level with the other, not only building a firm platform for the whole work and confirming the security of the superstructure by putting in foundations, but also reinforcing the whole with buttresses, quite steep and for safety's sake close together."[18] Lucian's description is in perfect accord with standard Roman practice of terracing.[19] Buildings in an untamed setting were not part of the Roman aesthetic, except perhaps in unforgivingly rocky or mountainous territory such as the thousand-foot seaside cliffs of Tiberius' Villa Iovis on Capri; but even there the urge to regularize the landscape was taken as far as possible. And the possibilities were greatly expanded in the Republican period with the widespread adoption of concrete in retaining structures.[20] Architects terraced their sites for at least two reasons. One was that horizontal surfaces made the surveying of foundations and walls much easier. Another was the Roman love of formal gardens. Shallow-rooted exotic plants required irrigation, which in turn demanded a nearly level watershed for maximum water retention. Grading of the terraces was therefore a matter of some concern and technical skill. Hadrian's villa near Tivoli, which once was home to hundreds of acres of gardens and groves interlaced with pleasure pavilions of all shapes and sizes, is terraced over much of its extent.[21]

In the premodern age, earth moving was a very labor-intensive and time-consuming stage in the building process, particularly if large amounts of earth and stone had to be removed from the site entirely.[22] Because of the lack of physical obstructions and the continuous and unskilled nature of the work, more individuals, human and animal, were likely to be at work now than at any later stage. From a design standpoint earth moving was not the most demanding phase on the architect. The main concern was efficient administration of the resources. Typically work crews would begin at the top, cutting back the slope first and then extending the terrace outward with the removed earth and stone. Excavated and transported downslope by men and beasts, the earth had to be continuously rammed down in thin layers. Otherwise it was liable to settle under the bearing pressure of the foundations (if they could not be extended down to the bedrock) or by natural subsidence over time. Loose rocks would have to be removed by cranes or levered downhill. Some construction, especially of retaining walls, may have been necessary at this stage. On steep sites, such as the Sanctuary of Hercules Victor at Tivoli and the nearby Sanctuary of Fortuna at Palestrina (Fig. 28), terracing and retaining walls constituted a large part of the overall construction plan. Access roads and ramps, materials depots, and workyards were given shape at this time as well. Their layouts and locations were all-important to the smooth progression of the project.

SETTING OUT THE PLAN

Now came the most important survey of all, the translation of the drawn plans or numeric measurements to the ground. This was done with a few simple tools: a set square (*norma*) for determining right angles, graduated rods for measuring, and sweeping cords for circle segments.[23] All the major structural features of the building's planimetry would be laid out not by inscribing the ground itself – foundation trenches would soon be dug directly underneath them – but by extending cords between stakes, which were fixed in the ground well beyond their mapped endpoints in order to remain clear of the trenches. Curves may have been rendered as polygons kept in place by short rays extending to stakes beyond the trench edges. For the most part, walls were probably designated by a single line, not a double one, since thicknesses could be easily communi-

cated later or calculated on the basis of the room size. However, if a wall or pier was complex – for instance, if it was of unusual plan, or destined to have statue niches or built-in waterworks – then its footprint would have been laid out more thoroughly (Fig. 29). The drainage and water-supply network, subterranean passages, cisterns, and any other planned underground features would be staked

28. Palestrina: model of Sanctuary of Fortuna. Fototeca Unione c/o American Academy in Rome, neg. 4348F.

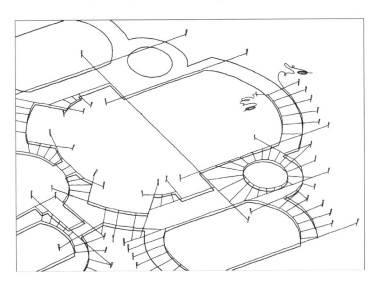

29. Dougga: hypothetical string layout scheme for the Baths of Licinius. Illustration: R. Taylor.

out at this time too. Since the lines would serve as both a plan guide and an elevation datum for the men in the trenches below, they would have been treated with some care. The possibilities for error were numerous, and there can be little doubt that a responsible architect oversaw or regularly inspected work at this phase. The sober consequences of inadequate oversight are occasionally legible in the archaeological record. Sweeping corrections made in the foundational alignment at military installations at Red House (Corbridge) and Hod Hill in Britain suggest that the architect absented himself during the setting out of foundations, returning later to discover the project botched; the extremely irregular foundations of the amphitheater at Caerleon tell a similar tale of absenteeism.[24]

Error, whether simple or compounded, was always a problem with hand measuring devices, particularly distance measures. Fortunately there were various methods of cross-checking distances by geometric means. Angles too, if they were done by a *traverse* (a polygon generated by a long incremental chain of angles and measurements, each relying on its predecessor in the sequence), could suffer from accumulated errors. Cross-checking was a routine part of Roman land surveying,[25] and the techniques developed by the professional surveyors of land apportionments may have been used on a smaller scale in the layout of complex ground plans.[26] It was best to establish a few logical datum points on the plan against which progress could periodically be checked by measuring angles and distances. However, as one would expect, the archaeological evidence around the empire shows a variety of standards at work ranging from punctiliousness to indifference. The importance of a project did not guarantee high standards. One example among thousands: For no apparent reason the great hall of the Markets of Trajan in Rome, a showcase of progressive architecture, is half a meter wider at one end than at the other.[27]

PRECISION AND ACCURACY

What then can be said in general about standards of error in Roman construction? Here we must pause to distinguish between precision and accuracy. In simple terms one is a means, the other an end. *Precision* is an inherent quality; it is the overall degree of refinement applied to a form or a system. *Accuracy* is a principle of transmission; it is the degree to which B transmits, or replicates,

A. A dishonest grocer can recalibrate a scale so that two pounds register as three. This is a gross inaccuracy, but it is not a result of imprecision. In fact, it has no bearing whatsoever on the precision of the scale, nor on the level of precision expected from it. Let us think in more architectural terms. When laying out a building's plan on the ground, a Roman surveyor might use instruments that allow high precision, say a margin of error of one inch for every hundred feet of distance. Yet he may still easily make an elementary calculating error resulting, for instance, in a wall five feet longer than planned – a gross inaccuracy. This is a failure in transmitting the internal relationships of the plan, not in the capacity of his instruments. It makes no difference whether his method produced an error of 5.1 feet or 5.0001 feet, it is a gross error all the same – and one that could easily be detected even on the small scale of the diagram. Precision may help to achieve accuracy, but it does not generate it. Even if the surveyor, again with his unusually precise instruments, were to set out his paper plan on the ground accurately, he would be doing so with false precision – the fallacy of presuming a degree of precision beyond the limitations of transmission, like "enhancing" an originally low-resolution image in a higher-resolution digital format. The surveyor cannot improve accuracy by using standards that exceed those of the diagram itself. So if the plan is on a 1:20 scale and has a margin of error of a tenth of an inch for every five feet, when transferred to the ground that ratio will properly remain the same, but on a larger scale: two inches for every hundred feet. This is only half the precision capacity of his instruments.

Choosing a method and its degree of tolerance is always significant. No Roman building required extreme precision in horizontal plan; the small distortions introduced by transmitting a paper plan to the ground with a warped measuring rod or a slightly elastic sweeping line might never be noticed and would have little effect on the building's structural integrity. Naturally, precision was maintained as much as possible within the limits of this method, but not to an obsessive degree. Accuracy – fidelity to the plan – was more important. The best way to guarantee the accuracy of *B* was to replicate the process by which *A* was created. Thus the Roman method of laying out the geometry of a plan at the drafting table was probably reproduced as exactly as possible on the ground. Where compasses were used on paper, cords (waxed, perhaps, to minimize stretching and humidity differentials) were swung around pegs on the ground. Where rulers were used on paper, pairs of graduated rods were leapfrogged alongside an extended cord. Where square rulers were used to make quick right angles, the *groma* – a vertical rod topped by a horizontal cross fitted with four plumb lines for the precise establishment of right angles – served for the surveyor.

Precision was most critical in *elevation,* though not necessarily as drawn on paper. There are numerous reasons for this, some psychological and some physical. Because we usually move about and examine things in the horizontal plane of our eyes, which is too close to the plane of the ground to decode its planimetric anomalies easily, we are more sensitive to *altimetric* aberrations in the upright dimension of walls and colonnades – particularly if a horizontal line goes crooked. For example, two or more columns within a colonnade can easily be (and often were) set further apart or closer together than the norm if an optical compensation is needed, but their heights must be precisely uniform or else the architrave above them will be perceptibly uneven. For *physical* reasons a column, pier, or wall, whether or not it corresponds exactly to the diagram, needs to be precisely vertical if it is to avoid buckling under its loads. This is why the plumb line and the leveling square were as familiar to the Roman mason as the trowel or chisel. The greatest degree of surveying precision in antiquity was applied to aqueducts. These too were the concern of architects, as Vitruvius and Frontinus attest. It did not matter much if an aqueduct channel was constructed a foot or two to the side of its projected course (and aqueducts *did* have drawn plans, as a well-known inscription from North Africa attests),[28] or if its continuous vault rose half a foot higher off the floor in some places than others – just so long as the floor maintained a precise, continuous, and carefully calibrated downhill gradient. In places, Roman technicians were able to produce gradients so precise and uniform – and not just in a straight line but along a sinuous course – that scholars are at a loss to explain their methods. A section of the aqueduct of Nîmes north of the Pont du Gard has a steady fall of only seven millimeters for every hundred meters of distance, even as it winds along the valley contours.[29]

In reality many Roman construction projects, especially those without continuous connections between buildings, seem to have been carried out without comprehensive plans. Lacking diagrammatic referents to one another, the isolated structures had no criteria for relative accuracy other than those laid out orally for the surveying team. The results were usually adequate for the buildings

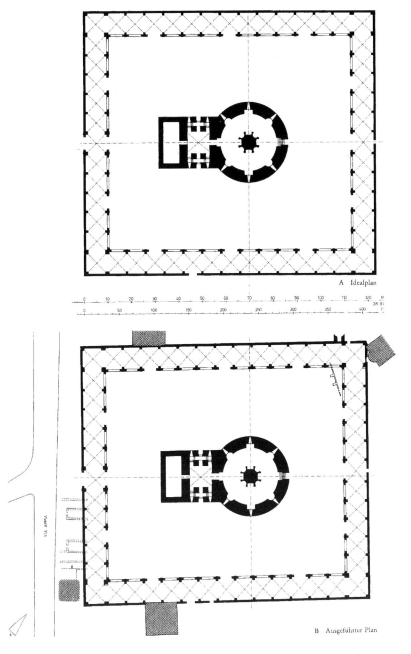

A Idealplan

B Ausgeführter Plan

30. Rome, Via Appia: ideal (A) and actual (B) plans of mausoleum at Villa of Maxentius. Rasch 1984. By permission of J. Rasch.

themselves, but when transferred to plans in modern times they show visible distortions. A typical example is the mausoleum at the Villa of Maxentius south of Rome (Fig. 30). The illustration shows the plan as it was probably envisioned ideally (top) and as it was carried out (bottom). The distortions in the actual complex are subtle but immediately noticeable, for we view the drawn plan in front of our eyes, not under our feet. They are virtually impossible to detect on the ground. The western colonnade is not quite square with the others, perhaps because of the oblique angle of the nearby road. But since it is on the entrance side the tomb has been aligned with it (albeit imperfectly). This decision has caused the tomb to be skewed slightly clockwise and south of center. Like many anomalies in plan, these are rather ambiguous. It is hard to distinguish error from conscious compromise; or which elements reflect the initial error (if any), which are additional errors compounding the first, and which are corrections made after errors were noticed. We must be careful not to *presume* error, for Roman architects understood the more forgiving "precision coefficient" in ground plans and exploited it masterfully.[30] In other words, we don't want to mistake conscious allowances of imprecision for unintended lapses in accuracy. One thing, though, is certain: Imprecision on this magnitude would not have been tolerated in the altimetric plane, either in the tilt of walls or columns or (most noticeably of all) in horizontal elements.

SITUATIONAL INACCURACY

The Baths of Caracalla, famous for the precision of their brickwork and the planar crispness of their masonry surfaces, offer a particularly instructive example of a plan where even accuracy is unambiguously compromised. Because of the extensive additive terracing of its platform, it may have been decided not to dig trenches into the completed terrace but to lay out a rough plan before the terrace fill was added, raising the foundations and substructures at the same rate as the ground level.[31] While having obvious advantages, such a method would have required the plan lines to be covered over and then reestablished about thirteen meters higher up by means unknown, with the attendant risk to accuracy. This approach is very problematic, and the evidence for it is ambiguous.[32] For one thing, short of time-consuming backsighting of every substructure wall from a level viewing instrument, how do the masons know where the floor level will be? Floor level determines the relative positions of the hierarchical voids that they are in the process of building: subfloor drains, hypocausts, service passages and intermediate drains, and so on. And how does one ascertain that a wall is going up straight when it is being progressively buried as it rises? Probably by some incremental method that suffers from incremental error.

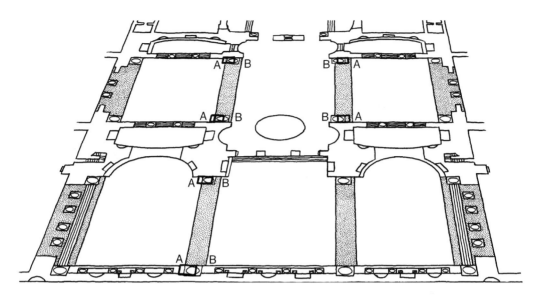

31. Rome: Baths of Caracalla, perspective plan of frigidarium and natatio with adjusted column positions. After DeLaine 1997. Illustration: R. Taylor.

Predictably, the later survey at the subfloor level revealed anomalies. One of the very first measurements set out at subfoundation level, the northern half of the modular 200-foot square, ended up at subfloor level to be only 96.7 feet wide instead of 100, an appalling error of 3.3 percent. This measurement must not have been cross-checked even initially. It threw off many of the other dimensions of the bath block that relied upon its (in)accuracy.[33] Various corrective measures were made at subfloor level to even out the distances – a sure sign that the initial error was deemed inaccurate by the builders. The remaining irregularities are still an affront to the measuring tape. And yet to the unsuspecting visitor most of them are invisible, utterly beyond detection by casual means. In short, the builders understood the limits of optical perception and lived within its laws. The result is a flawed floor plan that grew into a building of undiminished magnificence.

In one case, however, the line of casual perception was crossed. Although the error provoked a chain of compensatory measures that ultimately affected the proportions of the entire superstructure of the frigidarium, its only genuinely problematic aspect was in the vertical plane of walls, niches, and columnar screens. The subsequent attempt at optical correction – as opposed to mere correction of measurements – is instructive (Fig. 31). It was a simple measuring error, causing the foundation wall of the inner side of the eastern bays of the frigidarium and natatio to be laid out several feet too far from the outer wall.[34] The foundation is represented on the plan by the stippled areas to the left of the centerline. Its western counterpart (right of the centerline) was measured out accurately. This was a mistake of such gross proportions that it threw off the visual symmetry of the scheme, even though it made little difference to the building's ultimate structural success. The challenge to the builders was not to eliminate the error but to minimize its effect. There were two concerns: the visual integrity of the whole and the local symmetry of the parts. The initial task, it appears, was to re-think the positions of the massive columns and piers that would en-frame each of the bays. The second and more important task was to adjust the secondary visual elements within these compromised enframing elements. As DeLaine reconstructs the process, the four column bases on the substructure of the natatio and frigidarium were not set in their intended positions (marked *A* left of center), for that would have placed them too far off the mismeasured foun-dation. Instead they were positioned almost flush with the eastern edges (the corresponding positions labeled *B*), while in the frigidar-ium two of the bases were moved inward to the point where they teetered on the edge of the substructure (positions labeled *B* on the right side of the centerline). Obviously this second correction was done to approximate symmetry in the compromised frigidarium, for it was done at some risk to the columns' integrity. To maintain the strong axial symmetry of the bays, the enframed clusters of niches in the back wall of the natatio were redesigned to maintain rigid symmetry within the frames of the columns, although not with re-spect to each other. This is especially visible in DeLaine's recon-structed elevation drawing (Fig. 32).

Because of the human incapacity to judge certain kinds of plani-metric inconsistencies over long distances, the positions of the large columns in relation to each other was relatively unimportant. It was the columns' relationship to their neighboring elements (piers, pools, niches) and the effect on short-distance relationships that were of greatest concern. If two asymmetrically positioned columns are addorsed to symmetrical piers, the incompatibility will be imme-diately evident by the differing distances from the edge of each col-umn to the nearby edge of the pier. But it will take a great deal of effort to determine which class of elements – columns, piers, or both – are not true to the overall scheme. The builders instinctively un-derstood this. They also recognized that unobstructed visual axial alignment is far more detectable than obstructed alignment. It was

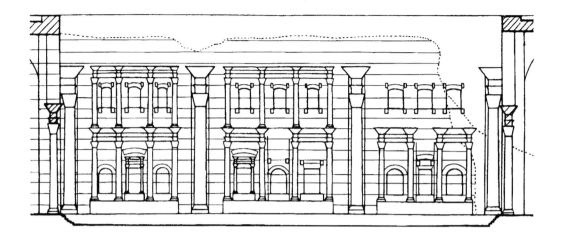

32. Rome: elevation of natatio facade of Baths of Caracalla. DeLaine 1997. By permission of J. De-Laine and *Journal of Roman Archaeology.*

not important that the four inner columns of the frigidarium were misaligned with those in the natatio, for they could not be seen in close relation to one another. Much more important was the centering of the niche schemes within each unequal bay of the natatio wall, for the bays were visible along a horizontal axis from more than seventy meters away through two enframing column screens.

Naturally these relational principles were useful not only in damage control but in building design as well. The correspondence of parts to the whole, particularly in large and intricate buildings, was often established through such hierarchies of enframement. Even Vitruvius' famous theory of symmetry and proportion, in which buildings, like the human body itself, require "a correspondence between the measure of individual elements and the appearance of the work as a whole" (3.1.4), presumes hierarchies of mensural relationships: column height to column width, column to colonnade, colonnade to overall height and width of the building. They were like notes of varying values, the whole notes maintaining their rigor by means of the eighth and sixteenth notes. A good architect was a master of rubato: He could maintain a solid sense of rhythm and unity while subtly stretching or contracting the note values within small cells.

PREEMPTIVE INACCURACY

Situations sometimes arise in which surveyors or builders must be intentionally inaccurate – not to correct errors, as in the cases discussed above, but to avoid them. The principle at work here I call *preemptive inaccuracy.* It might be useful to consider an analogy. Say you are a canoeist aiming for a specific landing point across a large lake. Unable to see the landing against the background of trees or rocks, you consult map and compass and then establish a sight-line to a prominent landmark in the vicinity of the landing. But you do *not* aim directly for the destination. Recognizing the limitations of your tools – there are many factors that compromise their precision – you intentionally aim either to the left or the right of your landmark. That way, when you reach the far shore, you can be reasonably confident that you have arrived on the *predicted* side of your destination, and you will know which way to turn in order to reach it. This may seem inefficient, but the alternative is even less so; if you aim directly for the landing and don't find it when you arrive, fifty percent of the time you will turn in the wrong direction to seek it out. By experience you have determined an acceptable margin of error, and you know that aiming, say, two degrees to the right always leads to a satisfactory conclusion, whereas a margin of just one degree occasionally has led you astray.

The same guiding principle can be seen behind some surveying and construction decisions. In elevation it found many uses, from drainage infrastructure to the carving of stone blocks to be set in serial (see Chapter 6). Good architects are attuned to such things, but it is generally the master builders and field engineers – those who have accumulated deep reserves of practical knowledge and experience with their tools and their work crews – who will use it most effectively. Preemptive inaccuracy is perhaps most necessary in addressing the rigorous demands of aqueduct design. The planned terminus of an aqueduct will be a certain distance lower than its source, sometimes an alarmingly small distance (e.g., a fall of 3 Roman feet over 10,000 feet of horizontal distance). The engineers or builders must be absolutely certain that a channel begun at the source will not end up below the terminus. The channel's gradient may be allowed a certain variability, but it must always progress downhill; there can be no upward "corrections." In such circumstances one must estimate, in mathematical terms, the precision of one's surveying effort on the basis of the instruments, the skill of the surveyors, the difficulty of the terrain, and so forth. If precision is determined to be on the order of $1:10,000$, for example, then the altimetric margin of error over a distance of ten thousand feet is one foot. Knowing that the terminus is only three feet below the source

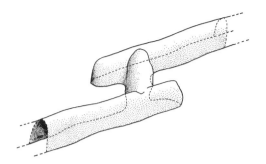

33. Bologna: analytical illustration of the juncture of two segments of the Roman aqueduct. Illustration: R. Taylor after *Acquedotto 2000* (Bologna 1985).

(and that information too is likely to be far from perfect) the surveyor must aim for a terminus at least one foot above the actual one. That way, if the error is at the maximum, and is all in the downward direction, the channel will still arrive at an acceptable level for the terminus. If, as is more likely, it arrives somewhat above the terminus (as much as two feet, if the estimate of imprecision was correct), there is no harm done.[35]

Similar methods were used for tunneling techniques that called for starting at both ends and converging at a point in the center. In such cases those working downhill had to aim slightly high, those uphill slightly low. Research on drainage tunnels in Etruria shows that the margin of error at the meeting point ranged from zero to over half a meter, but at least one abandoned project was found that dead-ends in both directions. In one case of extreme conservatism (and probably a poor understanding of the parameters of precision) a tunnel just 200 m long had a shelf at its center 2.8 m high, creating a little waterfall.[36] In aqueduct and drain tunneling, planimetric accuracy was almost as important as the altimetric, but not equally important. If two tunnels did not meet but were at acceptable levels, they could be connected even at right angles with no ill effect on the flow of water (Fig. 33).[37]

FOUNDATIONS AND SUBSTRUCTURES

Roman buildings made their greatest claim to permanence in their foundations. It is a common and mistaken presumption that the foundations of any given Roman building, following the published handbooks,[38] were sunk to a uniform depth. The danger of inadequate foundations was not primarily that the building would sink into the ground but that it would subside unevenly, causing the superstructure to crack and distort.[39] Uniform depth did not guarantee a remedy for either problem. The goal was to achieve even resistance to subsidence, and this was best done by digging down to a bedding of uniform consistency regardless of its vertical topography. Builders could not always have known how deep they would dig before they reached a satisfactory starting point for a foundation. Their uncertainty would always have been a wild card in the estimation of cost, materials, and labor. Ideally one hoped to reach bedrock. However, firm beds of clay, gravel, or other material could prove perfectly suitable for even very heavy buildings. (Pliny the Elder goes so far as to claim that the Artemision at Ephesos was earthquake-proof because it was built on a marsh.)[40] Roman practitioners, it seems, employed widely varying techniques suited to local conditions.[41] Some were remarkably counterintuitive; for instance, the suburban conduit of the Roman aqueduct at Caesarea in Israel evidently has no foundations at all, but sits with admirable firmness upon the surface sand – an audacious decision for an aqueduct, which must avoid even the slightest differential settling.[42] Others were failures, plain and simple. Describing a nascent theater project in Nicea, the younger Pliny laments,

I fear that it may be money spent in vain. For the structure is sinking and gapes open with huge cracks, either because the soil is damp and soft or the stone itself is poor and crumbly. It is certainly worth considering whether it should be finished, abandoned, or even demolished. For the foundations and substructure, by which the theatre was to be held up, do not appear so solid to me, although they are very expensive.[43]

The standard Roman foundation is a simple spread footing, a wall slightly broader than the superstructure it supports. Particularly heavy or many-walled buildings might have some form of a raft foundation, a solid or weblike bed of concrete or interlocked stone. The Colosseum is said to have a solid concrete raft under its travertine substructures, a feature made feasible by the prior excavation of much of the soil by Nero to create an artificial lake.[44] And the Red Hall at Pergamon rests on a raftlike foundation of concrete several meters wide.[45]

The construction of foundations and drains for Roman buildings was ordinarily quite different from the methods that have been suggested for the Baths of Caracalla or the Colosseum. It was initially a matter of digging vertical trenches down from floor level (or two

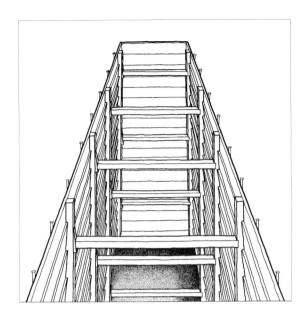

34. Wooden shutter-
ing for central-Italian
Roman foundation
construction.
Illustration: R. Taylor.

or three feet below it) to the chosen bedding for the foundation.
This created considerable instability, especially where trenches ran
narrow and deep, as for structural walls.[46] The typical Italian method, used for example on the Pantheon and the Basilica of Maxentius
in Rome, was to dig trenches shored up by a wooden framework of
posts and clapboards held against the opposing trench walls with
horizontal struts (Fig. 34).[47] Properly speaking this wooden shuttering was not formwork, as it is often called. It was designed structurally to resist pressure from without (i.e., the trench wall), not to
retain material from within (i.e., the concrete). Ultimately, however,
it accomplished both, and so it could not be removed either before
or after the pouring of the concrete. It was simply left in place, eventually to rot away. But the clapboard pattern remained in the vertical surfaces of the concrete, creating a jagged profile that bites into
the surrounding earth (Fig. 35). This keying effect was meant to
combat subsidence by maximizing the friction at the interface.

Using the ground-plan cords as a guide, workers dug their vertically walled trenches directly underneath, somewhat wider than the
wall plan. Upper struts or small gantries held pulleys for the buckets
of earth, which was either taken away in carts or added to the terracing; very little of it would return to the trenches. Periodically new
sections of shoring were added below the existing ones. Plumb lines
were referenced from the staked horizontal cords to ensure that the

trench continued downward on a vertical course. When a stopping point was determined (this could be anywhere from less than a meter down to fifteen meters or more), mortar and rubble were added in layers of about 30 cm, each tamped down to remove air pockets before receiving the next layer. In the trenches the concrete workers could operate without scaffolding, standing on boards extended between the struts or on the concrete rubble itself. Roman concrete exists in many formulas. Its classic formula is a slurry of lime and water well mixed with pozzolanic sand to form a reasonably consistent cement or mortar.[48] To this is added a coarse aggregate of stone or broken pottery or both at the time of application. Workers mixed these elements in pits or troughs at the construction site, taking care not to introduce dirt, ash, or other foreign substances.[49] Although I use the conventional term "pouring" to describe application, it is more accurately described as laying; it must to some extent be spread and evened out by hand. Pozzolanic concrete sets even underwater; thus it was possible to continue pouring in wet weather. Indeed, prolonged exposure to moisture and protection from temperature extremes, a process known as curing, improves the quality of the concrete dramatically. Temperature extremes and quick drying, not rain, are the nemesis of the concrete engineer.[50] Thus it was important to continue the pouring process throughout the day to minimize drying and temperature swings from the sun's radiant heat between pourings.

At some generally agreed-upon level, but still inside the trenches, the foundation wall ceased and a thinner substructure wall in finished masonry was begun on top of it. The masons, whether they worked from ladders or simply on rising earth fill, needed room to operate between the shuttering and the face of the wall they were erecting. This fact must have been taken into consideration when the foundation widths were established. As work progressed, the wooden transverse struts holding the shuttering in place were removed to make way for the walls, then replaced by earth or short struts set against the wall surface. Finally, when ground level was reached, the gaps on both sides of the walls were completely filled in. Substructure walls were often necessary in complex buildings because they, unlike solid concrete foundations, could be easily bonded and interpenetrated with other subterranean elements built in the same masonry technique, such as service galleries, cisterns, furnaces, hypocausts, and cryptoporticoes. Moreover, the interval between a

35. Rome: Palace of
Domitian, visible
concrete foundations.
Photo: R. Taylor.

substructure wall and the shuttering sometimes allowed room for
the construction of a parallel storm drain. Drains too were usually
done in traditional masonry.[51] Sometimes they were bonded to the
adjacent substructure and connected to lesser drains and downspouts that would continue up into the walls and floors above.[52]
Frequently a drain or a corridor would run directly through a substructure wall: One may often detect the position of a subfloor
storm drain by noting the relieving arch built into the wall just
above ground level.

   Drains that did not run parallel to walls were dug independently.
The main collector drain usually lay near the bottom of the foundation level, connected by vertical dropshafts to the secondary drains
at substructure level. It must often have been among the first elements completed, for even before it was connected to the building
it could have aided natural drainage of the site during construction.

WATER SUPPLY AND DRAINAGE

Abundant proof of high design in Roman architecture is the frequent presence of complex infrastructures that discourage evo-
lutionary changes in design during construction. Indeed the "genetic
map" of a grand building's form was seeded in the ground long be-

fore it would emerge into maturity. Many of the elements we asso-
ciate with modern infrastructure – water pipes and drains, flushing
toilets, central heating systems, service tunnels – existed in great
Roman buildings, their workings hidden underground, beneath
floors, and inside walls. From early times central Italians celebrated a culture of water. Like a cup under a funnel, Italian houses cap-
tured and cradled it in their depths. It was, in a sense, more central
to Roman life than fire. In time it became a prominent component
of architecture in its own right. Thousands of buildings in the Roman imperial period not only channeled and stored it but displayed
it abundantly. Water was a central and defining element of much
public and elite architecture – and not just baths and nymphaea.
Sculpture and sculptural niches were often fitted with fountain-
heads, water stairs, and overflow basins. Reflecting pools were stra-
tegically placed to mirror an attractive prospect or to divert a visitor
from a simple axial approach (see Figs. 148, 149). Elaborate networks of downspouts, gutters, and drains fed the subfloor drains,
where sometimes the concentrated volume was used to good effect
directly under latrines.

In extreme cases, as when a large public bath complex was introduced to a town, the entire water supply might have been planned
and constructed in conjunction with the building. More often water
was tapped from cisterns or an existing multipurpose aqueduct. In
any event, water management drew the architect's attention very
early in the design process, and the decisions made at this time were
essential determinants of the outcome. First he would need to determine the quantity of water available, how to get it, and how to reg-
ulate it. Once these extramural procedures were established, the
problems of distribution and drainage could be addressed. Roman
aqueducts operated on the principle of continuous flow. Distribution, achieved with networks of pipes branching out from subterranean mains to the waterworks in and around the building, was
a zero-sum game: More water in one part of the building meant
less in another. Problems of localized pressure and volume could be
solved at a later time. But to a large degree, decisions about distribution – particularly the locations and number of outlets, such as
fountains and pools – had to be made now, even before the laying
out of drains and supply conduits. In many cases the water supply
mains consisted of lead pipes installed along the inner walls of storm
drains running deep below the floor level, their branch pipes period-

ically penetrating the floor and continuing on their way to a terminus, which naturally was fitted with an overflow drain that eventually brought the water back underground.[53]

Inattention to the unglamorous matter of drainage has probably ruined more architectural projects than any single other failing. Once a building has been set upon a plot of land, one cannot simply presume the water that falls upon it, or is piped into it, will be absorbed into the earth. Good drainage is a science, but an inexact one. The problem is this: How does one ensure that all the water in a heavy, prolonged rainstorm – including the aqueduct water flowing continuously into the building – can be channeled off the premises without backing up or flooding? In many cases, as with some Roman temples set on high podia, no special measures were deemed necessary, and water was simply allowed to pour off the eaves of the building onto the ground. But other cases, especially in densely developed urban areas, where one large building's surface runoff could have inundated adjacent buildings, show far more attention to subterranean drainage. A treatise on aqueducts by Frontinus, the water commissioner of Rome under the emperor Trajan, reveals that the technology of the day allowed the measurement of water volume with some degree of precision. The architect needed to ensure that the principal collector drain(s) on the site, either existing or projected, would be adequate to handle the sum total of water. Their size, number, and distribution could be roughly calculated on the basis of the surface. But localizing water management was equally important: Working more from simple rules of thumb than from mathematical formulas,[54] the architect ensured that secondary drains feeding the principal drains likewise could handle the volume according to the surface area and hydraulic features to which they were assigned.

Our best sources of information on Roman drainage layouts are the buildings themselves. The Baths of Caracalla reveal a network of drains of various capacities, some principally for open courtyard areas and others to handle the water coming off the roofs in downspouts (Fig. 36).[55] The sixty-four exterior downspouts of the bath block, recessed in the walls themselves, were designed into the building from the beginning. They were set on average about fifteen meters apart all around the exposed surfaces of the building. Clearly a simple formula for volume of runoff had been established on the basis of the planned roof area.[56] Bowl-shaped buildings like amphi-

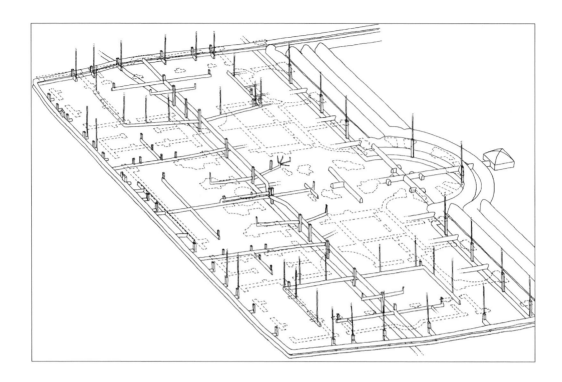

36. Rome: hydraulic and service armature of Baths of Caracalla, including downspouts and known drains. Dotted lines represent the plan of the walls at ground level. Illustration: R. Taylor.

theaters, circuses, and theaters, being especially vulnerable to poor drainage and even flooding, featured elaborate drain networks sometimes artfully tied in with the water supply. The Colosseum in Rome, like the Baths of Caracalla, received water in lead supply pipes attached to the inner walls of underground storm drains; that way, a subterranean leak would do no harm and was easily repaired. From there pipes ascended through the floors and vaults and up the walls to numerous fountains, some as high as the third level (see Chapter 3). The water traveled back along gutters and downspouts into the subterranean drains.

Perhaps the most carefully studied drainage system belongs to the large amphitheater of Pozzuoli, roughly contemporary with the Colosseum (Fig. 37, 38).[57] Rainwater falling on the outer parts, whether cascading off the facade or running into gutters and grilles positioned around the upper *cavea*, made its way into the radial outbound drains, marked *a'*, and then into deeper circumferential drains, marked *A*. Unlike their equivalents at the Colosseum, drains *A* are not continuous but end at each principal axis of the building. Amedeo Maiuri postulates that each of these four segments emptied into deeper radial drains *c'*, which led inbound to the principal

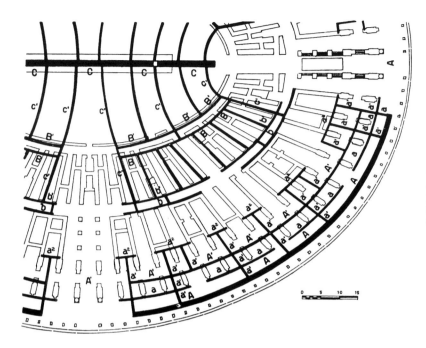

37. Pozzuoli: partial plan of Flavian amphitheater with drainage system. Maiuri 1955. By permission of Soprintendenza archeologica di Napoli.

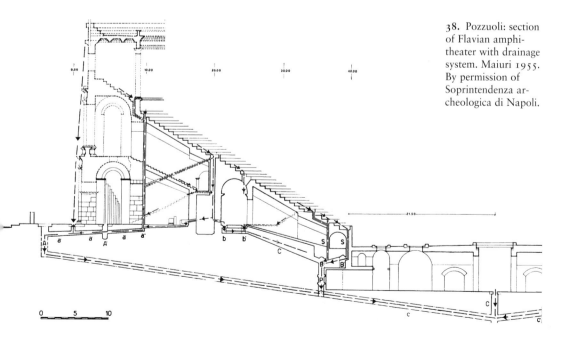

38. Pozzuoli: section of Flavian amphitheater with drainage system. Maiuri 1955. By permission of Soprintendenza archeologica di Napoli.

axial drain C at the center. In the lower part of the *cavea* the water made its way by various means to an independent network of radial and annular drains transporting the water inbound. At points *B* this water cascaded down about four meters into radial drains *c′*, where it merged with the water coming from the outer system. Axial drain *C* carried all the water from the precinct off to the sea. But this is not all: The amphitheater had no municipal water supply, and so the various fountains positioned within it were fed exclusively by cisterns that collected some of the rainwater from the upper *cavea*. Fountains and cisterns both would have been fitted with overflow drains leading down into the subterranean network. For the most part the drains, which are made of brick-faced concrete, parallel the foundations. The downspouts, being embedded in walls, would have been completely waterproof. In this case they were made of lead, but carefully mortared terra-cotta tubes could also have been used, as they often were in this region.

One may ask why a system as complex as Pozzuoli's was necessary. Why divert some of the rainwater outward only to have it flow back inward to rejoin the inbound water from another sector? Part of the answer is that the ratio of overall drain length to surface area does make a difference. A meandering course will accommodate more water at one time than a direct one. The gradient of the drains is not as critical as in free-flow aqueduct channels. A steeper system will not increase the volume of discharge (output always equals input, regardless of speed), but it will diminish the likelihood that the channels will fill with water and back up the system, and for this simple reason: When a given volume of water runs faster, it runs shallower. Despite the fundamental hydraulic difference between aqueducts and drains, the dimensions of both are similar. Collector drains of the sort featured at Pozzuoli, the Baths of Caracalla, and hundreds of other sites around the Roman world tend to be of a fairly uniform size, about 1.5–2 m high and roughly 1 m wide, to accommodate workmen for cleaning or repairs.

HYPOCAUSTS, FURNACES, AND SERVICE CORRIDORS

Roman subfloor heating systems, or *hypocausts*, play a less determinative role in a superstructure than do pipes and drains. Like floors, they are a static part of the building's design. Their disposition is essentially dictated by the superstructure and is thus un-

A. lime mortar
B. *tubuli*
C. crushed brick mortar
D. marble revetment
E. floor paving
F. mortar
G. subfloor mortar/concrete
H. tiles (*bipedales*)
I. brick pillars (*pilae*)
J. furnace opening
(*praefurnium*)

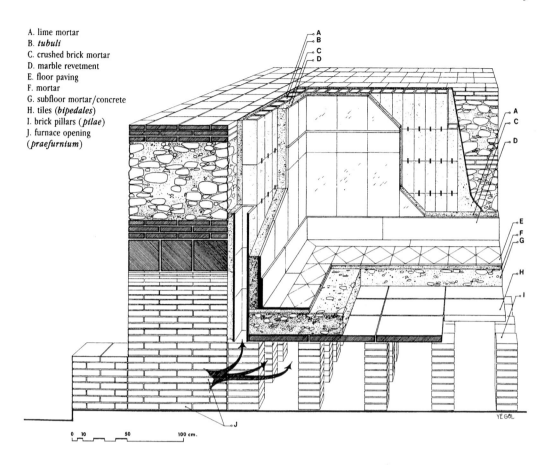

0 10   50   100 cm.

changeable after the substructures and lower walls have been set
out. Wherever the heated rooms are to be, there you will find the
hypocausts, along with their adjuncts: sunken furnaces, boilers, and
service galleries around the periphery, and bundles of interconnected terra-cotta tubes or "nippled" tiles (*tubuli* or *tegulae mammatae*)
covering the wall interiors and connecting the hypocaust's perimeter
to the chimneys above (Fig. 39). Very rarely an underfloor hypocaust system appears on a second level, as in the Fountain Court
West at Hadrian's Villa,[58] but its service system remains below
ground. The furnace(s) and adjoining galleries for service staff and
wood storage must be dug out and built at the same stage as the
substructures. The hypocausts and plunge pools themselves go no
deeper than about four feet below floor level, but the service corridors tend to begin at about the same level as intermediate storm
drains. In the Antonine Baths at Carthage unusually extensive service galleries formed an elaborate network of vaulted, six-meter-

39. Analytical cut-
away view of a
hypocaust system.
Yegül 1992. Courtesy
of F. Yegül.

40. Carthage: Antonine Baths, general view of subterranean corridors. Photo: R. Taylor.

deep underground rooms corresponding in plan to the rooms above (Fig. 40).[59] But usually furnaces and corridors were arranged around the outer periphery of the heated rooms, as at the Imperial Baths at Trier, Germany (Fig. 41). Ventilation of the service area was crucial, for fires without adequate convection would burn poorly. Air shafts, which also served as light wells, were therefore a regular feature of the galleries' vaulting. Hypocausts tend to cover the full extent of the floors above them, running just above the subfloor drains and forming a continuous void under the floors of the heated rooms (and sometimes the peripheral plunge pools as well). In effect, once the fires were lit the service galleries, furnaces, hypocausts, and wall vents all formed one labyrinthine continuum of voids channeling heat and air through the building's armature.

With the heating system two local issues concerned the architect: the even distribution of heat over well-defined floor areas and the regulation of temperature in the plunge pools. In the largest baths, separate furnaces controlled the hypocausts and the boilers. The capacity of each hypocaust furnace must have been gauged in terms of the maximum surface area, both of floor and walls, that it was expected to heat effectively. At the Baths of Caracalla at least twelve subfloor furnaces are thought to have served the hot rooms.[60] Because of the temperature limits of wood fires and their relative inefficiency at dispersing heat, the temperature of the rooms was more a function of the number and position of furnaces than of their size. The chimneys and furnaces must be relatively positioned such that

41. Trier: reconstructed cutaway view of imperial baths. Krencker 1929.

they draw the hot gases over as much distance as possible without dissipating the heat. While most hot rooms at the Baths of Caracalla settled for one or two furnaces each, the circular caldarium had eight furnaces directly under the central part of the floor. Numerous terra-cotta tubes connected to the hypocaust's peripheral walls ran up through the core of the piers; they formed a convection system like a spoked wheel, drawing hot gases from center to periphery.[61] Boilers too may have been gauged according to the water volume they could heat continuously at the desired temperatures.

The principal problem of heating, shared by water supply, is that the systems cannot be tested until the building is virtually finished. Architects must have designed flexibility into the system to allow for experimentation and calibration when the convection and boiler systems were in place. So conditioned were both systems by heat fluctuations and atmospheric conditions that they would have required continuous tinkering to perform their tasks well. There is no evidence that chimney flues were damped in any way, but there must have been ways to control air flow, perhaps by damping the furnace openings or the air shafts in the service corridors. Water was easier

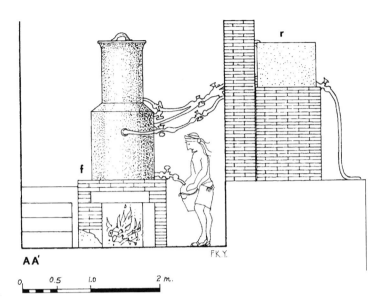

42. Boscoreale: Villa Rustica, furnace and boiler serving kitchen and baths. Yegül 1992. By permission of F. Yegül.

to control. Boilers and supply pipes all over the building would have been furnished with valves. A Roman boiler with a complex pipe-and-valve system found at a villa at Boscoreale near Pompeii gives some idea of what they were like (Fig. 42).

Most buildings with hypocaust heating had to provide three or four feet of subfloor clearance for the hypocausts and considerably more for the furnace network. In some cases the floors and even the hypocausts were built above ground level; Trier again serves as a well-known example (Fig. 43). But in many others hypocausts required earth removal and careful grading – though not necessarily at an early phase. Vaulted service corridors were typically built at the same time as the foundations or substructures, but hypocausts, being rather fragile and tending to obstruct work and traffic, must often have been left for completion until much of the heavy work on the superstructure had ceased.

FLOORS

Ground-level floors are the final feature of a building's sub-stratum. Unlike all the features that have gone before, they are essentially independent of the superstructure both physically and logistically. Having no substantial loads, they often have no foundations. Roman ground floors rest on rammed earth, the vaults of subterranean voids, or hypocaust pillars. Significantly, Vitruvius dis-

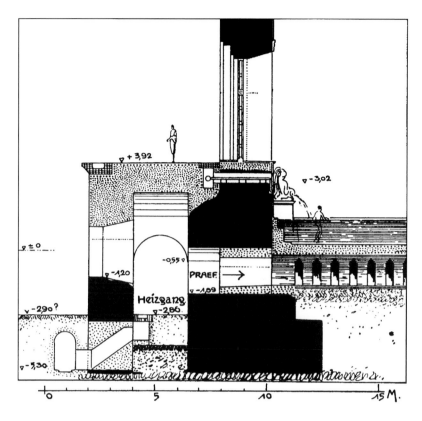

43. Trier: section through caldarium and external corridor of imperial baths. Krencker 1929.

cusses floors in his book on finishing – just before decorating techniques such as frescoes, stuccowork, and the like.[62] In planning, the floor is apt to play a subordinate role to a building's armature of walls, piers, and ceilings. Indeed, because it is essentially the liquescent matrix that conforms to the shape of any vessel into which it is introduced, it rarely influenced design or construction and must often have been laid after the majority of men, animals, and building materials had been cleared from the site. Still, in a sense the floor controls the plan and even the idea of a building. It is the datum level from which to measure and adjust vertical features; but more fundamentally it is the single feature – the *only* feature – without which no habitable building can exist. A building is a human artifact, and we are creatures of the ground. We feel the floor with every step as we perambulate a building. It informs our verticality and mediates the rightness of every element emerging from it or suspended above it. Anyone who has climbed the Tower of Pisa will come away appreciating the primordial necessity of a level floor, its importance in our spatial orientation and our sense of place. It is the thing upon which all architectural design is predicated.

In Roman buildings the floor is often massive, its thickness commonly exceeding two feet to eliminate or minimize subsidence and cracking. In effect, whether it rests on bare earth or on vaults or pillars it becomes its own raft foundation, deflecting and distributing weight in all lateral directions. Vitruvius' procedure for floor construction, though subject to much variation, conforms approximately to real life.[63] The first step, if the floor was to be laid on earth, was to ram the earth down and then grade it roughly to level, perhaps by shaving away at rises and ramming the shavings into depressions. A thick underlayer of mortared rubble was spread on top of this and rammed to eliminate air pockets and even out the surface. Above this was laid a thinner stratum of crushed terra cotta mixed with slaked lime to form a waterproof hydraulic cement. Having few large chunks of aggregate, this could be spread with a large flat trowel, much like modern cement. At this point Vitruvius exhorts the builder to lay the pavement "to the square and to the level" – not, however, to make it perfectly horizontal but to ensure that it has a subtle incline to facilitate the runoff of water or – in the case of the lower surface of hypocausts – the rise of the hot gases from the furnace. For the paving of upper-story floors he specifies an incline of 1:80. Floor gradients are not easy to see with the naked eye but are readily mapped out if we use Vitruvius' diagnostic tool, a rolling ball.[64] Skilled masons were probably able to lay a steady gradient approximating 1:80 with nothing more than their leveling squares and trowels, as Vitruvius suggests.

Suspended floors were likely to be as thick as those laid directly on the earth. For concrete pavements on joisted wooden floors, Vitruvius recommends an overall thickness of more than a foot. In baths and other heated buildings, the floors laid over hypocausts are up to a foot thick to prevent users from burning their feet.[65] Though Vitruvius recommends vigorously ramming the underlayer of pavements on ordinary wooden floors, this could not have been done on hypocausts, for the concrete was laid directly on a fragile layer of *bipedales* (thin bricks two feet square) which were propped upon the hypocaust pillars only at the corners (see Fig. 39). If the whole floor had been poured wet all at once, the weight of the liquid mass might have broken the bricks and sent the concrete crashing down into the hypocaust. The concrete must have been applied in layers, each adding to the floor's overall tensile strength as it set; or, as in the Trajanic latrines at the Forum Iulium in Rome, two layers of *bipedales* were used to add strength.[66]

Though in practice it may be completed late in the building process sequentially, in theory the ground floor is the datum of what lies both below and above. It is the goal and culmination of the substructure and the logical premise from which the superstructure emerges: the *terminus post quem* and the *terminus ante quem*. As this study follows a cognitive sequence rather than a strictly real one, we now may assume that the floor has been laid (though not yet decorated) and proceed to the next step in the sequence – the building of walls, piers, and columnar orders.

3

WALLS, PIERS, AND COLUMNS

The reciprocities established among materials [brick and concrete] and their functions both during and after actual construction were ingenious. Orderly procedures are necessary to all successful monumental construction, but the Romans mass-produced building materials and investigated their efficient and appropriate uses to a greater degree than any pre-industrial people. The ancient Latin principle of order, the instinctive habit of trying to put men and things in their proper places of service, lay behind this.[1]

– William L. MacDonald

The temples of Baalbek owe nothing of their quality to such new-fangled aids as concrete. They stand passively upon the largest hewn stones in the world, and some of their columns are the tallest from antiquity. There were once others at Cyzicus in the north which beat them by an inch or two, but Cyzicus is in limbo. Here at Baalbek we have the last great monument in the outworn trabeate tradition of the Hellenic world. And yet how new it is. . . . It is new because of its magnitude and of the challenge which magnitude has thrown to the architect.[2]

– Mortimer Wheeler

Either concrete or stone, often both, dominated the scene when a Roman building emerged from the ground. We begin with faced concrete. It is the material that opened the way for the Roman architectural revolution of the first and second centuries of our era – not, perhaps, because of its structural properties but because of its sculptural plasticity and responsiveness to architectural expression. The Baths of Caracalla are today one of the best-known and best-studied buildings in this medium (Figs. 44, 45).[3] And though they postdate the revolution, they follow essentially the same design principles, materials, and scale of one of the masterpieces of that era, the Baths of Trajan, built a century earlier. What makes the later baths so valuable is their combination of high complexity, a reasonably good state of preservation, and the exposure of the original building materials. Also, they continue in the Roman imperial tradition of high design: Their immense central bath block was completed in a very short time, no more than seven years.[4]

Let us then remain with this instructive edifice for our discussion of the generation of vertical features in Roman building. In a project of such complexity the joining of substructure and superstructure is a matter of great importance. Their line of connection constitutes a zone of transfer – not only of vertical loads but of the rising and falling of media exploited by the building's utilities, commonly water and the hot gases of hypocaust heating. Because the juncture usually coincides with a floor level, it is a zone of horizontal transition as well: the passage of human beings through doorways, corridors, and colonnades. Further above, there are additional planes and lines of horizontal interpenetration: upper-story passages and colonnades, windows, niches, and so forth. Obviously these vertical and horizontal transitions must not coincide unless by design; and so every drain, pipe, and heating duct respects the autonomy of every void, niche, arch and lintel, sill and threshold. The inception and construction of a Roman wall is not unlike weaving at a loom. Stretched vertically in the planner's mind are the warp strands, the wall's vertical solids and their infrastructure; shuttling between them, the artifacts of human extension: lines of vision and locomotion. Occasional mistakes can be traced in the patterned fabric, most often in the lateral jog of a downspout or flue around an unanticipated feature in the wall.[5] The digression always appears be-

44. Rome: Baths of Caracalla, reconstructed cutaway view. Illustration: V. Rauscher, 1894.

low the void, recording for posterity the sequence of recognition, reassessment, and remedy. Roman vaulted design is such that the voids can achieve a vastness all out of proportion to their function as perforations in the plane of a wall. Walls are frequently reduced to piers separating and defining the vast arched bays that came to dominate many monumental enclosures. In these cases the piers supported not only the vaults but much of the infrastructure as well; bundled around their surfaces and within their cores were the tubes of the building's vascular system.

In conventional Roman buildings walls and piers generally follow the foundation footprint up to the roofing level. This is true even in multistoried apartment buildings, such as the famous insulae of Ostia.[6] Relatively little surveying is needed above ground level. The issues of concern are in the altimetric sphere, and for this the surveying instrument, stadia rod, and sweeping line are rarely necessary. Only the measuring rod or cord is retained. The other tools of wall construction work on a more local scale. These are plumb lines, levels, and squares. Simply by measuring and aligning elements in the vertical and horizontal dimensions, builders were able to translate elevation drawings into upright features in brick, mortar, and stone.

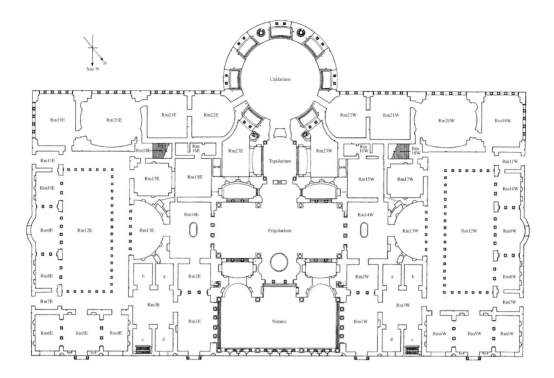

In a typical imperial bath building, walls and piers have at least four primary elements of structural design and many other secondary, or introduced, elements. The primary elements are

1 brick facing;
2 concrete core;
3 voids that pass through the wall's thickness, such as doors and windows; and
4 solids that pass through the wall's thickness, such as clear-span arches, relieving arches, and bonding courses.

The secondary elements, which usually do not affect the wall's structure, include

1 enclosed voids such as stairwells and narrow service passages;
2 downspout grooves and chimney flues in the brick facing;
3 terra-cotta downspout tubes and chimney flues in the concrete core for inner walls;
4 grooves for pipes and drains serving waterworks;
5 embedded carved stone elements for the columnar orders;
6 box tiles for the heating system; and

45. Rome: Baths of Caracalla, plan of central block. DeLaine 1997. By permission of J. De-Laine and *Journal of Roman Archaeology*.

7 putlog holes, roughly aligned gaps in the brick facing for anchoring the masons' scaffolding to the rising wall.

SECONDARY ELEMENTS OF THE WALLS AND PIERS

The secondary elements can be immensely complex. At the Baths
of Caracalla, at least seventy-eight vertical channels with various functions (downspouts, fountain drains, chimney flues) have
been identified in the wall and pier surfaces. Twenty-six others
have been recognized in the concrete core, and dozens more remain
unseen.[7] The putlog holes form an irregular grid over every brick
surface progressing from small perforations of the brick to larger
squared holes that pass through the entire thickness of some walls.
Box tiles once lined the inner surfaces of the hot-room walls and
piers for the circulation and convection of hypocaust heating. Narrow passages burrow almost invisibly inside the upper levels of
some of the walls and piers, bypassing both the wall-piercing transverse voids and the vertical tubes. Winding staircases bore upward
through some of the piers all the way to roof level. Except for the
putlog holes all of these elements depended on a careful plan of the
building's infrastructure, a "blueprint" that could be consulted and
refined during construction.[8] Downspout grooves and tubes were
rarely set with absolute symmetrical precision, but their placement
– already established at substructure level – relied on a confident
knowledge of the configuration of door and window voids and other obstacles that would emerge above. Each may have carried off
water collected on about 250–400 m² of roof surface.[9]

I label all these elements secondary because on the whole they do
not contribute to the building's visual design scheme and participate
only minimally in its structural regime. They are subordinate to the
masses and voids, and their design doubtless came second to the
more sculptural aspects of the building's form. In the actual building
process, they had to receive equal treatment; inattention to these details was likely to be costly later. To the mason, all interruptions in
the routine carried equal status. The continuous vertical elements,
once set into the floor plan at ground level, would require few additional reminders as the wall or pier was erected: Their continual imprint in the vertical progress of the masonry was reminder enough.
But in many cases their character was altered, if only momentarily.
For example, eight meters above floor level in the walls surrounding

three sides of the palaestrae, a continuous stone cornice that would support the barrel vaults was embedded into the walls. This forced the surface downspout grooves to retreat into the core of the walls in order to get past them, and then to return to the surface above.[10] The digression introduced four ninety-degree turns into each spout. Such interruptions are not unusual, and they are frequently so well resolved that it is hard to decide whether they are a situational remedy or part of the original building plan.

PRIMARY ELEMENTS OF THE WALLS AND PIERS

This chapter focuses on the primary elements of wall construction and the integration of columnar orders. The walls and piers of the Baths are built entirely of *opus latericium*, brick-faced concrete. Over time and distance the Romans used a number of different facing materials and techniques for their concrete buildings, but all shared certain properties. The materials consisted of small, portable elements hand-set with mortar to create vertical outer faces for the wall. These facings served as a mold into which the concrete or rubbled fill was introduced in layers. Various explanations have been offered for the Roman insistence on facings. The most likely reasons for their use are that they allowed the masons to build walls without wooden formwork, and that by retaining the moisture in the concrete core they aided in the curing process. Structurally, *opus latericium* has little to recommend it over the older Roman facing techniques, which consisted of small stones set in mortar. However, the brick-and-mortar skin provided better insulation for curing. And being thicker than its predecessors, it created a stronger, more rigid container during the pouring and setting process, when the liquid concrete generated outward thrusts against it. Superior retaining capacity allowed the concrete to be introduced in larger and less frequent batches. The process was not without danger: The masons might load more concrete on top of it before it was fully hardened, forcing the semiliquid core outward and deforming the brick facing. It has been suggested that "bonding courses" were introduced to deter just such a problem – an issue with which I deal momentarily.

The brick of *opus latericium* is fired clay mixed with various kinds of aggregate, usually pozzolana or ordinary sand. Brick of this kind was used in central Italy from at least the Augustan period,[11] and fired-clay roof tiles and decorative plaques had been in constant use for centuries before that. Yet fired brick was not the most familiar of materials to Vitruvius, who speaks mostly of adobe bricks and roof tiles modified into bricks. The vast potential of fired clay as a wall facing seems to have been widely recognized only in the following generation. Of the value of concrete Vitruvius was fully persuaded, if still somewhat cautious.[12] Technically, cured Roman concrete is a compound, not a mixture. In other words, it has uniform mechanical properties with no significant weaknesses of bonding between its components.[13] Brick and mortar are a mixture. The weakness of their bond is evident in the traditional practice of laying bricks horizontally in staggered rows. Dead loads tend to pull walls apart horizontally, generating vertical cracks. If bricks were laid vertically on edge, they would be vulnerable to separating from their mortar courses.[14] When laid in traditional overlapping fashion they resist vertical splitting by creating "stitched" vertical seams, which generate much more resistance to the horizontal tensile stress.

Fully understanding this principle, Roman builders took its logic one step further: If the bricks were well bonded to the concrete core, perhaps their resistance to cracking could be transmitted to the core as well. Or conversely, the core's nature as a highly coherent, monolithic compound could hold the bricks together. How then did one achieve the maximum bond between facing and core? Earlier techniques, such as *opus incertum* and *opus reticulatum,* led the way: Their elements were shaped like small cones or pyramids, the tapering end set inward to create a toothed bonding surface. With brick, Roman masons devised the method of sawing or breaking the square bricks diagonally and facing the hypotenuses outward (Fig. 46).[15] The opposite angles dug deeper into the core than the older facings, creating a toothed effect on the inside that increased the strength of the bond with the concrete. There was also an economic advantage: Compared to cutting and laying half-bricks orthogonally, the corner-to-corner diagonal face, being the longest cross section of the brick, reduced the overall number of bricks by more than 40 percent. Of course this reduction required a proportional increase in mortar and concrete fill, but these were cheaper and more readily available materials. By the Severan period, however, builders mostly had settled on roof tiles or *sesquipedales* (square bricks with one-and-a-half-foot sides) roughly broken on two or three sides to form trapezoidal shapes.[16] They offered enough variety to provide a strong bond with the concrete core.

46. Rome: concrete-and-brick construction method of the imperial period. G.-B. Piranesi, *Le antichità romane* (Rome 1756).

A *Mattoni quadrati, fegati a linee diagonali per formare i Mattoni triangolari. Di questi mattoni triangola-ri fono coftruiti i muri de'Portici dell'Uftrino; ficome ancora la maggior parte delle Fabbriche antiche. B Muro de'Porti-ci dell'Uftrino, compofto di detti mattoni triangolari, a riferva degli angoli, i quali fono formati di mattoni biflun-ghi quadrati. Di dentro egl'è riempiuto di calce, pozzolana, fcaglie, e pezzi di mattoni; polla ogni cofa fempre con av-vertenza in piano. C Superficie formata dai lati maggiori de'mattoni triangolari. D Superficie formata da corfi di grofsi Tufi tramezzati da altrettanti corfi di mattoni. E Muro della Fabbrica fuppofta del Magiftrato, coftruito di mattoni triangolari, e riempitura di calce e fcaglie. Offervafi la detta riempitura ogni tre palmi di altezza effere laftricata, e mofsa in piano orientale da un corfo di calce, e fcaglie minute di marmo F. G Muro dell'Abitazione de'Cu-ftodi coftruito di mattoni triangolari, calce, tavolozza, e fcaglie di Tufo.   Piranesi Archit. dis.se inc.*

Once the lowest course was set out, complete with recesses for downspouts and gaps for doorways, the survey lines and stakes could be removed. Much additional information would be necessary at higher elevations, but these could be carefully monitored by the master builders. Brick-faced concrete walls progressed quickly, but there were limits to the speed of progress due to the curing cycle of the concrete. This could take many days or weeks, during which time the bricklayers were able to occupy themselves with the next stage of the wall facing or with another part of the project. Let us now envision the routine procedure.

On both sides of the unfinished wall workers secured scaffolding to it by laying the bricks and concrete around and over the projecting putlogs, which were lashed to vertical standards (Fig. 47). The putlogs were not, as is often believed, jammed into the holes in the masonry; instead (whether or not they ran through the wall's entire thickness) the logs were erected in place before the masonry reached their level, and the masonry was laid around them.[17] When beginning a new level, workers set boards across a set of projecting putlogs just below the existing level of the top of the wall, creating the working surface. Before the new brickwork was begun, the scaffolding framework was extended up to the next level. This fulfilled two purposes: to hang pulleys on the outside for hoisting materials in baskets from the ground and to hang plumb lines on the inner side. To either side of a single mason's assigned workspace (perhaps little more than an arm span)[18] the plumb lines were suspended at a short, even distance from the wall surface to guide the vertical progress of the new brickwork. Two horizontal guidelines may have been run along the top as well, designating the stopping point. With a straight rod or a keen eye, the mason could periodically check his work against these lines. Each mason would lay down a full course of mortared bricks, ensuring that it met up neatly with his neighbor's work. At the edges of his workspace he might have to shorten the length of a brick to accommodate his neighbor; a couple of practiced taps with a hammer would do the job. Then another row of mortared bricks, and so on. Somewhere below the finishing point, the team of masons would install the next set of putlogs. These were aligned with the partial scaffolding that had already been erected for the plumb lines. Bricklaying proceeded up to a comfortable stopping point, perhaps chest or chin level. Because masons working on opposite faces had no need to interact except in the event of a through void in the wall, the exact number of courses they laid varied.

Methods of applying concrete were not uniform. The rubble aggregate was sometimes thrown in at random, at other times arranged horizontally.[19] In thin walls, the brickmasons themselves may have added the concrete to the core incrementally, after every few brick courses. Thicker walls and piers probably had larger and less frequent applications, during which alternate batches of fresh mortar and rubble were introduced into the gap. Workers standing inside or above arranged the stone aggregate evenly and rammed

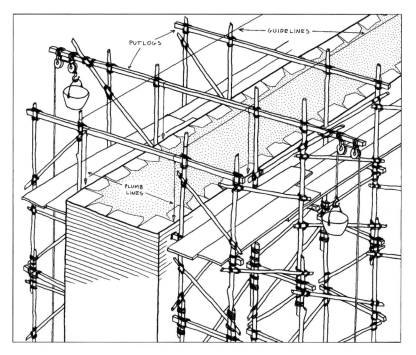

47. Roman scaffold-
ing with continuous
putlogs. Illustration:
R. Taylor.

the compound with timbers to remove air pockets. Finally, when the
concrete had reached the top, a final bonding course, or through-
course, of bricks was laid across the entire upper surface. The concrete was allowed to set, and then the whole process was repeated.

On a macroscopic scale, teams of brickmasons did not always
progress in perfect harmony. Examined carefully, Roman buildings
in brick-faced concrete show traces of different bricklaying styles
and materials. Periodically separate teams would meet up, usually
at corners or over large voids, cobbling together their incompatible
brickwork improvisationally. These seams reveal an uneven mesh-
ing of bricks, slight shifts in the heights of bonding courses, even
changes in brick color and thickness.[20] Joins in the middle of walls
are visible at the Markets of Trajan, where abrupt seams in the masonry work at horizontal intervals of about eleven feet have been
recorded.[21] Presumably these were the workspaces of pairs of masons operating from the center of each zone to the edges.

BONDING COURSES

Bonding courses, which are among the most distinctive elements
of imperial brickwork in central Italy from the Flavian period until the late third century, deserve a closer look. They are sin-

gle horizontal courses of large square bricks (*bipedales*) that run through the entire thickness of the wall (Fig. 48).[22] The length of their sides, and sometimes their color, makes them immediately recognizable in an otherwise featureless wall. They are usually set at vertical intervals ranging from three to five Roman feet. There are no consistent rules for their use at any period.[23] At the Baths of Caracalla, they are set about four and a half Roman feet apart, with some variation. Designed to support vaults over their intervening spaces, the walls are typically six Roman feet thick, requiring three *bipedales* in cross section. Thus only two out of every three bricks were bonded to the facing; the inner brick "floated" free in the core, resting directly upon and under the concrete fill. Bonding courses appear in many central-Italian imperial structures from the Flavian period onward. But Trajan's architects in Rome occasionally avoided them.[24] They were not considered essential to monumental construction, yet builders found them desirable. Why?

The problem is nicely summarized and refined by DeLaine.[25] The only thing on which most authorities agree about bonding courses is that they represent the interval between a concrete pouring phase and the laying of the brick facing for the next wall stage. Further explanations tend toward either the physical or the diagnostic. Physically, bonding courses served:

1 to prevent undue settling of a mass of wet concrete by creating new "floors" for each stratum;
2 to "top off" a day's work of bricklaying and concrete pouring, thus sealing in the underlying stratum while it was curing; and
3 as a convenient surface on which to place woodwork such as scaffolding putlogs and centering for arches and vaults.

Diagnostically, they served:

4 as guides to keep the walls truly vertical and their courses truly horizontal; and
5 as modular vertical measures so that the masons did not have to measure heights from the ground up.

Explanation 1 may have testimonial support. In the same letter that complains of the settling theater foundations in Nicea, Pliny gripes about a professional disagreement over the completion of a gymnasium: "an architect – to be sure, a rival of the one who started the structure – contends that the walls, even though 22 feet thick,

48. Rome: Baths of Caracalla, modern restoration of a cross section of a spur wall with visible bonding courses. Photo: R. Taylor.

cannot support the loads placed on them because the core, which is packed with rubble, is not overlaid with brick."[26] This report is more remarkable than it seems. The letter was written to Trajan, whose builders in Rome were not uniformly enthusiastic about bonding courses. Pliny seems to record a genuine philosophical disagreement within the profession during his time. It is interesting that the local dispute recorded by Pliny took place in Nicea, a town near the North Anatolian Fault. "Bonding" courses have the opposite effect in earthquakes, creating discontinuities in the concrete that can cause horizontal slipping and rotating.[27] Perhaps the initial architect of the Nicea gymnasium had this dynamic issue in mind when rejecting bonding courses, whereas his successor was more concerned with statics.

What static advantages does this feature have? By artificially stratifying the concrete in the wall's core, it is argued, bonding courses minimized deformation created by the settling of the unstable liquid mass while it was setting. An apt analogy is a warehouse, its many stories laden from floor to ceiling with contents that have a tendency to settle just after they have been put in place: The bonding courses are the floors, the concrete is the stacks of wares. But what possible resistance could a single layer of bricks, some of them floating free in the wall's center, have against the dead weight of the concrete above them? If the concrete was actually settling – and nobody has shown that it ever did – the bonding courses would have given way without resistance. Pliny notes that the walls were twenty-two feet thick; that makes them thicker than the Pantheon's, and subject to nine floating rows of *bipedales* within the core! The only static advantage that a bonding course could conceivably have, it seems, is compressive strength: Like travertine, brick bonding courses often appear at the springings of arches and vaults. This is more a perceived than an actual advantage.

Explanation 2 is also interesting. DeLaine has argued that four and a half vertical feet of brickwork followed by concrete work could not possibly have been achieved in a day. But the only important phase in this model is the concrete pouring, which could definitely have been done in less than a day, leaving time to top off the work with a protective layer of bricks. What were the bonding courses protecting the concrete *from?* Roman pozzolanic concrete benefits from a moist environment as it hardens. Its matrix is hydraulic cement, which sets underwater just as it does in open air, by converting water and lime into hydrated silicates. It does not shed water by evaporation,[28] and its core and surfaces harden at a relatively uniform rate if it is allowed to shed heat more or less uniformly. The more beneficial climatological effect of bonding courses was to keep out the sun or frost and to lock in moisture.[29] This would help to slow down the hydration process and maintain the entire mass of concrete at an even temperature, minimizing the expansions and contractions that can cause weakening cracks in a setting compound. Explanation 3 is perhaps the most comprehensive of the three, and it is strengthened by the frequent correlation between bonding courses and windowsills, arch haunches, and vaults, not to mention the putlog holes for scaffolding. It also meshes with 2, as DeLaine observes: While a section of wall is curing, the masons can give way to the carpenters for the erection of centering and the next level of scaffolding. Relieving arches in particular relied on

centering that must have been constructed through the full thickness
of the wall, and was most effectively set directly on a smooth and
even platform.[30] The third rationale also meshes with explanation
1 if we completely recast the bonding courses' role as compressive
elements (imposts for arches and vaults) rather than tensile or bending elements ("floors in the warehouse").

Now we come to the diagnostic properties. Explanation 4 presumes that bonding courses served as a visual aid to keep walls
straight and level. Keeping the courses horizontal longitudinally and
transversely was certainly desirable, since windowsills and lintels,
vaults, and so forth relied on them. But levelness of this sort could
have been achieved without a transverse platform through the core.
DeLaine suggests that one purpose of the courses was to ensure that
the walls were built to a true vertical.[31] If we discredit the old explanation 1 (bonding courses deter structural deformation), it is hard
to see how they would achieve this goal any better than a simple
plumb line. After all, a through course can be perfectly level yet still
project out or recess inward from the course below it, marring the
verticality of the face. (It can, however, assist in maintaining a uniform wall thickness.) Explanation 5, that the lines of *bipedales* function as vertical modular measures, is, I think, the most interesting
of all. But as DeLaine herself admits it cannot account for the origins of bonding courses, which in the Flavian period were set at irregular intervals with no evident mensural interrelationship. Nor
does it account for the "floaters" deep in the core of the wall. This
diagnostic function clearly evolved from a more physically oriented
purpose. In the Markets of Trajan at least one bonding course seems
to have been used as a benchmark and platform for surveying elements higher up.[32]

At the Baths of Caracalla the bonding courses should be seen not
only as linear measures but also as measures of quantity. They are
rather evenly spaced, not only in absolute terms (about four and a
half Roman feet apart) but also with respect to numbers of courses,
on average about twenty. The sides of the *bipedales* are two Roman
feet long, and thus the course can serve as a linear horizontal measure to complement the known vertical module. The amount of brick
needed for a section of wall could be easily estimated on this basis:
For example, twenty courses of diagonally halved *bessales* at twenty
linear feet would require about 850 units on both sides combined.
If the bricks were to be orthogonally halved, they would number

about 1,200. Concrete volume would have been calculated in similar terms. Most of the arithmetic could be dispensed with after a couple of trial runs: Those responsible for requisitioning materials would memorize the volumes and amounts needed per linear foot. Windows and doors are usually of a regular width in Roman feet, keeping the subtractive arithmetic simple.

It would appear, then, that the 4.5-foot module is the calculated result of a heuristic process. Begun as a perceived benefit to structural design, and apparently maintained as such for two centuries, bonding courses expanded their function when other benefits became apparent. By the Severan period they had become the carefully placed bookmarks suited to a number of parallel narratives: concrete pourings, scaffolding additions, centering for arches and vaults, and perhaps the regular requisitioning of basic materials. On a more global level, the regularization of bonding courses would have allowed the master builders to monitor overall progress.

RELIEVING ARCHES AND WINDOWS

Bonding courses are natural windowsills. One of their virtues is that they bring the work of opposing masons into temporary agreement on the leveling of their courses. The masons try to maintain this agreement through the entire height of a window void, since their courses must turn inward at the window's edges and meet in the center of the jambs. A subsidiary effect is that adjacent masons, if they are working on opposite sides of a door or window, no longer need to mesh their courses. As a result, they often get out of alignment and must be reconciled above the lintel or relieving arch. In effect, masons alternate between maintaining vertical consistency with their lateral neighbors and with their opposing neighbors. This tends to have a chain effect that regularizes the procedure over the construction of the entire wall. Thus bonding courses may contribute obliquely to building economics not only by providing a quick measure for estimating materials consumption but by actually contributing to the regularization of procedure that makes those models predictable. All masons working on a wall will learn very quickly what the desired thickness of a mortar bed should be, and how many regular courses should be laid between bonding courses.

It is no surprise, then, that many of the windows in the Baths begin at these courses. However, they do not end in a similarly predictable manner. Sometimes their lintel arches, or relieving arches above those, appear to spring from bonding courses, but not consistently. Ground-level doors are somewhat more consistent: Many of their lintels and relieving arches spring at or near the third or fourth bonding course above floor level. It would seem that the module was being used in two slightly different ways. Having only one variable limit in the vertical dimension, the top, the heights of doors were controlled by the module. Windows, however, were modular only with regard to position, not to height: They were begun at the nearest bonding course to their planned lower limit, but their upper limits were determined by measurements from the sill, not by the nearest bonding course to their planned height.

Every void and arch in the wall represented a break in the routine. To commence a window, the mason could have hung new plumb lines from the inner scaffolding. One of these would have been measured from a datum point, probably the extreme end of the room on which he was working. (Niches, doors, and windows tend to be measured in whole Roman feet from interior corners of rooms.) The jamb lines would be etched in the top surface of the bonding course after its perpendicularity to the wall's surface had been checked with a square. Opposing masons would begin work at the center of the jamb, each turning the corner with the right angle of a half-brick (either diagonally sawn or not). Progress on the void would continue upward through as many bonding courses and concrete pourings as necessary. Near the top, according to DeLaine's sequencing of tasks, arched wooden centering would be laid across the void, propped on the jambs, for construction of the relieving arch. (For this no bonding course was needed.) The lintel arch underneath it, forming the upper limit of the window, was completed afterward on separate centering. The zone between these arches was then constructed in ordinary *opus latericium*, its final upper courses carefully wedged into the curve of the relieving arch soffit.[33]

DeLaine's model, which rests on careful observation of the bonding of a few arches to the walls below, cannot have been the norm. In many other buildings, and even in the Baths, the arch curves can be highly irregular, suggesting that the brickmasons constructed them directly on top of the rising wall without centering. Centering is unnecessary and time-consuming, and requires cumbersome tasks such as infilling cut brick and concrete into the narrowing gap between wall and arch. However, sensational new evidence in Rome

49. Rome: Baths of Caracalla, niche in west oval room containing bowed arch. The brick facing is mostly modern. Photo: R. Taylor.

has confirmed DeLaine's sequence in one other famous Roman monument. In the recently discovered zone of the Golden House of Nero on the Oppian Hill encompassing the now-famous "city fresco," inscribed dates have been found on various parts of walls and arches. These leave no doubt that the relieving arches were built on centering before their spans were filled with masonry.[34]

In at least one class of relieving arches a centering scheme would have required elaborate formwork partially propped on the ground, whereas a layered sequence of construction would have caused no problems whatever. These are arches of the "bowed" variety. Though most arches at the Baths are in a single plane, a few are in cylindrical walls and thus have pronounced curves not only in elevation but also in plan. Arches of this kind, which date back at least to the mid-first century, almost never appear in stone except in very gently curved walls of considerable thickness, such as the facades

50. Baiae: reconstructed interior view of annex of "Temple of Venus." Wilson-Jones 2000. By permission of Yale University Press.

of theaters and amphitheaters. And with good reason: They are patently unstable. Any true arch whose crown projects beyond the vertical plane of its haunches cannot effectively transfer its load to that plane. It will tend to deform or fail unless it is part of a more or less monolithic mass that absorbs most of the load. The relieving arches in the corner niches of the south oval rooms fit the latter category, but their construction would have required some care. They describe a nearly 180-degree arc in plan as well as elevation (Fig. 49). Any putative centering would have exceeded the thickness of the arch itself, constituting in essence a half-cylinder over which the arch was draped in a diagonal loop. The front of the cylinder, saddled by the crown, would have required an independent prop from below until the infilling was complete. Bowed voids have survived intact in curved bath walls and (as semidomed niches) in the annex of the "Temple of Venus" at Baiae (Fig. 50).[35]

Relieving arches are a widespread phenomenon in Roman architecture. Their actual effectiveness is debated, but the intended purpose is obvious: The arches are meant to serve as load-umbrellas, deflecting downward thrusts to either side of a vulnerable spot beneath them, usually a void in the wall. To achieve this effect they must be physically differentiated from the surrounding wall. Here the knowledge that brick and mortar are a mixture, not a compound, may have been applied to structural design. Typically on the wall faces, complete square bricks (or orthogonally halved ones) and thin wedges of mortar were laid on edge upon wooden centering as if they were voussoirs, the independent wedge-shaped elements that constitute a classic arch. In the core zone, "voussoirs" of concrete alternated with brick dividers, also set on edge. At the Baths, brick was laid continuously through the core area, but whole bricks alternated with clusters of partial bricks, the remaining space being filled with concrete.[36] The weakness of the bond between brick and mortar was apparently thought to mimic the action of a true arch, whose independent voussoirs, by transmitting loads obliquely across the bearing surfaces with their neighbors, created an efficient compressive system while minimizing the kind of tensile and shear stresses that cause cracking in ordinary monolithic lintels.

Whether such rationalizations are valid is still a matter of lively dispute.[37] Mainstone suggests that no brick-and-mortar arch functioned as a true arch, observing that robbed brick arches leave the concrete vaults above them unharmed. This appears to be correct; indeed, the unexpected durability of even bowed clear-span arches in brick, mortar, and concrete, a durability that is never matched in other materials, remains for all to admire. Some ancient architects and builders must have intuited the redundancy of the brick arch within the medium of *opus latericium,* but there was never a universal formula for the application of *relieving* arches. They were slowly phased out over the third century as builders recognized their dispensability.

In the Baths, relieving arches were only slightly wider in span than the voids they "protected." But vertical distances between arch and void varied considerably. In walls that supported vaults, several tiers of arches were common. The rear walls of the palaestra exedrae, for example, carried three eight-foot-radius relieving arches in tiers over the doors, each springing from a bonding course. Indeed many arches of all kinds have radii of standard lengths (e.g., 30, 25, 12, 8, or 6 Roman feet). Many arched windows, including some very large ones, had no relieving arches. Instead, their upper limits consisted of double arches of *bipedales.*

The brickmasons' work on the Baths of Caracalla was all but complete when all the walls reached roof level. In preparation for the vaults the level of the walls was checked and a final bonding course was laid. But before we proceed to vaulting (in Chapter 5) we must consider the other major ingredient of the building's supportive armature: the stone columnar orders.

STONE ELEMENTS

As many great monuments around the empire attest, building in solid stone continued to flourish throughout the imperial period.[38] Stone carried special status. It sometimes came from exotic places and usually bore the brunt of a building's ideological message, whether in reliefs and inscriptions or the more intuitive geometries of *romanitas,* such as the massive squareness of a triumphal arch or the wedding-cake frippery of a multitiered aedicular facade. Stone was the only structural material that was also fully decorative, yet it was not therein an economical material. Instead its heft and substance betokened a similarly generous outlay of skilled craftsmanship, heavy engineering, and expense.

The subtlety and skill of the best Roman stonemasons still excites admiration. Particularly in the Greek-speaking eastern empire, artisans carried on the classical and Hellenistic tradition, but not without adapting to transformations of architectural culture and to the two economies of Roman building. The uneasy mix of stone and concrete led to an inevitable shift in traditional priorities and approaches to form. The architectural revolution of the first and second centuries carried the plastic arts to a new scale, that of the building itself. The medium of choice for this sculptural phase in Roman architecture was concrete. Stone followed in its wake. In the East and even in some regions of the West local limestones and sandstones were adapted to the recently canonized forms, literally substituting for the missing material in vaults and domes whose forms would never have existed but for the magical, malleable substance to which their builders had no access. In the concrete buildings of the privileged centers, stone was often cast in a subordinate role but a brilliant one nevertheless. Skilled stonecutters and sculptors were more in demand than ever, and the demands made of them more numerous. To be sure, the traditionally rectilinear canon of post, lintel, and pediment was to continue serving the cool, enigmatic, and orderly architecture of traditional religion, but it also found new and unexampled uses in the more secular aesthetic. Characteristically Roman architecture, it has often been observed, emphasizes enclosure, inclusion, interiority. And the tool of its embrace is the curve. Roman stone, with its repeated verticals and contoured horizontal accents, augments a building's sense of reach and flexure but also of enchamberment within its vaulted bowers. Romans must have appreciated the effect generated by column screens, an effect that was simultaneously inviting and cloistering. They encouraged one to look and move through them, to explore the partially revealed spaces beyond, but they also generated a satisfying sense of security and enclosure within each space. Even the famous thermal windows under the great vaulted ceilings were pillared with non-structural vertical elements to continue this effect at higher levels. The tracery of rows of column screens fading into cavernous, humid distances gave powerful realization to the aesthetic of bath buildings.

Some of the columnar orders at the Baths of Caracalla were introduced late, after the walls were essentially complete – but only when they were separated from the walls by a barrel vault.[39] We should never presume that stonework was an afterthought of the more sculptural process of modeling concrete. It collaborates with concrete masonry at the center of Roman design. In many cases the walls and piers, so prominent today, could better be regarded as the structural backdrop to the columnar stage. The laborious character of stonemasonry required that decisions about the application of stone be made very early, perhaps even before ground had been broken. At the Baths, the proportions of every columnar order were worked out well in advance of wall and pier construction. There were at least forty-six different column screens in the main bath block, each in a transitional zone where a pierced wall could have sufficed (see Figs. 44, 45). Their heights were carefully coordinated, the lower levels of some entablatures coinciding with the upper levels of others.[40] Many had no load-bearing function at all; their entablatures merely drew a thick horizontal chord under an arched void. In addition there were the sixteen colossal columns of the natatio and the frigidarium, each addorsed to a pier or a wall, and numerous aedicular colonnades enframing niches or doorways. The walls are full of sockets where stone columnar elements were once embedded. Every column screen carried a marble entablature, which was set into the walls at either end. The aedicules, sometimes carrying pediments on their facades, sometimes just horizontal entablatures, were usually anchored to the walls behind them at the column

pedestals and reentrant sections of the entablatures just above the capitals. Vestiges of the style are visible in the natatio of the Baths of Diocletian (Fig. 51).

The Greeks, pioneers in hoisting stone, developed large cranes with elaborate block-and-tackle systems operated from below and behind.[41] Roman builders inherited this technology and took it to new levels of efficiency and monumentality. For the most part, Greek engineers had ensured that elements were in their final orientation before they were hoisted. Thus their larger stone columns were made of stacked drums, each raised from the ground by attachments on its top surface and lowered into position onto the previous drum. Roman architecture, for reasons that remain unclear, embraced the practice of erecting monolithic column shafts in addition to the more traditional fluted drum shafts. Perhaps initially builders did not want to fracture the patterns of the exotic colored stones that were now available from the emperor's many quarries around the realm. Whatever the explanation, monolithic shafts soon became part of the imperial building culture even to the point where their real and ideological mass far outstripped the practicality of their production and transport.[42]

51. Rome: perspective view of natatio, Baths of Diocletian. G.-B. Piranesi, *Vedute di Roma* (Rome 1748).

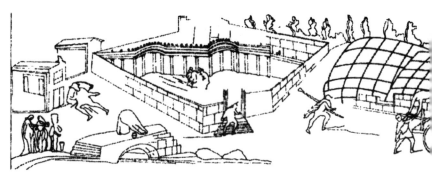

52. Stabiae: construction fresco from Villa S. Marco. Barbet and Miniero, eds., 1999. By permission of Centre Jean Bérard and École française de Rome. Illustration: L. Rega.

Stonemasons and architectural sculptors must have been a perfectionistic breed. They knew that a slip of the drill or chisel or a lapse in precision could destroy days of work, even jeopardize timely completion of a project. They often had to choose between two dangerous options: complete the delicate decoration of a stone element on the ground and risk damaging it during installation or in subsequent construction; or install it unfinished and risk making an indelible carving mistake in the fabric of the building. There is abundant evidence around the empire that both options were pursued according to the preferences of the builders; in either case, of course, damage could be patched, but with varying degrees of success. Pompeii, still rebuilding after an earthquake when it was buried under volcanic ash in 79 A.D., proves a particularly rich source of evidence for sequence and method, and a fresco from nearby Stabiae may show both practices in its depiction of a city under construction (Fig. 52).[43] The second option, it should be observed, required extensive scaffolding where it otherwise might not appear, around column capitals, entablatures, and pediments. To be sure, some minimal scaffolding would always have been needed for the workers who guided upper stone elements into place and secured them with clamps, but the incentives to minimize time-consuming and labor-intensive carving high above the ground were strong. At various sites around the empire, including Didyma, Baalbek, and Rome, templates for entablatures and pediments were etched into walls or floors to allow the stoneworkers to test the assembly of all the elements before they were hoisted into position.[44]

Others have dealt with the methods and tools of working stone,[45] and there is little need to dwell on them here. For our purposes, the most important aspects of the stoneworking are standards of preci-

sion. The square, level, plumb line, and straightedge were constantly in use as blocks and column shafts were being dressed. Stonemasons understood the importance of precise joints, particularly
between voussoirs or in the horizontal plane through which vertical
loads were transmitted. A joint in which both faces were not completely flat would distribute the load unequally. And flatness alone
was not enough. Especially on columnar elements, the bearing surface was made perfectly horizontal and perpendicular to the axis of
the column to avoid uneven loading. Surfaces of contact and their
edges were customarily dressed to standards of extreme precision.
But on these matters I have more to say in Chapter 6.

RAISING COLOSSAL COLUMN SHAFTS

The Greek practice of building columns in stacked segments
(drums) continued in the Roman period, but in many places
it gradually gave way to a preference for monolithic column shafts.
The surviving technical literature seems to presume the segmental
approach to column construction. Iron forceps, which were effective in lifting drums, were not much use on heavier oblong objects.
Hero of Alexandria describes a "crab," a forceps with three or four
arms that were hooked under the load and lashed together at the
sides with rigid bars.[46] But a "crab" too could hardly have been
manufactured on a scale to deal with granite monoliths of mature
Roman architecture. Furthermore, its use presumes that the shaft
has been tilted upright already, and there seems to be no practical
way to extract the claws from under the load after it has been set
into place. A simple and popular method of hoisting drums required
nothing more than rope looped or tied around large bosses on

53. Column drum
with lifting bosses.
Illustration: R. Taylor.

unfinished column drums (Fig. 53). Pompeian wall paintings show
that these bosses sometimes were left in place as a "rusticating" design element.[47] The best method of attaching crane hoists to monolithic column shafts or long drums was to lash ropes under a series
of projecting bosses or a collar projecting around the circumference
at a height above its center of gravity, a technique that may be represented in a relief from Capua (Fig. 54). Protective collars at the
extreme top and bottom were standard features of column shafts
in transport.[48] But as I will suggest below, hoisting may not have
been plausible for the largest column shafts, which weighed upward
of 110 tonnes.

Monolithic column shafts either were ordered from distant quarries in certain standard lengths up to fifty Roman feet or selected
from preexisting depots at major port cities.[49] In reality, batches of
a prescribed length were often slightly inconsistent in length. Such
was the case, for example, at the Severan forum complex at Lepcis
Magna. If the builders chose not to cut them down to exactly the
same length, the other elements would have to compensate for the
discrepancies. In this sense the capitals were the controlling, preemptive element in resolving inaccuracy. Prefabricated in roughed-
out state, they were not precisely trimmed at top and bottom until the shafts had arrived on site and their measurements had been
checked.[50] (The Roman imperial preference for shafts and capitals
of contrasting materials, and thus from different quarries, almost
ensured that they would not arrive in a single shipment.) Alterna-
tively, the shafts themselves may have been trimmed down to match
the shortest in the set; hence the uniform shafts of the Temple of
Antoninus and Faustina in Rome, all cut to something less than
forty Roman feet.[51] In the case of hypostyle buildings – that is,
buildings (such as many basilicas) in which colonnades supported
structural walls – it was therefore of utmost importance to have the
requisitioned stone elements on site at a very early building phase
so that an entire columnar order could be in place as soon as the
enveloping structure was ready for them. Even when installation
of the orders was deferred, intensive work on the stone decoration
would have commenced as soon as possible. It has been argued that
for large and important imperial projects, specialists in working
a particular stone would travel with the stone itself to oversee the
carving. Even so, mistakes were made; for instance, the concrete
core of the Severan temple podium at Lepcis Magna preserves a

54. Capua: funerary relief depicting tread-mill crane lifting column shaft. Adam 1994. By permission of Chrysalis Books.

number of marble rejects from other parts of the project possibly overseen by specialists from Asia Minor.[52] Because of the sheer labor of carving capitals and entablatures – especially relative to the simple masonry of foundations, walls, and piers – the stonework must have caused many a project to lag behind schedule. But this was the kind of work that could proceed through the winter while construction teams were inactive. We may hypothesize that for highly organized imperial projects skilled stone carvers were virtually ensured employment year-round.

Cranes and gins are not much of a presence during the construction of brick-and-concrete walls and piers, but they are essential to the introduction of stone elements that cannot be hand-carried. Their positions and movement must be envisioned throughout the design process, otherwise a building is apt to prove itself unbuildable. (We explore this issue in greater detail in the next two chapters; here it is enough to lay out a few general principles.) Cranes do not usually coexist comfortably with scaffolding, and so their heaviest use should not coincide with the erection of concrete-and-facing masonry or wall decoration. There must be clearance and physical means for the cranes' assembly, operation, and removal and (if necessary) room for them to be moved laterally; large cranes could not slide or pivot horizontally during hoists. Heavy objects must be raised in areas with clearance not only for the crane mast but also for its rear stay-ropes and capstans. Let us consider what was required at the Baths of Caracalla.

The sixteen great columns of the frigidarium and the natatio, each with a monolithic thirty-six-foot shaft of granite, present a dual problem: The shafts were very heavy, about ninety tonnes each,[53] requiring massive lifting engines, and they were placed very close to the walls and piers – difficult enough against a single surface, much harder in a corner. And eight of those columns were crowded into corners (Fig. 55; see Figs. 2, 22, 23). How was it done?

Roman engineers regularly faced a task that Greek architects had largely avoided: getting very heavy horizontal elements into vertical position. Every monolithic column shaft had to be turned upright before it could be set onto its base. Or such, at least, is the usual regime for small and medium-sized columns. But in the case of the larger column shafts, this two-part process – what we might call "standing" (tilting) and "hopping" (dead-lifting onto the base) – grew far more difficult. Hopping very heavy objects is difficult for obvious reasons: They are never easy to hoist off the ground or to control after they have been raised. Ropes can slip, even if they do not break or come loose, threatening damage to the stone and to the crane. But standing too becomes difficult. The ninety-degree shift in orientation presents mechanical complications, for the stresses on the material are uneven as the shaft is being raised. *Lewises* – expanding grips that were fitted into trapezoidal sockets cut into the top of the stone – are much easier to manage on horizontal elements where they can be used in multiple numbers, for too much weight on a single lewis will pull it free of the socket (see Fig. 81, *c*).[54] Even more troublesome is the prospect of fitting a lewis *sideways* into the socket of a recumbent column shaft and pivoting the column upward with it. This would generate shear stress on the stone around the socket – not enough stress, perhaps, to endanger smaller column shafts, but a great threat to the behemoths.

If the two-part process suffers a law of diminishing returns as weight increases, its advantages nevertheless are clear-cut. Presuming the crane is adequate to the task, a dead-lifted shaft can be guided down onto its doweled base with precision. If the crane is slightly out of position, the shaft can be swung, levered, or twisted slightly as it hovers over the base. Moreover, the whole operation can be done from a single direction; the crane operators work beside and behind the crane. But what if the bipartite procedure simply becomes too troublesome or time-consuming? The answer is to eliminate the hop altogether: The shaft is tilted upright directly onto its base. Such a procedure is simple in conception, immensely difficult in execution. Jean-Pierre Adam suggests that the task was accom-

plished with an ingenious pivoting device that could raise the shaft in a controlled and predictable fashion (Fig. 56). This process, unlike hopping, requires clearance on opposing sides of the base, one side for the column at rest and the other for the pulling teams. The shaft must be mated to the base perfectly: Its underside cannot be allowed to roll or drag, but must be rocked precisely into position

55. Rome: reconstructed view of frigidarium, Baths of Caracalla. C. A. Blouet, 1826–7. Fototeca Unione c/o American Academy in Rome, neg. 13017.

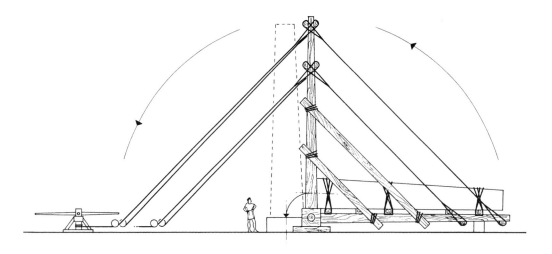

56. Hypothetical tilting mechanism for large column shafts. Adam 1994. By permission of Chrysalis Books.

in one try. Even the best effort is likely to chip the stone on both the base and shaft unless some kind of a catch, perhaps a row of bosses or collars on the shaft hooking it firmly to the cradle, keeps the joining surfaces apart until the shaft is nearly vertical. (No catch appears in Adam's illustration.) To ensure that the catch does not slip, and to avoid toppling at the end of the procedure, the shaft must be securely lashed to the cradle.

Could the builders of the Baths of Caracalla or similar buildings avoid tilting? Did they have cranes that could dead-lift such heavy weights? There is no definitive answer yet. Column shafts, unlike horizontally disposed elements, could be hoisted only by one crane at a time, and modern engineers are reluctant to suggest that a single rope-and-timber crane could achieve such a heavy lifting capacity.[55] Even if it could, the shape and orientation of the column presented difficulties, as I explain below. The great Helleno-Roman sanctuary at Baalbek serves as a fine laboratory for investigating methods of moving colossal stone elements (Figs. 57, 58, and see Fig. 9). The porch ceiling blocks of the Temple of Dionysus, which have double clusters of lewis holes at either end of their top surfaces, relied on two cranes hoisting concurrently, or on wide compound cranes with multiple treadmills and a large clearance area for rigging (Fig. 59).[56] They are proof that the necessity to distribute the weight over the top surface of the block, and among many lengths of rope from which it was suspended (their tension evened by a compound pulley system), was fully understood.[57] Such a system is visible in the Stabiae fresco (see Fig. 52).

57. Baalbek: flank of Temple of Dionysus before archaeological intervention. D. Roberts, *The Holy Land* (1843). By permission of Duke University Museum of Art.

Clearly lifting colossal monolithic column shafts was not simply a matter of their dead weight. Nobody denies that the sixty-tonne marble entablature blocks above the great columns of the Baths of Caracalla were hoisted into place.[58] The builders of the Temple of Jupiter at Baalbek raised even greater weights to the top of fifty-six-foot column shafts, as can readily be seen in an illustration with

58. Baalbek: recon-
structed view of same
part of the temple.
Wiegand 1921–5.

59. Baalbek: analyt-
ical view of roof-
construction method,
Temple of Dionysus.
Wiegand 1921–5.

weight estimates of each element (Fig. 60, 61). The difficulty with
shafts, as opposed to horizontal elements, lay in the concentration
of stresses in a very small area. Horizontal distribution of the weight
was impossible at the top of a shaft or a tall drum, and at a certain
order of magnitude the concentration of stresses in this area during
lifting became intolerable. Indeed, there is no trace of lewis holes in
any of the sections of the three-drum shafts at the Temple of Jupiter

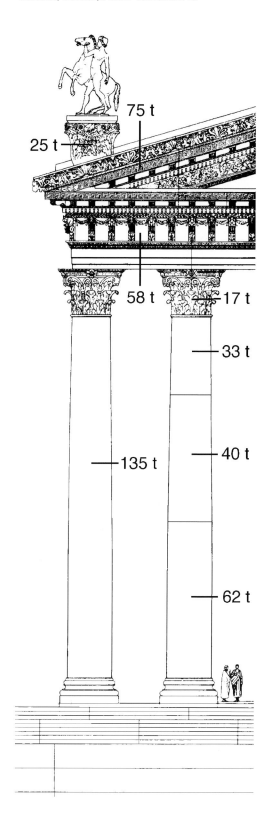

60. Baalbek: facade of Temple of Jupiter with estimated weights of elements. After Ragette 1980.

61. Baalbek: corner block of pediment, Temple of Jupiter. Deutsches Archäologisches Institut, neg. 58.2884. Photo: Herbig.

at Baalbek, nor (to my knowledge) in any monolithic Roman shaft of thirty-six feet or more. Yet they are numerous on the pediment and entablature blocks of Baalbek, some of which are exceedingly heavy.[59]

The Baths of Caracalla preserve two very interesting details that I believe provide strong evidence for tilting. First, DeLaine has recognized a discontinuity in the masonry at all four corners of the frigidarium (Fig. 62).[60] It seems that the transverse spur walls were built against, and therefore after, the longitudinal faces of the piers. This sequence is best explained, I would suggest, by the need to allow longitudinal clearance on opposite sides of the corner column bases for tilting the columns into position.[61] Second, all the column bases are spaced far enough apart that the shafts can be rested horizontally between them, parallel to the room's longitudinal axis. Set in this fashion, with their crowns facing inboard from their bases, all the shafts could have been tilted up into position with adequate clearance for the pulling crews on the outboard side. Only then would they have been hemmed in by the transverse walls.

How was tilting consistently achieved in antiquity without the risk of irreversible error? In a horizontal position, the column shafts would have been dead-lifted off their delivery carts directly into the cradle of the pivoting mechanism by medium-sized cranes working in parallel. The cradle must have been positioned very precisely

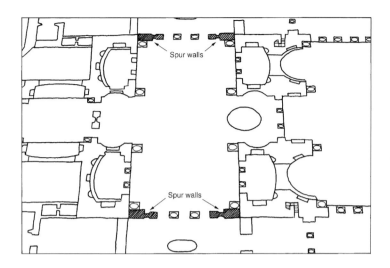

62. Rome: perspective plan of frigidarium of Baths of Caracalla with breaks of continuity in masonry. Illustration: R. Taylor after DeLaine 1997.

along the axis with the base, and at exactly the right distance from it. Workers would then drill holes for the dowels that would anchor the two elements together. Dowel-hole drilling is not usually done so late, but in tilting there is no way to twist the shaft into position if its holes are slightly off alignment with those in the base. This way a single template could be applied to both surfaces along the shared pivoting axis, ensuring that the holes would be in perfect alignment. On the largest shafts the holes number three and are spaced evenly around a central compass mark (Fig. 63). Pouring channels would be chiseled into the base surface leading inward from the edge to

63. Baalbek: contact surfaces of monumental column base and shaft. Wiegand 1921–5.

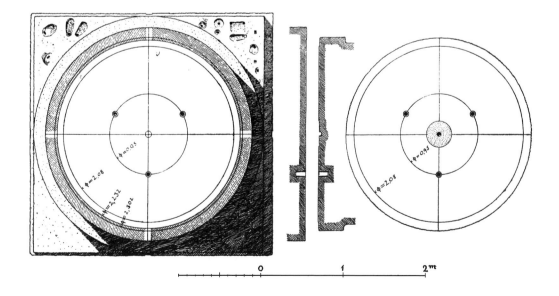

each hole. Short iron dowels would be cemented into the holes in the shaft with molten lead. These would be mated to the holes in the base as the shaft was pivoted into place. (Dowels can be quite short, since their sole purpose is to counteract the horizontal action of earthquakes.) Finally, with the shaft in position, molten lead would be funneled into the channels at the edge of the base to encase the lower half of each dowel.

The pivoting would have been confined to a narrow zone of activity on the north and south sides of the room. Only when the column shafts were in position, and their massive capitals hoisted onto them with large cranes and doweled to them, could the great projecting entablature blocks have been installed. In the frigidarium these were not merely decorative elements; they supported some of the weight of the vaults whose long, slender haunches emerged from them. And though the piers behind them bore most of the vault thrusts, the sheer weight of masonry soaring up from them would have raised concern: They were, in effect, the ancient equivalent to the Gothic *tas-de-charge*. It is highly unlikely that these sixty-tonne marble supports could have been inserted into the wall sockets before the columns were erected beneath them, as has been suggested.[62] They were load-bearing (not to mention load-producing) elements, and they needed the support provided by the columns. Furthermore, even if they did not impede the task of tilting the shafts upright, they most definitely would have obstructed the cranes hoisting the *capitals* into place. It is one thing to lower a gigantic marble capital into place from above. It is another thing altogether to slide it in horizontally under a covering element. There is no way to dowel the elements together on their surfaces of contact. The crane's access to the top of the capital must be eliminated. And how does one generate the necessary lateral movement? Swinging, no simple task with a ponderous pendulum, does not maintain the necessary vertical and lateral uniformity; nor does levering. Better not even to consider the option. We must be satisfied with the common-sense sequence: piers and walls up to entablature level first; column bases and shafts second; column capitals third; projecting entablatures fourth; piers and walls encasing the entablatures fifth; vaulting sixth.

If the entablature blocks were not intended to prop the vault haunches over empty space, why, then, were they embedded so deeply in the walls and piers (Fig. 64, and see Fig. 108)? Rome is subject to occasional earthquakes, some of which probably helped

64. Rome: Baths of Caracalla frigidarium, socket left by robbed entablature block. Photo: R. Taylor.

to bring down the vaulting of the Baths of Caracalla, the Basilica of Maxentius, and many other monumental buildings in the Middle Ages. These blocks, anchored in the piers and doweled firmly to the columns below, were meant to protect the columns from seismic shocks. Incidentally, this is where monolithic column shafts are at a distinct advantage: Pinned firmly at the bottom and top, they do not suffer the shear and slippage of stacked column drums.[63]

Two final observations deserve to be made about the giant columns of the Baths of Caracalla and its sister buildings around Rome and the empire. First, *there is no inherent reason why the column shafts could not have been erected before the walls and piers were begun.* The complete lack of barriers to the pivoting process would have been a significant advantage. But let us recall that in this particular instance the surveying errors in laying out the substructure of the Baths was evidently not detected until the superstructure had been begun. Only after this time were the giant column orders erected in their slightly irregular positions. Second, *it is not strictly nec-*

65. Rome: Basilica of Maxentius, southeast wall exterior. Vertical crack corresponds to the wall's bond with the eastern pier forming the corner for one of the monumental columns. Photo: R. Taylor.

essary to tilt column shafts into place without obstructions. If the piers – that is, the longitudinal elements – were given time to harden, they themselves could be the point of purchase for the pulling ropes. Completed at least to the height of the column shafts, they could be fitted on top with rope guides, either grooved wheels or greased slots. This method introduces a new point of friction into the process, but also offers the benefit of a simplified cradle (without Adam's right-angled element) and a sure barrier against overshooting the vertical position. Again, though, the physical evidence from the Baths seems to exclude this option.

The same applies to the Basilica of Maxentius. A superficial, keyed-brick bond exists between the southeast transverse wall and the south corner pier, which is rabbeted to receive it (see arrows in

66. Rome: Pantheon, view of facade. Photo: R. Taylor.

Fig. 21). A long vertical crack on the other end of this wall, corresponding to its juncture with the east corner pier, is visible from outside (Fig. 65). This too suggests a weak bond between the two corner surfaces that embraced the column inside, one built before the other.

THE COLUMNS OF THE PANTHEON FACADE

I f pivoting was the method of choice – and perhaps the only viable method – for raising the colossal orders at imperial baths and temples, then it must have been used to erect the porch columns of the Pantheon (Fig. 66). The Pantheon porch, it seems, originally was intended to have fifty-foot monolithic shafts forming sixty-foot columns overall, including base and capital. Instead the builders settled for forty-foot shafts and forty-eight-foot columns erected on the same plan (Fig. 67).[64] We do not know why the original design came to grief, but its failure must be related to the logistical difficulties of moving such gigantic cylinders of granite. Quarrying the shafts and transporting them from the mountainous quarries of the Aswan to the narrow streets of Rome would doubtless have been a staggering task. But the same task had been accomplished quite recently for the great northwest structure of the Forum of Trajan (traditionally identified as the Temple of the Deified Trajan). I want to suggest that the problem had nothing to do with procurement. Instead, it was

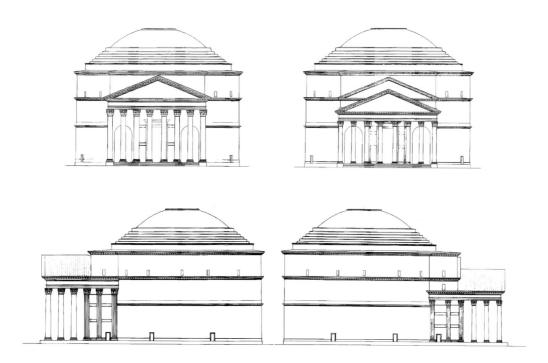

67. Rome: Pantheon, elevations as intended (*left*) and as built (*right*). Wilson-Jones 2000. By permission of Yale University Press.

realized too late that the columns as originally planned could not be tilted into position. The great rotunda and part of the intermediate block were already well on their way to completion, creating a southerly barrier to the pulling teams. There was no way to sequence the erection of the planned fifty-foot column shafts without creating a hopeless snarl. The shafts were simply too long to be positioned on the floor in a workable configuration, regardless of sequence. The problem was most acute with the four inner columns defining the three bays of the porch. They could not be laid diagonally in any of the bays. Nor could they be raised orthogonally, parallel with the facade, for they would interfere with one another. (Recall that a minimum of fifty feet of clearance was needed on both sides of the base, and preferably much more on the pulling side.) But with forty-foot shafts there is enough room in the central bay to lay out each shaft diagonally in turn. Presuming that the porch at this stage was surrounded by a level surface of earth fill to create a generous pulling zone on three sides, the columns could have been raised in three stages, working from south to north (Fig. 68).

The method I suggest leaves unlimited pulling range for all the columns. In the first stages all the column shafts were positioned diagonally, always either southeast or southwest of the bases. In stage 1

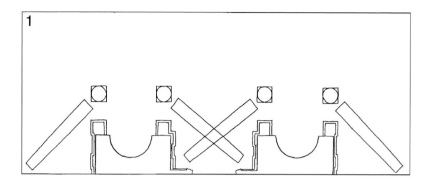

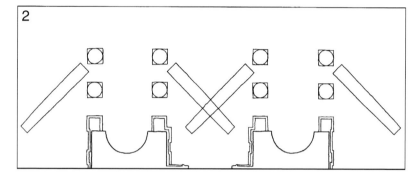

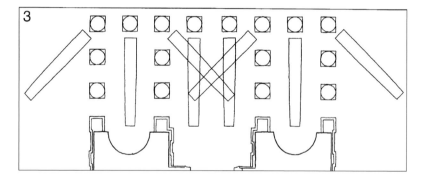

68. Rome: plan of Pantheon porch with three hypothetical phases of column positions. Illustration: R. Taylor.

the four southernmost columns – those nearest the entrance – were raised. Each of the two inner columns was placed diagonally in the central porch bay and raised in sequence. The two outer columns were raised from positions outside the porch. Stage 2 was a repetition of stage 1 but for the next rank of columns to the north. The third and foremost rank required two stages: another repetition of the configuration of stages 1 and 2, then the orthogonal placement of the four facade column shafts corresponding to the bays. These would have been set out facing due south in the bays and raised into position from the north.

We have concerned ourselves in this chapter with moving structural solids into self-sufficient equilibrium, the condition of standing upright. But a complete building goes beyond free verticality. It must negotiate the tension between uprights and the elements that bind and cover them. In each of the next two chapters we consider a case study of the two elemental conditions that Roman architects imposed upon verticality: first, binding schemes of unprecedented complexity and ingenuity; second, concrete coverings.

4

COMPLEX ARMATURES

> They [the Romans] conceived cups and bowls and troughs of
> space, so shaped as to funnel the spectator's attention toward
> each distinct, formal pattern of spectacle, so perforated as to
> channel the flow of large numbers expeditiously in and out,
> to and from their assigned places, so presented as to assert the
> public importance and dignity of the proceedings and to invite
> penetration to the core of space. The appropriate figure of each
> spatial concavity was directly reflected in the curved or straight
> contours of the exterior. Each was supported by an ingenious
> structural web of radial and concentric vaulted passageways.
> Each presented to public view tiers of open, enframed arches,
> so spaced and proportioned as to suggest, from a distance,
> timeless stability in a continuous, fugitive negation of perspec-
> tive and, close to hand, irresistible attraction.
> – Frank Brown[1]

Having considered a building process in which the planimetry varies relatively little with changes in elevation, now I wish to consider a very different process
for a different form, the amphitheater – and in particular, the Roman amphitheater par excellence, the Colosseum (Fig. 69). As with
other freestanding building types designed for spectacle, its altimetric and planimetric schemes are so tightly interwoven as to be in-
separable. In cross section an amphitheater is a visible metaphor of
this collusion of axes. Its most powerful line is not the ground line

or the towering facade, but the diagonal hypotenuse holding the horizontal and vertical in uneasy equilibrium. Like the vector of two perpendicular forces, that diagonal is the felt consequence of divergent impulses collaborating on a task. Carried into a third dimension, these impulses encounter a further scheme of obliquity: a ground plan of radial spokes emanating from points along the building's principal axes. The result is a tour de force of rational planning, always anticipating the convergences and collisions of lines, planes, and volumes. The form is intensely logical and indeed *processual:* The spectator could only be amazed at the massive armature and fragmented voids and the demiurgic mind that created them. This geometry was revealed in inverse proportion to one's social status: The emperor and senators had little measure of the building's miraculous structure, for they took a straight course through the short axis of the building to their front-row seats, barely departing from the ground floor. The rich and powerful were granted the prerogative of indifference. But those wending their way through the labyrinthine succession of corridors and stairways to the upper tiers could not help but admire the structure's ability to arrest the white-hot energy of this exploding star in cool concrete and stone.

CONSTRUCTING THE COLOSSEUM

L et us try to envision the outlines of a process by which the Colosseum came into being. I present the following hypotheses not as fact but as parallel and sequential processes that *might* have worked. The most important element of the narrative is not its absolute accuracy or its provability but its coherence as a narrative. Our task it not to plot a certain path from conception to completion, merely to propose a plausible one. Every building proceeds in one way and one way only – yet it could have arrived at its finished state in any number of ways. Architectural contingency thereby extends the principle of statical indeterminacy into the dynamic world of cause and effect. Complicating the issue is the path of compromise from intention to reality. In large and unprecedented projects, as also in many simple and routine ones, it is impossible to avoid failures of concept or unanticipated complications. A good architect or builder is not a determinist but an opportunist. He or she must

69. Rome: Colosseum, aerial view. Fototeca Unione c/o American Academy in Rome, neg. 10575F.

be prepared for setbacks, and even embed the certainty of uncertainty into the planning of a building. Often we can observe changes of plan in a building. Its fabric is a cartography of invention; it maps out the improvisations that would rarely be visible in working drawings, even if they survived.

The Colosseum's very familiarity tends to obscure its architectural distinction as the most complex structure ever successfully completed in antiquity. It is surpassed in daring, originality, and beauty by other buildings, but as a monument to architectural process it stands alone. As John Ward-Perkins has remarked, the building is notable not so much for its form and methods, which were a well-developed staple of Roman architecture by this time, as for its sheer scale and complexity: "the outstanding characteristic of the building is the skill and foresight with which the unknown architect can be seen from the very outset to have marshalled the whole gigantic enterprise towards its predetermined conclusion."[2] In a single, fairly continuous narrative, this chapter offers a distillation of that enterprise.

The Colosseum measures 188×156 m in plan, with eighty radiating walls. Its four-story facade rises to a height of 50 m above grade, higher than the Pantheon's dome and the Pont du Gard's aqueduct. If we are to believe the single Latin source that comments on the duration of the Colosseum project, the Chronographer of 354 A.D., that amphitheater was built in an amazingly short time span, perhaps five years.[3] It was begun by Vespasian and after his death in 79 was virtually completed by Titus, his son and successor. Titus died in 81; by this time, the chronicle says, five levels had been completed.[4] Influenced (perhaps unduly) by this information, modern scholars have divided the seating tiers into five sections.[5] An inscription of the Arval Brethren from this period refers to four seating areas: *maenianum primum*, the first sector; *maenianum secundum imum et summum*, the lower and upper second sector; and the *maenianum summum in ligneis*, the upper wooden sector. It appears that the inscription excludes the *actual* first sector (*primo settore*), the lowest area accommodating members of the senatorial elite.[6] (These areas are labeled in the upcoming Fig. 74.)

Titus staged the amphitheater's inaugural public spectacle, a mock naval battle, in 80.[7] It is hard to envision filling the arena as we know it today with water; thus it is widely believed that the mazelike substructures of the central arena were not completed until Domitian's reign. I will presume that the arena remained undeveloped during the early phases of construction of the *cavea*. As such, it provided a convenient workyard and depot for materials.[8]

Those materials included an unusual amount of quarried stone. The Flavian era saw the emergence of brick-faced concrete as the material of choice for large Roman buildings in central Italy, but the Colosseum – perhaps because of its unprecedented size and structural loads – followed a more conservative dictate, reserving large parts of its fabric for squared stone laid without mortar. Some idea of the proportion of stone to concrete, especially on the lower levels, is conveyed by Gaudet's analytical drawing of 1875 (Fig. 70). Giuseppe Cozzo has estimated that the building consumed a hundred thousand cubic meters of travertine alone. This was used almost exclusively in large blocks requiring lifting devices. Tufa was also used extensively, sometimes in blocks of comparable size but also in smaller sizes. The joining surfaces of stone were cut with a preci-

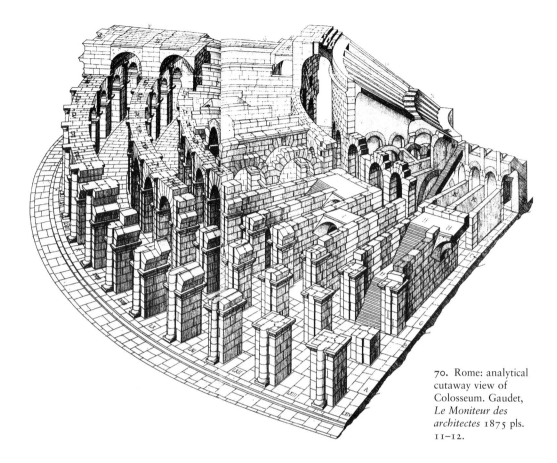

70. Rome: analytical cutaway view of Colosseum. Gaudet, *Le Moniteur des architectes* 1875 pls. 11–12.

sion equal to the finest Greek stonework. Concrete, brick, and mortar, the only truly portable materials used in the building, were relegated mostly to the vaults and the upper tiers. How could such a huge and unprecedentedly complex building be completed in only five years when the bulk of its fabric required the time- and labor-intensive art of stereotomy? A murky legend that fifteen thousand prisoners from the Jewish War were put to work on the project, even if it holds a grain of truth, offers little relief to our puzzlement. While they might have joined the slave forces transporting materials and pulling ropes, they could not have augmented the highly skilled and specialized workforce of craftsmen working these local materials in local fashion.[9] More than a dozen guilds of specialists in the building trades are attested in the construction of the Colosseum, and many more went unrecorded.[10]

We shall never have the full answer to our question, but we may presume that it includes an impressive efficiency model as well as a genius for exploiting unskilled and semiskilled labor with maximum flexibility. There were many tasks, such as measuring distances and angles, mixing mortar, laying concrete, sawing stone, levering stone blocks and cranes into position, and so on, that could be learned by any able-bodied person in a short time.[11] One of the master planner's responsibilities, no doubt, was to keep a large force of slaves, free agents, and even temporarily idle specialists on hand to tackle the task of the moment. As for materials and skilled labor, logistics and contracts must have been worked out well ahead of the project. Bricks must be cured and fired. Quicklime must be slaked months in advance of its use. Stone must be quarried and delivered, wood, rope, and hardware made available for cranes, scaffolding, and centering. Skilled laborers of all kinds must be available in adequate numbers; stonemasons, in particular, were at a premium. During construction, legions of artisans were shaping the thousands of stones to be fitted precisely into the fabric of the Colosseum. Arches would be laid out on templates, blocks carefully measured, sawed, and chiseled according to detailed specifications either of the architects or of a master stonemason working from plan and elevation diagrams. Final dressing was probably done after the stone blocks were safely in place.[12]

THE GROUNDWORK

The drawing-board plan used for the foundations would have been laid out with ropes swung from carefully established points serving as the eight centers of curvature for each of the circle segments constituting its shape (Fig. 71). Such a method would have been sufficient at this stage, but the method decreased in accuracy proportional to the length of rope: The outer circumferences suffered from the greater play, or "creep," in the longer ropes used to draw them. Over lengths of several hundred feet interrelated details of planimetry such as uniform width of seating rows would have become a real problem. After the substructures were complete, all subsequent annular lines were probably defined by an alternative method, using shorter lengths of rope, of measuring back from the edge of the arena instead of the original points. Because the seating areas of amphitheaters maintain the same width and profile around the entire arena, the same method can be used repeatedly around the periphery. This procedure carried three implications:

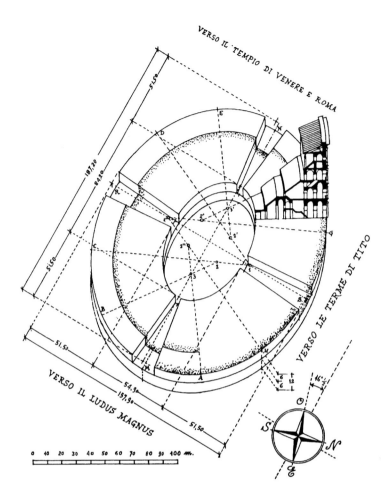

VERSO IL TEMPIO DI VENERE E ROMA

VERSO LE TERME DI TITO

VERSO IL LUDUS MAGNUS

71. Rome: Colosseum, axonometric plan depicting raft foundation and radii of curvature. Mocchegiani Carpano 1977. By permission of C. Mocchegiani Carpano.

1 Rather than a sweep, it was a more laborious connect-the-dots exercise.

2 The measuring lines always had to be held perpendicular to the tangent of the arena perimeter. At the Colosseum all the radiating elements follow this rule of perpendicularity, and thus they could have served as quick visual guides for the measuring lines.

3 Abandoning the original points of reference allowed the arena itself to serve as a zone for activities that otherwise would have obstructed the sweeping lines.[13]

The outer periphery of the *cavea*, though perhaps less accurately drawn than the inner edge, could also be used as a point of departure for measuring lines inboard, especially to cross-check particularly critical outboard measurements. Probably all of the annular lines were redrawn in this way, for in fact the Colosseum *cavea*

72. Rome: Colosse-
um, analytical model
of infrastructure,
Museo della Civiltà
Romana. Deutsches
Archäologisches
Institut, neg. 73.1063.

appears to be remarkably uniform in width. The width of its outer
ambulatory deviates only a few centimeters from the ideal.[14]

Schematically the Colosseum, like all freestanding Roman amphitheaters, follows a design that (consciously or not) mimicked the
cosmological map of the universe: a net of radial and annular lines,
which when applied to the surface of a globe (as on the Pantheon
vault) become meridians and parallels. At every intersection of this
grid, from the top of the foundations up to the third story, rose a
forest of travertine piers ascending like tree trunks up through the
foliage of connective architecture (Figs. 72–74). These were the
main structural or load-bearing elements of the edifice. At various
levels they intersected with floors, forming a regular network of
nodes interconnected in various ways. In plan, the nodes are spaced
more or less evenly along eighty radiating spokes. At ground level

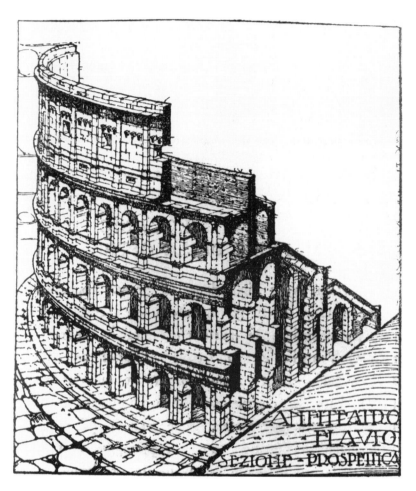

73. Rome: Colosse-
um, section view after
Cozzo. Deutsches
Archäologisches
Institut, neg. 56.177.
Photo: Moscioni.

each spoke has seven piers made of solid travertine blocks (Figs.
72, 73). These are usually assigned numbers from outside to inside.
Most of the supporting structures inward from Pier 7 were of concrete faced with diagonally halved *bessales*, the characteristic technique of Flavian builders in Rome. Not all are freestanding, of
course; many are joined together by solid walls. Except along the
four major axes, the pattern of structural elements is uniform at this
level. The two outer rings of piers are unobstructed, creating vaulted annular corridors, Ambulatories 1 and 2. They are followed by
four piers embedded in walls of tufa. Then between Piers 6 and 7
there is a third vaulted annular passage, Ambulatory 3. Beyond this
the travertine gives way to smaller squared tufa blocks and brick
and concrete, presumably because the superior compressive strength
of travertine was not considered necessary to support the lower seat-

ing tiers. Initially there is a wall, then a fourth vaulted corridor, followed by a thin ring of irregular and poorly preserved chambers, some of them evidently latrines intended for the senatorial elite, and then a small passageway giving access to them, Ambulatory 5.[15] One travertine block survives on the inboard side of Ambulatory 5; the podium separating the ambulatory from the arena seems to have been at least ribbed with this material.[16]

In elevation section, the *cavea* is traditionally divided into four floors or levels corresponding to the four columnar orders on the building's exterior. At first the correspondence may seem arbitrary, but in fact the floor of each level begins at exactly the same level as the column base on the facade (Figs. 73, 74). Levels 1 and 2 are easily identified: They each end at the vaulting above the outer ambulatories. Level 3 actually encompasses two stories of ambulatories, and Level 4 is defined by an inner order of columns, as well as the

74. Rome: Colosseum, section elevation with author's numbering system. Rea 1988. By permission of Edizioni Quasar.

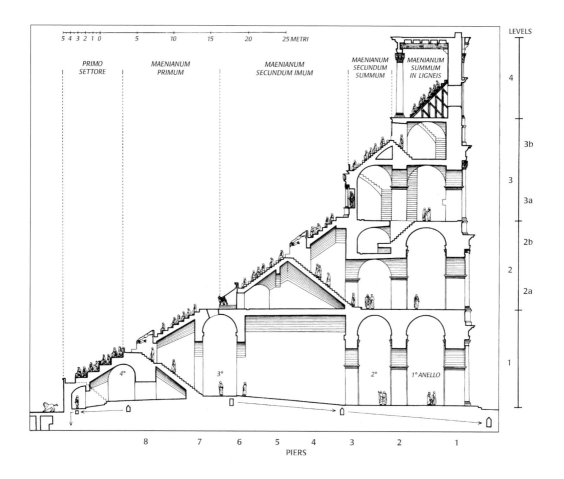

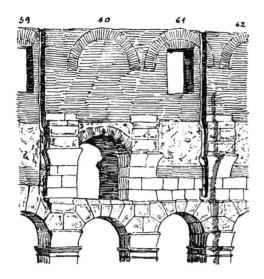

75. Rome: Colosseum, podium of Level 3a and remains of supporting structure seen from inside. Von Gerkan 1925.

pilasters on the outside. The five segregated seating tiers correspond roughly, but not perfectly, to the floor divisions. To avoid confusion I stick to references in elevation by floor, not seating tier. When elements are introduced at the lower or upper part of a floor division, they are designated by the letters "a" or "b" (e.g., Level 2a, Level 3b, as shown in Fig. 74).

On the two main axes of the building there are numerous corridors and chambers for the gladiators, staff, and animals just below ground level, mostly constructed of the same massive blocks of travertine as the armature of the superstructure. Off the axes, the travertine substructures extend down only about 90 cm, below which the massive concrete raft foundation, ringed with a thick band of brick around the periphery of the *cavea* and the arena, extends perhaps 13 m below grade (see Fig. 71).[17] Following a pattern similar to that at Pozzuoli, a multilevel water supply and drainage network weaves its way through the foundations.[18] The downspouts, gutters, and water-supply pipes numbered in the hundreds, and each was positioned roughly according to its estimated capacity. Downspouts and gutters – both open and covered – would be assigned to a reasonably well-defined area of watershed, while water-supply lines were routed to the network of fountains all the way up to Level 3a (see Fig. 89). The walls and piers were veined with downspouts, most commonly in surface recesses where maintenance crews could get at them (Fig. 75). But pipes and drains would also have to pass through the thickness of vaults, where they were inaccessible. Re-

cent research suggests that there were perhaps twenty-eight fountains at ground level, sixteen on Level 2a next to the stairs, forty at
Level 2b (and latrines as well, although their stacks have yet to be
identified), and, by one estimate, seventy-six on the third level.[19] All
of these, of course, had not only supply pipes but also drains.

Within the concrete foundations was embedded a spiderweb of
large subfloor drains. Short segments of drainpipe and water supply
pipe projected up from them to floor level, ready to be integrated
into the walls. Now the builders faced a number of options. Because
of the repetitive nature of the Colosseum in circuit, it was far more
efficient for the specialized work crews to operate circumferentially,
repeating their particular task all the way around the arena before
moving to the next assignment. However, the planners would also
want to keep as many people at work as possible at any given time.
Circumferential repetition is fine up to a point, but it is useful to
ensure that various parts of the building are in different stages of
construction so that, for example, the stone-hoisting crews are not
idle while the concrete vaults are going up. It is impossible to say
anything in detail about how this was done. My own reconstruction
of the process is artificially schematic. It views the process in cross
section, making relatively few observations about how construction
may have progressed circumferentially. I divide the tasks into discrete regimes only for simplicity's sake, not because it reflected reality. These follow a logical sequence of sorts, but it is not the only
possible sequence, and there can be little doubt that the overlapping
of tasks in real time was much more complex than I suggest – and
unpredictable even to the overseers of the project, who could only
roughly estimate the relative time needed for a thousand different
tasks.

From the standpoint of radial movement, it was illogical to start
at the inner and outer boundaries and work toward the core, for
this would create external barriers to the heavy lifting equipment
and encumber the delivery of the materials. Vertically, it was most
rational to complete an entire level before moving on to the next,
allowing the cranes to rise along with the building. However, these
advantages must be weighed against the obvious efficiency of working upward in a single material. Since some of the travertine stonework rose uninterrupted to Levels 2, 3, and 4, there was at least
the option of continuing upward without pause as far as the cranes
could reach. Every pause to "top off" a level with stairs and vaults

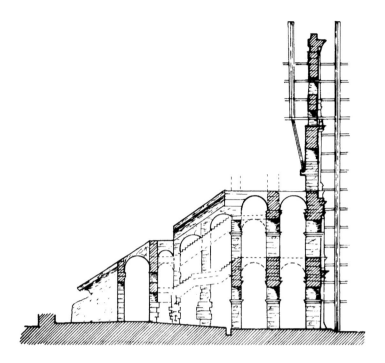

76. Rome: Colosseum, Cozzo's proposed construction scheme for upper levels. Sear 1989 after Cozzo. By permission of F. Sear.

forced the removal of cranes that would have to be reintroduced later to complete the work at a higher level.

COZZO'S PARADIGM

Cozzo has offered an influential version of the more vertically oriented model.[20] He noted that each radial row of Piers 3–6, extending all the way up to the raking vaults of Level 2, was joined together just below the vaults by brick arches (Figs. 76, 77, and see Fig. 72). The space between the piers, up to the arches themselves, was filled in at Level 1 with walls of squared tufa in large blocks, cut and joined just as carefully as the travertine, and at Level 2 with brick-faced concrete. Together with the piers these walls defined the radial stairwells that supported the dozens of staircases connecting Level 1 to 2a and Level 2a to 2b. To Cozzo this raised a puzzling question: Why would brick arches have been laid directly on top of those massive walls of brick-faced concrete? Relieving arches are necessary only over voids or other points of structural weakness. He concluded that the "filling" had all been added later, and that the piers were raised as freestanding elements. They were spanned by arches, he believed, so that the raking vaults above them, which sup-

77. Rome: Colosseum, view of the crowning arches and infill of Piers 3–6 at Level 2. Photo: R. Taylor.

ported the seating banks of the second level, could be completed at the earliest possible stage in construction. This way, he reasoned, a fair amount of later work, including the dressing and installation of the tufa blocks connecting walls and stairs, could be carried out under the protection of the vaults during rainy or cold weather. Cozzo's logic creates an artfully sequential, rather than strictly parallel, developmental relationship between a building's skeleton and its tissue. It would allow the builders "to complete the project rapidly by developing space for preparatory work and by creating a large surface of superimposed planes arranged in such a way as to subdivide and approach the tasks at various points."

Yet Cozzo's model for Level 1 is wanting both structurally and constructionally.[21] As Lynne Lancaster has recently demonstrated, the verticality of the travertine piers was only approximate, and

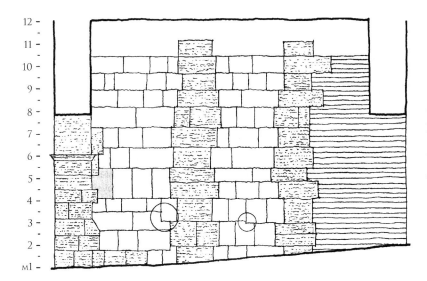

78. Rome: Colosseum, configuration of blocks between Piers 3 and 6. Lancaster 1996. By permission of L. Lancaster.

would not have borne loads safely as freestanding elements (Fig. 78). Furthermore, the tufa blocks could hardly have been shaped and inserted into the interstices between these piers. Both travertine (hatched) and tufa (white) were cut to meet the needs of the moment. Such interstitial "backfilling" as Cozzo proposes rarely happened except in repair work. We must appreciate just how time consuming it is to cut blocks to be slotted into a confined space. Take, for example, the tufa block shaped like a T turned sideways at the left side of Fig. 78 (shown shaded). To make it fit precisely between preexisting blocks of travertine above and below would have required hours of meticulous labor on the five faces of contact with the pier, and if it was the last block to be laid in its row, it would somehow have to be pounded in sideways rather than lowered from above.[22] More likely, it was notched to fit the travertine block to its lower left, set into place just after the travertine blocks to its immediate left had been laid, and then notched again when the next course was laid on top of it.

What about Cozzo's efficiency model? It is brilliant, but for one thing: It deprives the stoneworkers of their lifting advantage. The large tufa blocks constituting the walls filling in between the travertine piers were on a scale similar to or only slightly smaller than those in the piers themselves, which averaged about four tonnes apiece and were equipped with large lewis holes.[23] How would they have been lifted into place under a canopy of concrete and amid the cramped forest of uprights? There simply was not enough room

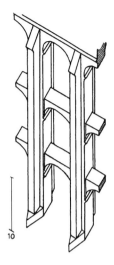

79. Segovia: aqueduct design with cross-braced arches. Giovannoni 1925.

for cranes of adequate lifting capacity, which required a clear zone in which to manipulate their rigging, to work in this space. As so often happens in architectural history, but rarely in successful architectural planning, the problems of interaction among movable, temporary elements (cranes, centering, people, animals, materials depots, etc.) and the immovable and permanent building to which they contribute have not been adequately considered. This more dynamic view of building is the source of a great deal of creativity in architectural design, because no single sequence of contingencies is necessarily the *right* sequence. There are many roads to the same destination, some short and flat, others steep and winding. Cozzo's path is at best a tortuous one, at worst a dead end with no exit. The arches that troubled him are not as superfluous as he claims, for those spanning the inner two piers of the four-pier sequence, 5 and 6, actually do have a void below them. This is the landing where the stairways turned the corner as they wrapped around the solid walls connecting Piers 3–5 (see Fig. 76).[24] It is possible that specialists in aqueduct engineering had been called in to design these pier armatures. Their design reflects a form well known in aqueduct studies, the cross-braced arcade (Fig. 79).[25] The brick arches may therefore have served as lateral braces for the travertine piers at this level, not as load deflectors. After all, the piers at Level 2 would have gone up independently before the bricks were laid between them.

LEVEL ONE

There can be little doubt that the initial intent at ground level was to raise the armature of travertine piers and tufa walls to a certain height, probably the deck of Level 2. Essentially the same techniques of dressing, lifting, and clamping applied to both stone types, so there is no reason to suggest that each material was handled by different crews. One initial task was to create wooden templates for Piers 1–3, which have complex footprints accommodating engaged columns or pilasters (Fig. 80).[26] With these provided, stonemasons could stencil out each course of stones.

Wall construction normally proceeds upward uniformly, course by complete course. There are several reasons for this. It is simpler to construct scaffolding in superimposed rows than in adjacent columns. A complete row of stones can be checked more comprehensively for levelness and plumbness than a few stones at a time.

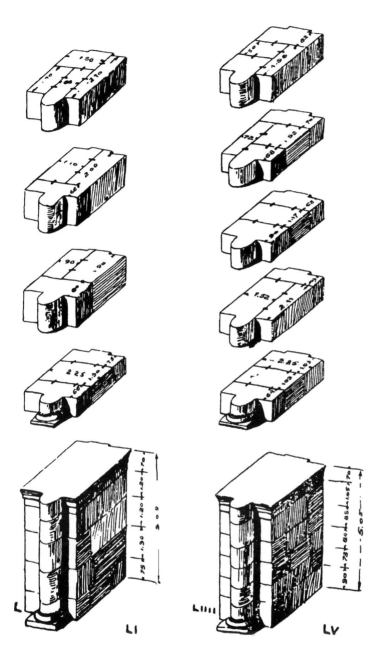

80. Rome: Colosseum, exploded view of the travertine courses forming piers. Cozzo 1928.

Starting at one end or at the center, the blocks, completely dressed on their surfaces of contact but left unfinished on their visible surfaces, were lowered by cranes onto the bearing surface, where workmen would slide and rock them precisely into position with levers. The joining surfaces would all be checked and corrected with a flat chisel if necessary. The block's upper surface would be tested for levelness, both inherent and in relation to the other blocks in the course, and made roughly plumb with the wall faces (the most structurally critical of the three dimensions of ashlar masonry). Most corrections could probably be made either with the block in place or by tilting it with the help of the crane for additional dressing. As a row of blocks was being set in place, clamp sockets were cut across the upper joints and they were clamped together with iron and lead.

The single-row method does introduce a certain rigid linearity that can slow down the process. In a multilevel approach, work on various courses can proceed simultaneously, provided that there is room for more than one crane and crew. In a project as intensive as the Colosseum's, we can presume that an adequate number of prepared blocks was available at all times and that there were as many crews installing them as could possibly be accommodated on site. With this in mind, we may envision any number of time-saving arrangements. For example, two or more cranes could work alternately either side-by-side or opposite one another, or both. The workhorse of Roman cranes was a shear, or A-frame, type that provided great stability for lifting heavy blocks (Fig. 81, upper right). It could tilt forward as much as thirty-five degrees from vertical or more;[27] thus an exceptionally tall crane twenty meters high had a clear reach of perhaps thirteen meters. Its disadvantage was that it could not be pivoted horizontally during lifting: The reach was strictly linear along the crane's vertical plane of operation. In between lifts, then, a crane often had to be slid or turned with ropes and levers to align it with the new target. There is, however, a partial remedy for this time-consuming problem. The crane, rather than operating in a plane perpendicular to the wall, can be aligned with the wall, putting the entire target along the axis of its reach (Fig. 82). Although the end of a rising wall will incrementally obstruct the crane's mast, the problem can be minimized by raising the wall highest in the center and then completing it by working outward toward the upper corners. Another problem is that as a crane's angle digresses far from vertical, its stresses increase. At thirty degrees, the tensile stress on the stay cables becomes equal to the load itself, and beyond that angle it exceeds it.[28] The upshot of this principle is not decreased lifting efficiency (it is no harder to raise the load at this angle, since the hoisting mechanism is separate from the staying system) but that it requires concentrated resources behind the crane. The ropes, posts, and capstans used to control the angle of the mast – as well

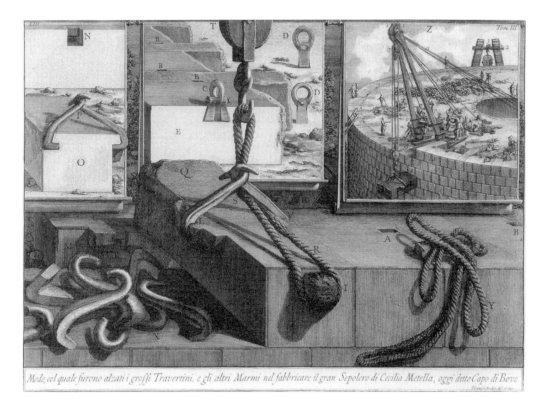

Modo, col quale furono alzati i grossi Travertini, e gli altri Marmi nel fabbricare il gran Sepolcro di Cecilia Metella, oggi detto Capo di Bove.

as the men and animals operating them – may have stood in the background of the masons, but their need for working space was just as real. And the space needed was considerable, for stay cables angling down sharply to the ground are not as efficient as, say, a horizontal clearance twice the length of the mast. It is rarely pointed out, though crucially important, that the capstans used to operate shear cranes were nowhere near as portable as the cranes themselves. Their liability was not their bulk but their need to be firmly anchored – often against many tonnes of tensile stress. Indeed, unless a building site was specifically designed to accommodate heavy capstans, there was no choice but to anchor them in the ground. Thus the entire lifting regime of a building had to be mapped out in advance, lest a crane crew should paint itself into a corner where it could no longer do its job simply because it lacked a clear line of access to its capstans outside the structure.

It was only natural to want to tackle the heavy lifting first, and at Level 1 this would mostly have been in the zone from Piers 1 to 7. Presumably there was then, as today, a good deal of clearance around the Colosseum precinct, allowing plenty of room for the

81. Analytical illustration of lewises and two-piece forceps with a hypothetical reconstruction of their use on the tomb of Caecilia Metella near Rome. G.-B. Piranesi, *Le antichità romane* (Rome 1756).

stay cables leading to the capstans. The central arena was also available for building materials and activity. Large cranes with long stays could therefore have been positioned along the radial axes just inboard from Pier 6 and outboard from Pier 3 (Fig. 82, a). Together each opposed pair of cranes had enough reach to complete the composite travertine and tufa walls without ever moving their footings. Just enough clearance was left between the cranes and the ends of the wall to accommodate the carts transporting the blocks. At Level 1 no consistent effort was made to draw a severe vertical drafting line between the travertine and tufa sections. In some places the lines were maintained, but in others the courses interlocked in a loose crenellated pattern. The tufa courses usually, but not always, corresponded in height to their neighbors in travertine. This fact does not, as Cozzo argues, imply two distinct building phases. Indeed, the quoinlike interlocking suggests quite the opposite. The masons simply improvised according to their own traditions. In general, they probably worked outward from the middle of the wall, so as to avoid the need to slot a block between two others. To make the most of the cranes' reach they may have chosen not to complete the wall course by course but, rather, to set the blocks in a roughly pyramidal pattern up to the top course of Level 1 and then, no longer in need of a crane reach to the center of the wall, to work outward. It is uncertain whether they needed any scaffolding at all, since the wall was thick enough to stand on comfortably.

Piers 3 and 6, being at either end of the walls, were rather more complicated than the others. Both supported circumferential arcades that would define the entranceways on either end of the corridors. The arcade of Pier 3 was of uniform height, considerably lower at the arch crowns than the overall height of Level 1. (The level of the crowns would in fact serve as the springing points for the annular vault of Ambulatory 2; Fig. 82, b.) The arches at the other end of these corridors had two heights: pairs of short arches under a stair landing followed by pairs of taller arches where there were no landings (Fig. 82, c). Again, the taller arches defined the springing level for the annular vault, this time of Ambulatory 3. The imposts for all these arches projected transversely from their host blocks, and to a great extent these arches and the walls above them had to be built at the same time as the radial walls. The arch voussoirs were set on simple semicircular wooden forms either propped on the cornices (as in position b) or on the ground (as in c). The voussoirs are

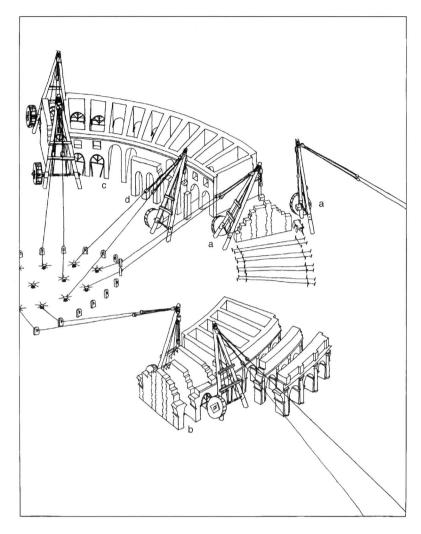

82. Rome: Colosseum, construction of Level 1. Illustration: R. Taylor.

elements of considerable subtlety, following not only the obvious curvature of the arch radius but also the very slight curvature of the circumferential plan.[29] These and everything above them was off-axis from the radial walls, and to hoist them the cranes would have to be angled slightly off their initial positions, a simple enough task with levers. Later the arcade surfaces would be thoroughly dressed. This required light scaffolding and could be done at any later phase. However there seems to be a general rule all around the Colosseum that wherever concrete was to meet stone, the surface of the stone was deeply scored or left rough to receive it.

One interesting aspect of the building sequence to the Colosseum is that the corridors formed by these walls remained clear and permeable, both horizontally and vertically, throughout the process of their construction up to the top of Level 1, even though roughly three out of every four of them were destined to be stairwells. The major stairways below Level 3 – all of them radial, none circumferential – were designed to be added after the completion of the stairwells. Their absence allowed a stream of men and materials to move in and out with ease and rapidity. Among these were the hydraulic engineers; as walls went up, they were installing carefully gauged pipes in recesses cut into the piers, overflow basins, and annular gutters leading to the preinstalled drainpipes. At irregular intervals around the circumference they ran supply pipes up the tufa walls behind Pier 3 (see Fig. 89). These were of a sufficient gauge to handle the volume for all the fountains at upper levels.[30]

The travertine-and-tufa walls, then, could be completed quickly. Now the large cranes probably assumed more widely separated berths, one moving to Ambulatory 4 and the other outboard of Pier 1. The inner crane would be responsible for the construction of Pier 7 in travertine (Fig. 82, *d*). One out of every four of the aisles formed by these walls would be an inboard stairway mounting to the seating area. The others gave direct access to Ambulatory 4. The outer crane would be occupied with the erection first of Pier 2, then Pier 1, each in travertine. Both of these piers, as also Pier 3, carried crisply dressed cosmetic surfaces that had to be treated with care. As before, there were many complex joints to be cut and fitted on site. Any elements requiring careful measurement or matching to their neighbors (and there were many) must have been dressed on site, where the stone carver could check his progress against the standing elements and the diagrams or instructions given him by the architects. Here again the circumferential arcades were erected in a fashion similar to those along Piers 3 and 6. The famous decorative scheme on the outer facade, all one with the travertine blocks, consisted at this level of an engaged Tuscan column, its entablature, and above these the dado for the next superposed columnar order (Fig. 83). The top of this dado, as also with Levels 2 and 3, corresponds perfectly with the flat deck atop the vaults, which forms the floor for the next level. It is thus the perfect stopping point for Level 1.

The innermost parts of the *cavea* – the latrines, Ambulatory 5, and its fronting podium – were in brick-faced concrete. They could have been constructed at any time, though not in such a way as to

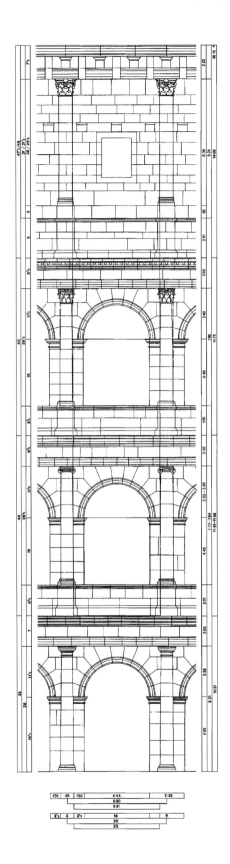

83. Rome: Colosseum, the facade orders. Wilson-Jones 2000. By permission of Yale University Press.

get entangled with the stays of the larger cranes in Ambulatory 4.
Now that all the stone elements of Level 1 were in place the next
step logistically (though temporally it must have overlapped the
first) was to apply the concrete vaulting, including the radial vaults
supporting the stairs and lower seating tiers. Strictly speaking, vaulting is a topic for Chapter 5, but the relatively small vaults of the
Colosseum did not present any significant problems of the sort we
explore there. Nor are they protective coverings; they are simply
part of the internal connective tissue of the organism. At this stage
the cranes would be removed and timber formwork and scaffolding
introduced. Now began the process of blocking most of the radial
passages, with the inevitable accumulation of wooden trestles and
scaffolds needed for this radically different building technique. The
patterns of transport and circulation were changed as well. Fewer
broad corridors of passage to the points of construction were needed to maintain the stockpiles of mortar and rubble. But because of
the speed of progress and the relative lack of skill necesary to mix
mortar, many more men and beasts would have been involved in
transport and fewer in the production. Materials could be hauled
up the scaffolding manually in buckets. The mixing of mortar in adjacent pits was a time-sensitive task that served the immediate needs
of the vaulting crews.

All five ambulatories, each radial corridor, and every length of
stairway required a concrete vault. The annular vaults over Ambulatories 1–3 were all designed to be laid on flying centering so that
the space below could still be used for the free passage of men and
materials. The centering, consisting of nearly semicircular wooden
frames set transversely at regular intervals around the ring and covered by lagging strips running along the axis of the corridor, could
be constructed and installed very quickly. These were set at the relatively short intervals of half a bay, so that no lagging board would
have to be flexed to accommodate the curve.[31] The concrete stairways and the radial sections of the two lower seating tiers, all of
which would be supported on diagonal vaults, were more challenging. Because of the slightly wedge-shaped plan of each corridor,
compounded by the upward diagonals of the stairs and seating
areas, these were no simple barrel vaults but rather sections of flattened cones. Before erection of the centering, three guides needed
to be in place: one each for the upper and lower limits of the vault
intrados, to ensure the correct placement of the centering frames;

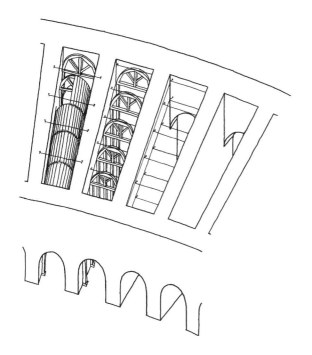

84. Rome: Colosseum, hypothetical string guides for establishing vault dimensions. Illustration: R. Taylor.

and an upper guide for the vault's extrados, to ensure the proper thickness of concrete (Fig. 84). They followed a line that ran precisely thirty degrees from the horizontal – one of the few drawing-board angles visible in elevation section, a clear sign that the design began at the bottom. The stairways' guides were inscribed as diagonal profiles on the walls. Where the concrete vault supporting the stairs was to come in contact with the wall, the stone surface was gouged or left rough. The centering frames would all be simple half-circles of different sizes and set at incremental heights on wooden props. In the stairwells it may have been simpler to complete the upper vaults before installing the stairs, so that the stair treads would not have to support any centering.

With the lagging in place, workers would apply horizontal layers of mortar and rubble to its surface. In the outer ambulatory vaults, ribs of brick and mortar were added, often at regular distances (Fig. 85).[32] They started at the lowest points and worked upward, taking care to keep the concrete mass in balance along the vault's axis. The concrete would be built up gradually into planar or stepped surfaces, its surfaces checked periodically with a leveling square.

As the extradoses of the tier vaults began to develop into the smooth surface of the *cavea,* the seating rows were carefully measured out from the edge of the arena. Perhaps their lines were inscribed in the wet concrete. The rows do not seem to have been shaped in concrete; instead, they consisted of solid blocks of marble beveled to fit the slope and crane-hoisted into place. These were all cut to a modular length and shape and presumably altered as necessary on site.[33] At three levels entranceways pierced the *cavea* surface periodically, all opening on radial spaces, either stairways or level passages. Inside the stairwells, the stair risers were finished in travertine. Beside them ran gutters in the same material. These would handle the runoff of both rain and fountain overflow.

Where were the architect and master builders during all of this? Theirs was, at this stage, an overwhelmingly supervisory and informational task. They were constantly canvassing the site, checking progress against the diagrams, conferring with crew foremen and among themselves about emerging problems, and ensuring as much consistency in materials and techniques as necessary while not insisting on absolute uniformity. It has been suggested that the four quadrants of the Colosseum were built by completely independent teams in order to maximize speed and efficiency.[34] Still, the notion of absolute independence between sectors is not in itself efficient. The project overseers and their assistants would have assigned specialized crews who had completed a task in one sector to similar work in another. Lancaster notes that each quadrant has distinctive stair vault profiles at Level 1, but does not identify quadrant-specific work at higher levels.[35] Indeed one would expect to see the greatest amount of segregation of labor early in the project, that is, at ground level, when all the crews were starting in different sectors. As the project progressed, and schedules began to diverge, some crews that had finished their initial task may have been moved to different sectors while others remained in place. Such minor complications (the thirty-degree angle dissolving into less pure geometry above is another example) can help us understand why buildings did not have the paradigmatic force of a poem, a painting, or a sculpture. Unpredictable contingency influences not only the form but the means of realizing the form. Management strategies that took an overly long-range view were apt to founder upon their projections and estimates, whereas midrange strategies and short-range tactics founded on flexibility and adaptability probably worked rather well.

85. Rome: Colosseum, outer ambulatory of Level 2, with visible ribs in the vault. Iron tie-rods are modern. Photo: R. Taylor.

At the end of the first stage of construction, two seating zones led up to a flat working surface extending all the way from Pier 7 to Pier 1. This floor was not entirely without encumbrances: Some of the stairwells, being incomplete, left oblong radial voids in this surface (Fig. 86). To avoid accidents, these may have been covered with planking. From this stage onward, many of the hoisting tasks would be divided into multiple stages: raising the material to the work surface ("supply" hoisting), moving it to the necessary crane, and then raising it to its designated place ("position" hoisting). Probably much of the supply hoisting took place around the periphery with cranes set on the ground. If so, it had to be done with great care in order to protect the travertine facade. Some protection would have been provided by the scaffolding that served the stonemasons working on the surface details and finish.

THE UPPER LEVELS

The only stone elements at Level 2 were piers and arches. The travertine Piers 3–6 would abandon the crenellated pattern of the lower level and become conventionally straight (see Figs. 72, 73, 77). The three cross-braced arches connecting them, which I discussed above (at the end of the section "Cozzo's Paradigm"), were probably laid out on centering, for in about one quarter of the walls the inner arch actually spanned a void, a stair landing at Level 2a between Piers 5 and 6 (see Fig. 74). The walls beneath these arches, which had been of tufa on the ground level, would be continued in brick-faced concrete here; the familiar putlog holes associated with Roman brickwork are still visible in them. But construction of the piers and their stone arches took priority. The stay cables had to be kept clear, and thus each crane would have progressed sideways or backward, probably from the outside inward (see Fig. 86). Backward movement was the most efficient; the stay cables never had to be disengaged when the crane's frame was moved, and the capstans could be employed to drag the whole crane inboard for repositioning. Special care was taken to ensure that the cranes did not fall into the stairwells. Most likely, the bottom of each crane's frame was securely attached to stout transverse timbers long enough to span the stairwell voids. In this fashion Piers 1–3 would be raised all the way to the deck of Level 3, whereas Piers 4–6 were raised to progressively lower heights.

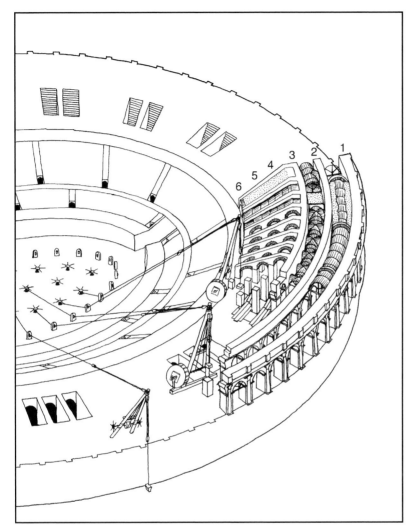

86. Rome: Colosseum, construction of Level 2. Illustration: R. Taylor.

Apart from the piers and arches, all construction at levels 2a and 2b was to be done with brick, mortar, or concrete, on scaffolding or centering and without cranes. The small, light materials of brick-and-concrete construction are easily handled but generate more traffic than stonework does. The work often progresses quickly, requiring higher volumes of material in shorter time spans.[36] Mortar is applied wet and must arrive in small, frequent deliveries. Bricks must be sawn or broken to fit, baskets shouldered, buckets loaded and hoisted – all at or near the center of action. The architects had ensured that cornices or imposts projected from the piers at all the critical places to support flying centering, thereby keeping the pas-

87. Rome: Colosse-
um, ambulatory of
Level 2b. Fototeca
Unione c/o American
Academy in Rome,
neg. 12183.

sages beneath the emerging vaults clear (see Fig. 86). Level 2a had
standard molded cornices; 2b had simple inward-curving imposts
for the very low vaulting (Fig. 87, and see Fig. 75). The various stairway schemes were constructed in about the same manner as before.
One feature of note is the different heights of Ambulatories 1 and
2, necessitating a cross vault, rather than a barrel vault, over the
lower inner ambulatory (Fig. 88, and see Fig. 74).

At every phase the plumbers were among the first on the scene
(Fig. 89). Water pipes ascending behind Piers 3 divided at deck level,
one branch digressing circumferentially, another continuing upward
inside the brick wall to the cornice level, where it emerged and
snaked around the top of the cornice to the front of the pier. From
here it headed up through the cross vault to Level 2b. Twenty or
more of these "pipe trees," all rooted in the same annular subterranean main, sprang up around the Colosseum, and apparently no
two were the same. The engineers were given discretion to lay pipe
as seemed most appropriate at the moment. But they were always

attentive to the overall network; though every tree was unique, each filled out its designated space.

Now we get to Level 3 and a controversy. Among the most puzzling features of the Colosseum are the large travertine corbels that project into the ambulatory from the outer piers at Level 3 (Figs. 90, 91). In the preserved Flavian section of the building, these are of quite regular height and thickness. But in the areas restored in antiquity after a damaging fire, they are inconsistent, and several are missing altogether.[37] They do not appear on any other level. Cozzo maintains that they supported the interior scaffolding for the great travertine attic that was erected above this level (see Fig. 76).[38] Obviously this model – in keeping with Cozzo's other "verticalist" hypothesis discussed above – presumes that the entire attic was erected before the vaults of Levels 3a and 3b were added. As others have noted, this scenario is deeply flawed.[39] For one thing, the corbels are unnecessary for the task assigned to them. It was easier, and indeed safer, to raise scaffolding from the deck of Levels 2, 3, and 4 succes-

88. Rome: Colosseum, inner ambulatory of Level 2a. Fototeca Unione c/o American Academy in Rome, neg. 6001.

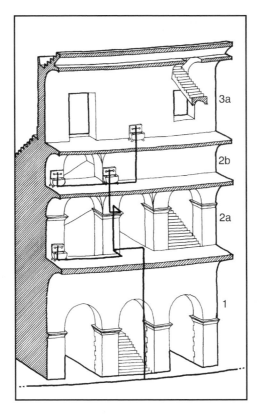

89. Rome: Colosseum, section of Levels 1–3 with typical water-supply scheme. Illustration: R. Taylor.

90. Rome: Colosseum, stairway of outer corridor of Level 3a. Anonymous lithograph, ca. 1860.

sively: Certainly there could be no perceived danger that light scaffolding would jeopardize the vaults below. Apparently cognizant of the real problem, the matter of adequate footings for the heavy lifting apparatus, Cozzo seems to suggest that this was no ordinary scaffold but rather a structure sturdy enough to hoist the travertine blocks of the attic. No effort is made to explain how this was done. Where were the capstans or windlasses anchored? How were the blocks moved laterally after they were raised? The whole scheme is in fact absurd. Not only is it needlessly precarious, but it seems to imply that large cranes would have been too constricted or heavy at the upper levels to do their job. There is plenty of material evidence to refute such a presumption: most obviously, the large columns with seven-meter monolithic shafts that once stood around the inboard side of Level 4. There was only one way to get the columns in place, and that was with large cranes.

The difficulty with the corbels is not that they were useless but that they did not seem to address the foremost problem of heavy

91. Rome: Colosseum, interior surface of outer wall from Level 3a to top. Fototeca Unione c/o American Academy in Rome, neg. 528.

lifting. This is puzzling, for there is enough evidence at higher levels to suggest that the builders did not trust the concrete vaults to resist heavy point-loads. Although the Colosseum required no shoring up during construction, we may reasonably suppose that at this stage evidence of the building's internal stresses was emerging. The builders well appreciated that an amphitheater must stand up not only to static loads but to those of cranes lifting several tonnes at a time, and ultimately to fifty thousand human beings in rhythmic movement. The heavy cranes may have caused cracking in the lower vaults, particularly at the crowns and around the surface of contact with the vertical travertine elements, shaking confidence in the strength of the lateral bonds and in the planned thicknesses of the vaults. Whatever the precise inducement, these corbels at Level 3a may have been the first reactive measure taken, but with uncertain practical applications. In themselves, with jutting cornices directly above them, they could not support cranes or vertical props of any kind. Whatever their purpose originally, the third-century reconstruction was accomplished without their help. So desultory are the replacements (some, we recall, are missing altogether) that the rebuilders plainly had no understanding of their function.

Let us then restore the corbels to the status of an unsolved mystery and resurrect the cranes, now hauled up the *cavea* surface, or dead-lifted by smaller cranes, to Level 3 (Fig. 92). We are reduced to a much narrower floor, pierced by stairwell voids and light shafts, and just two rings of travertine piers, 1 and 2, which would have been extended upward in the same way as on the previous level. The attic does not actually begin until Level 4. At the top of the Level 3 facade there was merely a higher band of dadoes and recesses above the arcade entablature, all of which would receive the same treatment as Level 2 but with small square windows in alternating bays; these looked out from Level 3b (Figs. 92, *a; 93*).

Most of the rest of the work at Level 3 was in brick, mortar, and concrete. Some have argued that the bewildering array of vaults and stairways of Levels 3 and 4 was partly an afterthought, the consequence of later restorations, but there is no compelling evidence that the scheme was changed from the original Flavian plan.[40] Now there was no room for radial stairwells; all available space had to be given over to annular circulation. In Ambulatory 1 of Level 3a, brick-and-concrete staircases hugged the inner arcade (see Fig. 90). In Ambulatory 2 of the same level, symmetrically converging stairs

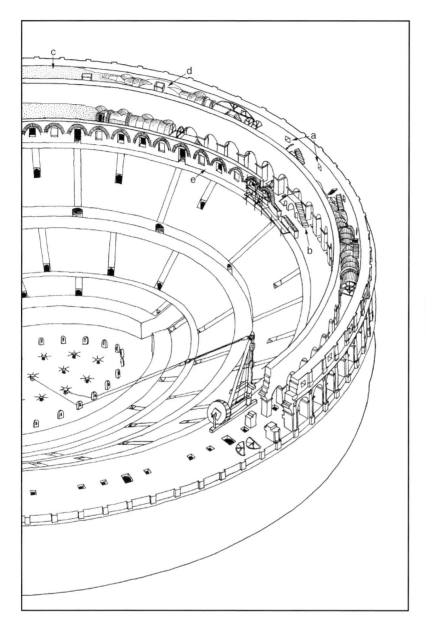

92. Rome: Colosseum, construction of Level 3. Illustration: R. Taylor.

hugged the other side of the same arcade, but only up to a landing just below cornice level (see Fig. 92, *b*). From there, the architects had recourse to a most unusual feature in premodern Western architecture: a flying or rampant staircase (see Fig. 74). This leapt overhead, ascending inbound to the penultimate seating tier. The stairways in Ambulatory 3b – which can still be seen outlined against the inner brick skin of the outer wall – were smaller but almost iden-

93. Rome: Colosseum, view of exterior from the north. Fototeca Unione c/o American Academy in Rome, neg. 6261.

tical in design (Figs. 94, 95). Their visible remains appear to be a third-century restoration that reflects more or less faithfully the Flavian model.[41] Rather like coat hangers on wall pegs, all the staircases at this level were supported by single travertine corbels projecting inward from above the piers. This measure evidently was intended to relieve the vaulted floor of the stairs' loads. One can still see the stumps of the travertine treads embedded in the concrete that lines the interior of the attic beginning at Level 3b (see Fig. 91). In the reconstruction, at least, the stairs were not built after the walls, as in lower levels, but seem to have been completed at the same time as the attic at this level. The symmetrical stone steps and their central "pegs" could actually have been finished before the vault below them, thereby briefly claiming distinction as the first cantilevered stairs on record until they were shored up by the concrete floor capping the vault. The great number of staircases at Levels 3a and 3b – thirty-two for access to the tiny penultimate seating sector and twenty-four leading to the equally constricted wooden tier of Level

94. Rome: Colosseum, "flying" staircases of Level 3b. Illustration: R. Taylor.

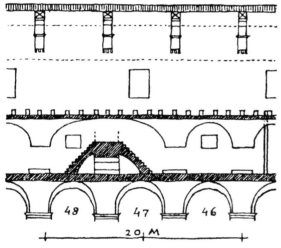

95. Rome: Colosseum, inner elevation of Levels 3b and 4. Von Gerkan 1925.

4 – is a function of their delicacy. These were stairs to be climbed single- or double-file.

At this stage, the vaulting technique needs little comment. However, one particularly imaginative feature is introduced. Over the flying staircases embedded in the wall, the standard single-bay cross vault is stretched over two adjacent bays (see Fig. 95). Thus the vault, though remaining semicircular in radial cross section, becomes a broad, sweeping half-ellipse in circumferential cross section (see Fig. 92, *d*).

Over Pier 3 was erected a high brick podium separating two seating sectors (see Fig. 92, *e*). It would be richly decorated with marble. Pier 2, probably completed in brick, also supported a podium at the top of the stone seating area. Extending to this podium were the cross vaults of Level 3b. Very thin at their crowns, they caused sufficient worry to induce extraordinary measures. These took the form in the third-century restoration – and probably in the original building campaign as well – of a double floor. From the upper podium to the brick-and-concrete inner skin of the attic, radial joists were extended directly over the concrete floor (Fig. 96, and see Fig. 92, c), presumably topped with wooden planking. Their sockets are still visible in the brick (see Figs. 91, 95). The footings for the columns, however, would have been solid stone or concrete resting on the podium below. The double floor provided excellent support for the cranes, which were to see some of their heaviest work at this level.

There were five classes of elements to be lifted to Level 4, each in its own logical sequence: bases, shafts, capitals, entablature blocks, blocks for the attic (Fig. 96). Almost certainly the first elements to be set in place were the composite columns upon the upper podium. In this cramped environment, the cranes could not operate as before, by sliding backward and inboard between tasks. Their progress was exclusively lateral, the cumbersome but inevitable dictate of circumstance. Presuming that the elements were lifted from the ground outside, there was no way to hoist and position them in a single operation. Within work units, two treadmill cranes were probably used in staggered succession, moving circumferentially – the first hoisting elements from the ground to the center of the deck, then sliding laterally to the next position while the second moved in to swing them inboard into position (Fig. 96, a and b). The two cranes necessarily would have faced in opposite directions, outboard and inboard, respectively. Every column comprised three elements: base, seven-meter shaft, and capital (some later replacements of these capitals exceed a meter in height).[42] All were lifted by the first crane from an upright position on the ground and carefully set, still upright, onto the wooden deck. These elements mostly lack lewis holes; they must have been encircled by hoisting ropes. The elegantly minimal capitals, with smoothly pierced volutes, seem specifically designed for a rope girdle, but the shafts must have had lifting bosses.

Both cranes would have to be moved into place with great care in order to avoid upsetting the column shafts, which may have been steadied with wooden props or ladders for the workers disengaging

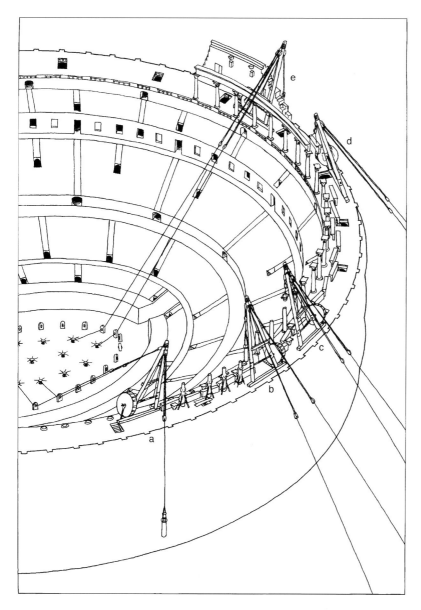

96. Rome: Colosseum, construction of Level 4. Illustration: R. Taylor.

and engaging the ropes during the transfer of cranes. The main encumbrances were the circular treadmills, each perhaps four meters in diameter. Detaching them must have been a simple matter of extracting a couple of axle linchpins and rolling the wheels out of the way between moves. Ultimately, the two tasks of supply and position hoisting may have consumed roughly equal amounts of time, with one crane dedicated to the first task and three to the latter. Raising all the elements – nine-tonne column shafts and entablature blocks, as well as bases and capitals – forty meters into the air was no small task, equivalent perhaps to mounting the shafts on the bases and the capitals on the shafts, accompanied by the insertion of iron dowels and the careful pouring of lead to anchor them in place (Fig. 96, *b* and *c*). A similar procedure was followed *between* radial axes for the positioning of the marble entablature blocks spanning the intercolumniations (Fig. 96, *d*).

With the columns and entablature in position the task of raising the attic could begin (Figs. 96, *e*; 97). Though fairly thin for its height, this great sheet of clamped travertine blocks was stiffened by its curvature, much as a piece of paper, when set upright on a tabletop, acquires strength and structure if it is rolled into a vertical cylinder. The blocks of stone were raised as before, though the stay cables for the cranes had to remain above the intervening columnar order. But now they formed a solid wall punctuated by rectangular windows. As always, the crew foremen were faced with dozens of intricate tasks to compete with their broader, more administrative concerns. The course of blocks above the windows was particularly challenging: three projecting corbels were to be set at equal intervals between each pair of engaged pilasters on the attic facade (see Figs. 83, 93). In the alternating bays with windows, the center corbel doubled as a keystone for the flat arch crowning the window. The single voussoirs on either side of the keystone would have been held in place on wooden centering – perhaps just a few upright timbers of equal length – until the keystone was dropped in place. These corbels would serve as the props for wooden masts that carried the great canopy over the *cavea*. At a higher level, inwardly projecting corbels would support the roof beams of Level 4 (Fig. 96, *e*).

Only when the attic was raised to its summit fifty meters above the ground, and crowned with the heavy perforated cornice through which the canopy masts would be threaded, was the timbering accomplished at the upper level. The crane used for the attic could also be assigned this task, but only if the radial joists could be swung far enough to one side of the crane. A small windlass custom-designed to fit in a stairwell could pull the load laterally until it was clear of the crane's mast, then it could be eased down into place, one end on the entablature and the other on the corbels projecting from the attic's inner face.

97. Rome: Colosseum, inner surface of attic. Fototeca Unione c/o American Academy in Rome, neg. 529.

This chapter has dealt exclusively with a specialized type of Roman building, the amphitheater. It belongs to an isolated class of buildings in antiquity encompassing theaters, stadia, and circuses as well. In one respect this genre is unique, for it embodies a structural design that is both grand and intimate. The visitor, if not too constrained by class divisions, was able to communicate at close quarters with its physical armature nearly from top to bottom and on nearly every surface. Nothing, except the distant visual prospects and the serpentine spatial logic, is far out of reach. Frank Brown envisioned amphitheaters as cups and bowls; one might further characterize them as exquisitely permeable sponges of humanity.

5

ROOFING AND VAULTING

Should the builders around the . . . stonemason Epigonos, con-
tractors for the part of the theater over which Ulpianus Heros,
prophet of the god, has charge of the work, and for which
Menophilos the architect has let the contract – should they deck
out the piers with the arches and four-sided vaults, and bring
them to fruition, or look for another contract? The god responded: "For skill and wisdom in the art of building, as for
the counsel of even the very cleverest man, it is meet to obey
those whose offerings appease Pallas Tritogeneia and mighty
Herakles."
– Greek inscription from the Roman theater of Miletos[1]

We are lucky to have three related buildings in Rome
with very different structural histories. The Baths
of Trajan, attributed to Apollodorus of Damascus,
have been leveled nearly to the ground. The similarly scaled Baths
of Caracalla have lost most of the vaulting in every room of the bath
block, but many walls, arches, and fragments of vaults still stand.
Finally the Baths of Diocletian on the Esquiline Hill, also roughly
on the same scale, retain many vaulted spaces intact – including the
great hall of the frigidarium, converted into the transept of S. Maria
degli Angeli (Fig. 98, and see Fig. 2). It is clear which building had
the more successful structural design, and yet we pay little attention
to its structure because the Roman fabric is hidden under a Renais-

98. Rome: Baths of Diocletian, now Church of S. Maria degli Angeli. Vault of frigidarium. Photo: R. Taylor.

sance veneer. We may hope that soon these great buildings, along with the hulking Basilica of Maxentius – an inflated epigone of the others that took structural design to the edge of the Faustian abyss – will be profitably subjected to comparative study with the help of modern materials analysis and computer modeling tools. Even today we have little idea why the first two halls failed and Diocletian's did not. Was some advance in bath design or technique made in the nearly two centuries intervening between Apollodorus' masterpiece and the anonymously produced structure commissioned by Diocletian? Did a single architect, after examining the older buildings, experience an epiphany of structural design? Or can we attribute their various fates to sheer luck or the destructive whims of posterity?

The physical success of premodern vaulted structures still arouses more intuitive speculation than scientific investigation. Ancient architects and builders knew much more than we do about the actions of masonry buildings. In an era of prestressed, reinforced concrete and steel-frame buildings, we have forgotten the lore that accumulated with centuries of careful observation of pure masonry structures. But in recent years, thanks to the efforts of historically informed structural engineers, the clouds have begun to disperse.[2] Concrete vaults, it is now recognized, act very much like vaults in other less cohesive techniques such as brick and mortar or cut stone. The one real structural advantage of concrete is that its rubble aggregate can be gradated from heavy stone at the base to lightweight volcanic stone at the crown. Roman builders took full advantage of this virtue.[3]

Centering for concrete presented special problems, for any deformation of the wooden form would be transmitted to the vault. It was important to begin casting the vault at the bottom; this would minimize, though not eliminate, the actions of dead weight upon the centering. The masons applied the concrete in roughly horizontal layers. As it set the concrete would develop its own stonelike homogeneity, and its strength and coherence would increase while its deadweight loads upon the centering were much reduced. This is easily envisioned if we replicate the process on a scale model with plaster. At first the plaster has no coherence, depending for its form on the wooden mold beneath it, upon which it bears down with all its weight. But soon this ceases to be the case: We can remove the formwork, even if the vault is left incomplete, and the plaster will stay in place, hanging out over the void. The formwork, in effect, has compounded the statical indeterminacy. This fact does not mean that it is relieved of all external loads, for during the application of concrete it will have deformed to some degree under the weight and become wedged in place by compression and friction. The important point to remember, though, is this: As in the application of cement on a thin brick layer over the suspended *bipedales* of a hypocaust, the mode of application – layered and incremental, or abrupt and unphased – matters tremendously to the amount of stress endured by the underlayer.

However, the centering under any large concrete vault – especially a dome – never bore more than a small fraction of the full deadweight of the concrete applied to it. Concrete begins to hydrate, or harden, as soon as it has been mixed, and it continues to do so at a decreasing rate as long as it is kept moist and held within a given temperature range.[4] It is important to recognize that hydrating concrete, even if still moist, is not liquid like freshly mixed concrete. Wet concrete at lower levels will be much more rigid than the wet concrete laid more recently on top of it and will begin to exercise tensile and compressive strength. The full strength of concrete accumulates slowly. Setting, which is accomplished in a couple of hours, accounts for only about 10–20 percent of strength; curing, which continues for years, but is mostly complete after two or three weeks, accounts for the rest.[5] The upshot of this phenomenon is that no Roman concrete vault of great size generated a continuous dead load over the entire surface of its centering.[6] As the lower parts were strengthening, the formwork in that area was being relieved of some of its load while the higher parts were taking on the greater burden of liquid concrete.

Whatever deformities developed would be a permanent blemish on the vault. It may have been common practice to compensate for anticipated deformity, which in domes and barrel vaults is usually manifested as a flattening of the profile, by heightening the crown of the centering above the position it would take after loading. The measure of a good supporting framework was the extent to which it resisted deformity. Few surviving arches, vaults, walls, or piers in Roman buildings show obvious deformations that took place during vault erection, though many vaults, when plotted photogrammetrically, are revealed to be a few centimeters short of a perfect half circle.[7]

Builders must have recognized that a vaulted building in progress lacked the equilibrium that it would gain when completed. Complex vaulting systems, especially of bath buildings, therefore required a fully conceived construction plan. Any lapse in logic or confusion of sequence could spell doom. One example of logistical thought visible in structural form is the vaulting of the apodyteria in the Baths of Caracalla at Rome (see Fig. 45, rooms 3E and 3W, with bays *a–d*). The spur walls dividing these rooms into bays are unusually thin, indicating that they were meant to take the counteracting thrusts of two identical vaults over the bays that they divided.[8] The builder's first inclination might be to save labor and materials by centering one room, completing the vault over it, then reusing the centering in the other room to construct the companion vault. But this would have endangered the vault, projecting unopposed horizontal thrusts on the thin dividing wall before they could be counteracted by the second vault. The workers probably vaulted the two rooms concurrently, working symmetrically to keep the dividing wall in balance. Some Roman bridges were built in a similar fashion in order to keep their piers balanced; they were early ancestors of the modern cantilevered bridge.[9]

There was no mold for the exterior of the vault, and thus the profile of its thickness was a matter of judgment or careful measurement. Wet mortar, having the characteristics of a viscous liquid, would tend to pool into lower areas and its upper surface to settle into a horizontal plane. This tendency may account for two common Roman practices. First was the thickening of the vault toward the bottom, which in effect reduces the pitch of its exterior near its base and eases the difficulty of laying mortar on a near-vertical surface. Of course this tends to have a stabilizing effect too, but it has been pointed out that Roman domes are much thicker than they need to be.[10] The step rings of the Pantheon, which may have relied on formwork, are now thought to be a structural liability.[11] The second Roman tradition was the mixing of very large amounts of rubble into the mortar, in effect creating concrete (see Figs. 35, 110). The chunks of stone and terra cotta caused enough of a damming effect that the mortar could be shaped to some extent like a truly plastic material.[12] Although the aggregate was laid horizontally in intervals, allowing for partial setting between applications, the portion of the new layer forming the outer surface would have to retain its oblique surface without help. But precisely how the vault's thickness was monitored is unknown. Perhaps one of the advantages of brick ribs, used widely in Roman concrete vaults in the third century, is that they served as thickness gauges.[13]

DESIGNING CENTERING

The unsung heroes of Roman architecture are the carpenters. In the construction of large, vaulted buildings everything depended on their skill and intelligence. Even more than the master masons, they must have been intensely aware of structure, sequence, and process. Their understanding of the tolerances of timber, and of the most efficient means of manipulating and joining wooden members, was essential, as was their ability to build complex geometric shapes high in the air and across vast open spans. This wooden formwork, essentially the mold on which the vaulting was to be laid, had to support many tons of stone or concrete without too much distortion. The wooden facing then would be removed out from under the pressure of the dried concrete or stone masonry, but without necessarily bringing down the timber framework holding it in place; for under large vaults the framework would serve as scaffolding for the plasterers, mosaicists, and other decorators. The carpenters and rigging specialists ensured that at every step appropriate places were available for positioning the cranes, gantries, booms, or pulleys that would raise and lower the timbers, and for positioning the men who would guide them into place.

Centering techniques in antiquity are undocumented except to the extent that they are visible in the buildings themselves. The only suitable material for centering was wood, aided under tensile stresses by metal fasteners or rope. The shaping and constructing of timber formwork was costly and time-consuming. Efficiency was all-important, demanding innovations at which we can only guess. Certainly Romans perfected the use of flying centering, a kind of formwork erected not from the ground up but from the springing points of the planned arches or vaults. Flying centering of large buildings was probably constructed in modular units on the ground and at least partially preassembled to ensure that all the members fit together correctly and could be assembled from the available platforms. Special lifting devices might have to be devised in order to make the best use of the cramped space on the highest completed parts of the support structure. Once the crane components had been hoisted up on pulleys and assembled on platforms or piers, then the centering timbers, either partially preassembled or marked individually for quick reassembly, were lifted into place. If unmortared stone was to be used, the voussoirs themselves could be laid upon the experimental centering to ensure a precise fit before the entire ensemble was reerected on the structure itself. On the Pont du Gard near Nîmes a numbering system is still visible on some of the bridge's voussoirs, suggesting that they were fitted together experimentally before becoming components of the bridge (Figs. 99, 100).

Only experienced carpenters understood the demands of scale on timbers of varying sizes, wood species, and configurations. The effectiveness of joints, so essential to the success of the whole, depended on knowledge of the actions upon them such as tension, compression, torsion, or shear. A primary consideration of joints in centering is that they must be easy to disassemble under trying circumstances. For this reason they are not likely to resemble joints

99. Nîmes: Pont du Gard. Photo: R. Taylor.

in, say, shipbuilding. Hero of Alexandria recommends rope lashing rather than fasteners for the joints of large lifting engines.[14] Indeed the carpenters must have relied heavily on a combination of hewn joinery and lashing techniques, but joints in tension were sometimes best served by iron bolts, which I discuss below (in the section "Building the Pantheon Dome"). Nails or spikes were used mainly to hold members in place, not to create a genuine joint. Flying centering relies principally on a system of tension (triangular trusses) or of compression (polygonal wooden arches). The largest projects, such as the Pont du Gard, the Basilica of Maxentius, the great bath complexes, and the Pantheon, combined both, but with an emphasis on compression. Arches and barrel vaults are entirely compressive, while semicircular domes are fully compressive in their upper areas and circumferentially tensile in the lower. Centering, however, will undergo complex shifts in stresses as the masonry accumulates on top of them.

The principle of the truss, where the load bearing down in compression upon an angle of a triangle creates tension in its opposite side, could be used effectively to counteract the flattening and

100. Nîmes: Pont du Gard, mason's marks designating s[inistra], m[edia], d[extra] ("left, middle, right") and I, II, III, IIII, V. Photo: R. Taylor.

spreading tendencies of an arch or a vault until it was stabilized by the masonry around it. Evidence for the Romans' widespread use of the truss is strong; in addition to numerous apparent examples depicted in the reliefs of the Column of Trajan, we have documentation of a trussed roof over the porch of the Pantheon (removed in the Renaissance). To this can now be added a funerary relief in Rome showing an ashlar stone structure with a trussed roof system (Fig. 101).[15] Jean-Pierre Adam reconstructs the centering of the Pont du Gard as two compression systems (the butted chords directly under the intrados of the arch and the large angular struts at the bottom) enmeshed with a tensile system; this is the isosceles triangle extending from the two upper stone corbels to the crown (Fig. 102). John Fitchen proposes a lighter structure with a com-

101. Rome: relief discovered in the vicinity of the Palazzo della Cancelleria depicting a structure with complex timber roof. Musei Capitolini. Illustration: R. Taylor.

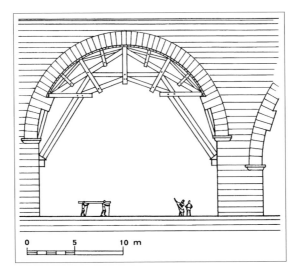

102. Nîmes: Pont du Gard, hypothetical centering scheme. Adam 1994. By permission of Chrysalis Books.

pound horizontal tie beam subjected to tension and compression in successive nodes (Fig. 103).[16] The part above the upper corbels would have been able to support only a single set of voussoirs; thus the framework had to be moved twice to complete the arch, which is three voussoirs thick. Whatever the means by which the centering was moved – the process probably was achieved with the help of ropes suspended from above – lightness was indispensable.

Indeed it is often presumed that whenever possible a single centering framework was used repeatedly in a building under construction. A diligent student could identify repeated patterns of wood grain impressed into concrete barrel vaults at dozens of sites. But in the largest projects such economy was patently impractical. Speed and the demands for structural equilibrium required that many vaults be built concurrently. And then there is a matter that is too often forgotten or dismissed: Over particularly lofty spaces, the centering necessarily served as scaffolding for the decorators. This was of little concern on bridges, but it was supremely important in monumental buildings. Without waste, delay, and expense, centering over great halls would not often have been fully dismantled until the construction *and decoration* of the upper vaulting were complete. Both purposes were factored into design of the carpentry.

Centering must undergo an intermediate stage between loading and dismantling. In this phase, known as *easing*, the supporting framework is made to drop away slightly from the surface by the removal of wedges from joints between compressive elements.

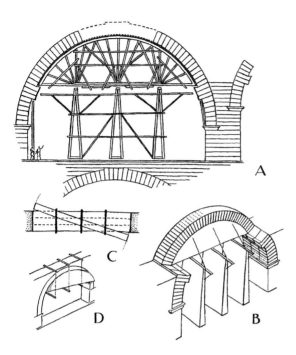

A

C

D   B

103. Nîmes: Pont du Gard, hypothetical centering scheme. Fitchen 1961. By permission of University of Chicago Press.

Wedges could be set under the feet of the centering or in intermediate positions between crown and feet. Blocks of serrated compound wedges, such as those proposed by Fitchen, could have made the task easier.[17] Without this stage, the entire structure would have remained lodged tightly under the masonry vault with no means to work it free short of a bonfire. Easing tested the vault's integrity while avoiding complete disaster if it should fail. Once eased free of the vault, the surface strips, or *lagging,* of the centering were removed from the support framework. Then a makeshift scaffolding for the decorating crew could be lashed to the remaining framework.

Medieval churches were vaulted with thinly mortared stone that could be laid directly on a surface of spaced lagging strips or even without lagging altogether. Concrete, obviously, must be applied to a continuous, impermeable surface. This presents two problems. First, smooth, continuously curved surfaces are difficult to create in wood, especially for forms with double curvature like hemispherical domes. Second, concrete can adhere tenaciously to sawn wood. This is of little concern with small vaults, which often show the imprints of wooden planks laid edge-to-edge. But who could guarantee that when the wedges were sprung from under a much larger vault, the whole framework wouldn't remain glued to it?

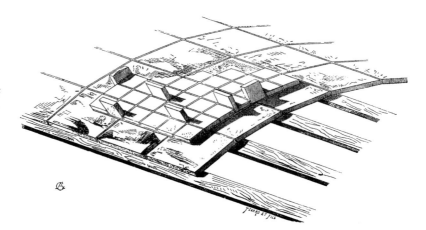

104. Rome: Baths of Caracalla, hypothetical centering scheme for vaults with tile lining. Choisy 1873.

Builders of the imperial period found a ready solution to the second problem. Many large vaults were entirely lined with one or two layers of brick, which had been set flat against the surface of the centering before the concrete was laid. Auguste Choisy argued long ago that these served to close the gaps in widely spaced lagging (Fig. 104). They also ensured that the concrete would not come in contact with the wood.[18] But where linings were not used, the situation required continuous rather than spaced lagging. If any space whatsoever was left between the boards, cement would have crept into the interstices, holding the centering in a ferocious grip. Strips of wood were laid flush against each other like floorboards; sometimes their imprint is still visible (Fig. 105). Typically, they are horizontal on barrel vaults and vertical (meridional) on domes. Jürgen Rasch has mapped almost the entire centering imprint of the "Mausoleum of Helena" at Tor de' Schiavi (Fig. 106). Here the lagging boards were shaped irregularly but fitted to one another precisely. Because they were flat, in order to approximate domical curvature they had to be rather short – in most cases less than a meter. This required a heavy armature of circumferential rings, ten in all. All surfaces exposed to the concrete may have been planed smooth and sprinkled with some loose organic material to ensure disengagement during easing.[19] The lowest zone, subject to friction during easing, could have been coated with wax. When melted away it would leave a thin void as in the lost-wax process of bronze casting.

Decentering was another concern. One did not want to risk pulverizing stonework, cracking a floor, or crushing the drains underneath it by bringing the whole framework crashing down (a procedure that, at any rate, is hard to envision without loss of life). It

105. Rome: Basilica of Maxentius, barrel vault preserving imprint of centering. Photo: R. Taylor.

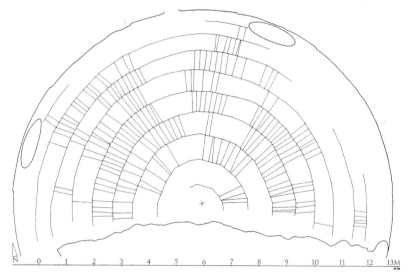

106. Rome: Tor de' Schiavi mausoleum, pattern of lagging boards impressed into dome. Rasch 1991. By permission of J. Rasch.

must have been accomplished by various ingenious means, many of them heavily dependent on cables or struts. The decentering process, which was confined to activity from below, did not necessarily resemble the centering process, during which lifting and suspension devices could be freely employed from above. No cranes for decentering: this harsh fact bore heavy consideration when centering was being designed.

There are fundamental structural differences between barrel-vault and dome centering, just as in the masonry forms themselves. Dome centering, because of the principle of the compression ring, can be

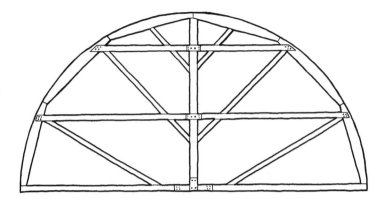

107. Semicircular
centering rib that can
be dismantled in
stages. Illustration:
R. Taylor.

built and dismantled without any elements spanning the entire vault
or propping its crown from below. Like a dry masonry dome, a
wooden framework on a radial plan can be constructed and dismantled in layers without collapsing inward. A barrel vault does
not have this advantage. If its crowning element is missing, a thin-
shelled barrel-vaulted framework has no choice but to drop inward
unless it is artificially supported. The same problem applies to its
centering. To control each frame during disassembly, one could extend transverse horizontal beams across the span at various height
intervals (Fig. 107). When the centering was complete, these timbers
acted in tension, serving as the chords of a truss across a central
king-post. But during decentering they acted in gentle compression,
serving as struts to hold the two sides of the incomplete arc in place
as it was dismantled from above.

For the Baths of Caracalla DeLaine has proposed semicircular
flying frames that may have been too massive for the decentering
task.[20] The weight of individual elements and the likelihood they
would do damage when dismantled are the pivotal considerations,
along with the facility of dislodging wedges during easing. The
whole job is made much easier if the frames are lighter and more
numerous. At about seventeen tonnes, DeLaine's frames would have
tested the capacities of two medium-sized cranes working together.
The notional mass of each frame can be reduced substantially by
diminishing the cross sections of its elements and simplifying the design (Fig. 108).[21] The number of frames can then be increased in
proportion to the reduction in their weight. In turn, these closely set
parallel ribs will offer much more even support for the lagging laid
across their exterior, and the lagging itself can be made thinner and
lighter (Fig. 108, *a*). In this case, complexity ultimately simplifies.

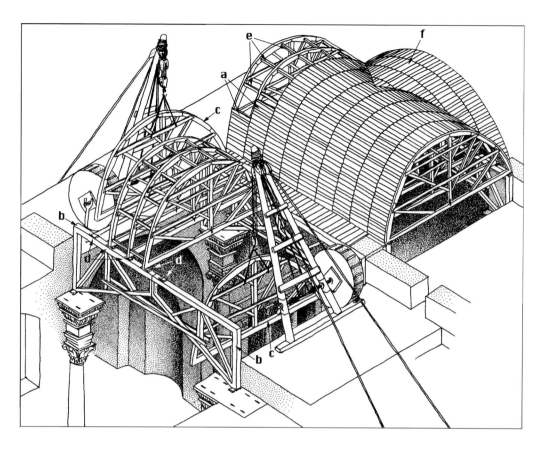

Treadmill-operated cranes were set up on the platforms above the barrel-vaulted bays to hoist the entire preassembled frames into place on large supporting beams that extended across the main space. Clearly cranes of considerable height and strength were needed to hoist a heavy object nearly halfway out over the span. With lesser frames to lift, they could have been fairly slender and easily slid laterally between tasks. Among the heaviest single elements were the transverse beams or trusses on which the semicircular frames were to rest, each with substantial wooden props at the ends to raise them high above the cornices on which they rested (Fig. 108, *b*). These could have been lifted by two opposing cranes hoisting either end and guided into place with ropes and levers. Each frame for the three parallel transverse vaults, whether entire or in tiers, was hoisted and positioned by a single crane (*c*). Between the beams and the frames were placed wedges (*d*), which could later be sprung with sledgehammers – helped along, perhaps, with liberally applied grease. Spacers were installed to connect the frames to each other

108. Rome: Baths of Caracalla, hypothetical centering scheme. Illustration: R. Taylor after DeLaine 1997.

(e). They would ensure that, after the lagging was removed, the flying frames would remain upright and rigid. They also served as the supports for scaffolding, which now would be lashed to them and to the ribs to allow later access to the surface area from below. To the frames were nailed the surface lagging strips (a). Finally the frames for the longitudinal barrel vault were applied directly on top of the flanks of the transverse vaults (f).

After the vault masonry had been applied and was completely dry, the wedges were sprung and the lagging knocked loose by workmen on the preinstalled scaffolding. Decoration was no easy task, and even under the best of circumstances probably would have been achieved in very cramped quarters at the lower levels. No easing mechanism separates the centering appreciably from the *lower* part of the vaulting. The lagging strips, however, could have been thicker here, which, combined with the hypothetical wax layer, allowed a wider gap when they were removed – a gap that could be further widened with drawknives or chisels.

With the barrel vaults, dismantling of the frames and scaffolding would begin at the top. Small timbers could simply be dropped to the floor, but in the case of large timbers, or elements near the walls, more caution was required. Adjacent frames could serve as anchors for pulleys. Each unit of timber would be attached at both ends to a cable – one cable serving as a stay, the other as the lowering line.[22] With particularly troublesome members, stay cables and even lowering lines could have been controlled, through the great lunette windows, by workers on the lateral platforms. The horizontal struts of each frame would keep it from collapsing inward once each level had been removed. When the frames had been removed, there remained only the massive cross beams and their props. These must have been lowered with pulleys tied to the piers at their ends. Guiding ropes would twist them diagonally to ensure that they did no damage on the way down.

The procedure at the Baths of Caracalla seems hard enough. Yet these were smooth vaults; the difficulty was compounded when coffers were introduced in a vault's intrados as in the case of the even larger Basilica of Maxentius (see Figs. 21, 22, 105). Coffers are lauded by art historians for their graphic potential to exploit surface geometry, and by engineers for reducing the dome's overall mass. But they are troublesome for the engineer who must ease and decenter the carpentry. Coffered vaults, because of the complexity of their surfaces, were not lined with bricks as smooth vaults

109. Rome: Basilica of Maxentius, analytical view of coffered vault. Choisy 1873.

sometimes were. Their surfaces were mostly rubbled concrete or brick and mortar laid edgewise; the Basilica of Maxentius has both (Figs. 109, 110). It has often been presumed (most prominently, by Viollet-le-Duc) that the coffer molds, the ziggurat-shaped bosses applied to the surface of the centering to create the recesses in the concrete, were firmly fixed to the lagging. In fact, this was impossible, for engaged coffer molds would have snagged the downward motion of the centering as it was eased. The molds were entirely free to slide about on the surface. Each must have been held in position by removable pegs only until the lower part was embedded in concrete to a sufficient degree to hold it in place. Then the pegs were removed and the mold completely covered with concrete. The molds offered no resistance when the centering was eased from below.

BUILDING THE PANTHEON DOME

Now let us turn to a domed form with coffers: the Pantheon of Hadrian, built nearly a century before the Baths of Caracalla and two centuries before the Basilica of Maxentius (Fig. 27, 66). No dome of remotely comparable size had ever been attempted, and it must have been understood that techniques used on smaller domes would not necessarily work on a larger scale. To the extent possible, the details of design must have been tested in rehearsal. The centering would have been the result of considerable experimentation, all carried out in a clear area where a mock cornice could be laid out on the ground and the assembly rehearsed with cranes and rigging; for it was the Pantheon's upper inner cornice that would support the principal timbers. With the help of a sweeping cord anchored at the center to ensure a hemispherical surface, various configurations of centering could be tried out on the ground-level cornice. Even without the ultimate test, a simulated concrete load, this would have been the surest road to success. Equilibrium under pressure was of course a great concern, but procedural criteria such as ease of assembly and especially of disassembly were also critical. When the engineers were satisfied with the design, the centering would have been carefully dismantled and its members marked for easy reassembly on the building itself.

The choice of light ribs in great numbers, rather than fewer heavy elements, is a superior strategy in most centering schemes of extraordinary size. Let us review their advantages:

1   they are easier to assemble and position far above the ground;
2   they are easier to dismantle;
3   being more numerous, they distribute the vaulting loads more evenly; and
4   they probably simplify the task of the decorators, who can work around small timbers more easily than large ones.

110. Rome: Basilica of Maxentius, fallen fragment of coffered vault revealing construction materials and techniques. Photo: R. Taylor.

These advantages hold for domes as well as for barrel vaults, but, as I have already explained, dome centering has its own advantages stemming from the compression-ring principle. One advantage is the option to include an oculus at the crown, which simplifies decentering. A peculiarity of dome centering is that the lagging boards are not all of a uniform length, but conform to the more complex rib structure of double curvature.

Now we must take account of some recent hypotheses about the construction of the Pantheon. The maximalist approach – consisting of a forest of timbers extending up from the ground – has always had a following, but few accept it today, partly because it is unnecessary and partly because it would impede activity inside the rotunda. Two scholars have recently suggested that the centering of the Pantheon was built in stages, progressing upward as the dome rose with it. Rowland Mainstone proposes that the coffers were used as footings for the timbers of higher levels; this must mean that each tier of centering was removed as the work progressed upward.[23] Jürgen Rasch offers a more detailed proposal for Roman concrete domes from the early second century onward.[24] He suggests that their construction was revolutionized by Apollodorus of Damascus, Trajan's chief architect and putative author of a surviving treatise on siege engines.[25] According to this hypothesis Apollodorus adapted the design of his siege towers to the problem of cen-

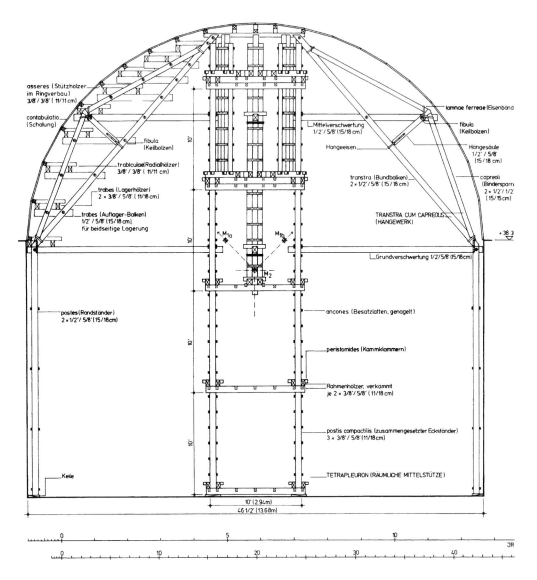

111. Rome: Tor de' Schiavi mausoleum, hypothetical centering scheme. Rasch 1991. By permission of J. Rasch.

tering the Pantheon dome. The resulting design, a central wooden tower (*Mittelstütze*) reaching to the crown of the dome from which the centering frames radiated, introduced a skeleton that was so rigid that the profile would hardly flatten at all under the dome's weight. The rigidity of the frame, Rasch argues, actually allowed the lagging to be applied in a single tier at a time, like shuttering, then after the concrete had been poured and set, removed and reused for the next tier (Fig. 111). This model is problematic from a logistical point of view, for it would have compelled the masons and carpenters to alternate cycles of productivity and idleness.[26] The seeds of

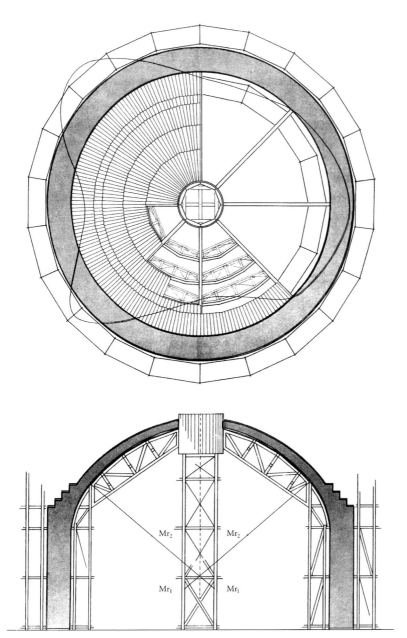

112. Hypothetical tower centering scheme for large domed rotundas. Rakob 1988. By permission of F. Rakob.

this idea lie not in any Roman evidence but in Alberti's *Ten Books on Architecture* (*De re aedificatoria*), which prescribes a similar method of "hanging centering."[27]

More seductive than Rasch's suggestion of spot-lagging is his notion of a central tower itself. A similar structure is proposed by Friedrich Rakob (Fig. 112),[28] but neither he nor Rasch discusses all the implications of a tower support. Could such a structure have worked on the Pantheon, or even the smaller late-antique Italian domes that Rasch meticulously documents? The greatest advantages of a tower would be the rigidity it conferred upon the centering and the relative ease (theoretically, at least) with which each radial frame of centering could be set in place. This latter issue is not a trivial one, for the scenario I present below requires the use of many cranes concurrently and a great number of guy lines to hold the ribs in place, whereas a tower would allow a single crane, or a few cranes working independently, to install the top of each prefabricated rib snugly into a waiting slot on the cylindrical surface of a compression ring at the summit of the tower. No guy lines would be necessary to protect the ribs from falling out of alignment. Other advantages have been claimed for a tower: It could be used for raising elements of the centering into place; it could also be of assistance in the decentering process. Neither of these functions is very important in the event. In all likelihood, the only purpose for the tower was to support the cylinder before the ribs were inserted. Once this was engaged, the tower could be dismantled. The command post for decentering was the edge of the oculus, which unlike the tower threatened no damage to itself during the disassembly of timbers.

That the engineers in Rome could build great wooden towers is certain. A derrick taller than the Column of Trajan had been built just a few years earlier to erect that monument,[29] and there is little doubt that engines of similar size were used for the erection of colossal statues. Surely a 43-meter behemoth with a 4.5-meter-diameter summit cylinder (the size of the oculus) was within reach of Apollodorus or his successors. Why not accept the tower hypothesis, then? The problems lie first in its capacity to be disengaged from the centering, and second in its necessity.

Let's begin with necessity. A freestanding tower of such proportions was a huge undertaking unto itself, demanding much more timber and "engineering" than a simple shell centering. Rasch is persuaded that the development of the tower support is responsible for virtually deformation-free domes in late antiquity. These stand in sharp contrast to the dome of the Augustan "Temple of Mercury" at Baiae, which flattened considerably under the concrete loads during construction, presumably due to centering that had no adequate support at the crown.[30] But as I already explained in the opening section of this chapter, no wooden vault centering must necessarily be subjected to vast liquid loads all at once. If concrete is applied in relatively thin layers and at a measured pace, merely adequate centering should not suffer gross deformation. This is especially true in domes, which as they rise create in effect a series of self-supporting compression rings. Perhaps, then, the simple precept of thin layering was the difference between early deformation and later success, further refined by the introduction of gradations of aggregate. Some flattening at the crown was to be expected, certainly more than a tower would permit. But the designers could easily have anticipated this and compensated by pinching the centering upward into a slightly ovoid profile.

Then there is the difficulty of compression upon a tower. Whatever the extent of the deformation, the static loads on the centering were substantial and unavoidable. As the concrete accumulated the compression around the crown increased, jamming the ribs of the centering inward against the tower's summit cylinder. The ribs would not be able to slip downward during easing, and the whole project would fail unless the cylinder itself was structurally independent of the tower. This would have been a great challenge for many reasons. First, it (or the whole tower) must be set on top of wedges; for the ribs would not drop unless the cylinder dropped. Second, it had to be positioned exactly in the center of the rotunda, just as it had been in rehearsal, otherwise the ribs would not fit in place. With the help of small cranes built into the tower it could conceivably have been adjusted laterally until it was centered, but only with the greatest difficulty if it rested on wedges. Another possibility was to design some *vertical* wedge mechanism into the cylinder itself, which when dislodged by a pile driver would cause the whole cylinder to collapse inward slightly. But it has one very troublesome requirement. If the ribs are to fall inward, they must all be independent of one another. Any connective material joining them laterally, such as lagging and circumferential struts, must be removed. Neither of these expedients protected the cylinder from being knocked off center by a frame as it was being hoisted into position. Wedges under the entire tower, on the other hand, would have endured such stupendous point loads that they could not possibly have been sprung.

The most widely accepted centering scheme for the Pantheon derives from the nineteenth century. In his monumental dictionary on medieval architecture, Viollet-le-Duc proposed a centering scheme

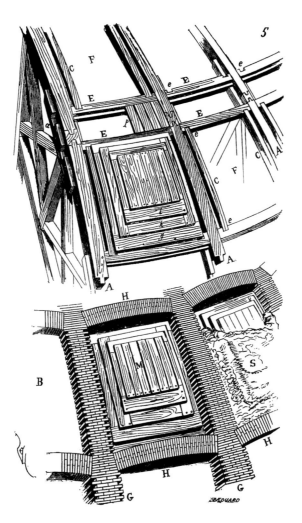

113. Rome: Panthe-
on, detail of hypo-
thetical centering
scheme. Brickwork in
phase B is incorrect.
Viollet-le-Duc 1875.

that gains acceptance even today.[31] In essence it consists of horizontal rings of struts joined at several levels to twenty-eight ribs, forming a cagelike pattern of parallels and meridians corresponding to
the grid around the dome's coffers. There are no massive supports
anchoring it to the ground (Fig. 113, 114). The scheme is elegant
and persuasive in general conception. However, from the perspective of the design and construction process, it is deeply flawed. The
reconstruction is vague about joinery. The coffer molds are fixed
firmly to the framework, a logistical impossibility. Unconvincing
details abound, such as the odd cantilevered timber resembling a
hammer-beam embedded in the masonry between the two bottom
rings of coffers, or the lack of lagging. Most important, the sequence
of construction or installation seems never to have been given ad-

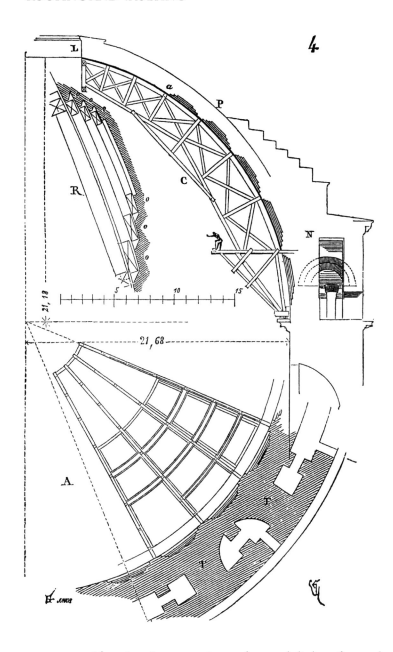

114. Rome: Panthe-
on, hypothetical
centering scheme in
plan and elevation.
Viollet-le-Duc 1875.

equate consideration. I propose instead a much lighter frame design
in two parts divided horizontally and installed sequentially (Figs.
115, 116), and discuss its merits in light of some of the shortcom-
ings of the nineteenth-century design.

   First, the entire centering scheme remains structurally disengaged
from the dome. Viollet-le-Duc's "hammer-beam" is a misbegotten
detail, for it renders the easing process virtually impossible. The con-

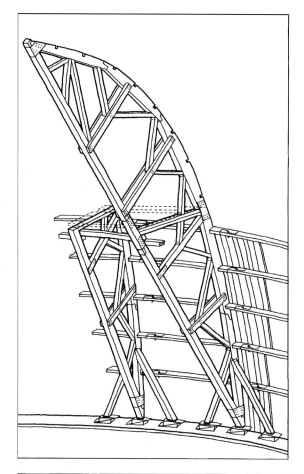

115. Rome: Pantheon, author's proposed centering scheme, analytical view. Dotted lines represent a temporary working platform. Illustration: R. Taylor.

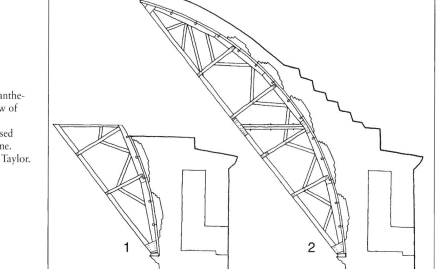

116. Rome: Pantheon, section view of two phases of author's proposed centering scheme. Illustration: R. Taylor.

crete fabric of the Pantheon dome remained hidden behind its cosmetic layers of plaster until the late 1920s, and until then revealed
only fragmentary evidence of putlog holes in the masonry.[32] As it
happens, there are indeed squared holes at the base of the dome,
which were known to Piranesi in the eighteenth century; but their
complete pattern and origins are uncertain. These and other holes
visible in an 1898 photograph of three stripped coffers are sunk into
concrete, not into horizontally laid brickwork as in the traditional
fashion[33] (Fig. 117). There is no chance that these supported scaffolding during construction. Concrete required a mold: It could no
more have been laid like brick from a scaffold than oatmeal (with
or without an aggregate of raisins). And having a mold, it could not
receive putlogs. Roman concrete domes, whether or not they included brick relieving arches, as did the Pantheon dome in its lower
zone, demanded formwork from base to crown. The holes in the
Pantheon surely were made in the early modern period, in preparation for a restoration of the dome surface. In the eighteenth century
Piranesi proposed a hypothetical scaffolding scheme for repairs that

117. Rome: Panthe-
on, base of dome
stripped of plaster.
Fototeca Unione c/o
American Academy in
Rome, neg. 3595F.

uses putlogs in precisely these positions.[34] Somewhat earlier the painter Panini recorded a pattern of holes at the intersections of parallels and meridians in one sector of the dome's intrados (see Fig. 27). Since these are clearly visible, whereas the brick arches of the lower levels are not, we must conclude that they pierced a cosmetic layer of plaster, much in need of restoration by Panini's time. The plaster certainly is not Roman; therefore neither are the holes driven through it.

The only practicable easing mechanism consisted of wedges beneath the ribs. Naturally, the ability to remove them depended in part on the lightness of the ribs. Viollet-le-Duc's proposed ribs appear to be about 60 × 60 cm in cross section and the stiffening trusses nearly as thick. Given that the framework would never be required to support more than a small fraction of the dome's weight at any given time, these dimensions are excessive. Smaller, lighter timbers, perhaps 30 × 40 cm, would more than halve the weight of the frames and still provide sufficient strength for the task. To distribute the loads upon the wedges, the ribs could have been forked at the bottom with lateral struts attached to them by lap joints (see Fig. 115). This tripling of the number of loading points not only would lighten the load on each respective pair of wedges but would help to distribute the loads more evenly upon the thin, vulnerable marble cornice. As for the circumferential struts, they should be reduced greatly in weight and increased proportionally in number. We saw above (in the section "Designing Centering") that at Tor de' Schiavi strut rings were built about a meter apart on average. On the much larger Pantheon the rings could have been roughly two and a half meters apart, and they were light enough to be installed by two or three men without machines.

Viollet-le-Duc's circumferential beams appear to have no joints at all with the ribs. They are simply fitted into recessed blocks nailed to the sides of these members. He understood the struts to be exclusively compressive elements; taken as a whole each parallel hoop formed a compression ring. But as has already been explained, one of the peculiarities of domes, even temporary wooden ones, is that when fully hemispherical they will experience compressive stresses only in their upper two thirds. The lower third will experience hoop stresses, tensile forces that try to expand the circumferential elements holding the dome together in that zone.[35] The lower parallels would have acted as tension rings, not compression rings. Thus the segments of each ring had to be anchored firmly either to one another or to the ribs. It is a further peculiarity of domes that these stresses become fully manifested only when the structure is nearing completion. During construction when the upper parts were not yet in place, the lower parts of the wooden dome would in fact have acted under compression. The lower strut rings therefore had to resist both compression and tension. They probably were joined by means of a splayed indent scarf fitted into a halved joint in the rib (see Fig. 115).[36] Each scarf joint must have had transverse keys, two small wedges driven into a square hole at the center to tighten the joint, so that it could be loosened later. To keep the keys accessible the joints were positioned just to one side of the ribs.

Let us now briefly try to envision the stages of conception, construction, and dismantling of the centering. One of the earliest decisions would involve material. Most likely the master carpenter chose a wood with a high ratio of strength to weight, such as fir or spruce, with as little deflection as possible.[37] Only well-cured wood without blemishes would be selected. The centering frames could be built with straight timbers, even rather long ones for the truss ties, but the *cradles*, that is, the meridional elements of the frames, as well as the parallel struts connecting them, followed the curvature of the dome. This fact limited the effective length of their members.[38] But one wanted to minimize the number of joints, each of which was a weak point in the frame's structure. The joinery of the frames themselves would have been as simple as possible. The cradle segments may have been connected by simple scarf joints strengthened by through bolts. Where possible, sawn or chiseled carpenters' joints were avoided altogether. It has been observed that the best way to construct trusses is simply by overlapping two or three timbers, drilling holes through them, and running them through with metal rods or cotter bolts.[39] Reliefs on Trajan's column clearly show the round heads of metal bolts at the joints of trusses, as do Renaissance drawings of the Pantheon's original porch trusses.[40] Hardware of this sort, conjoined with iron ferrules or fishplates to combat torsion and splitting at the joints, must have been favored widely for their strength and simplicity. Nevertheless, plenty of lubricant would have been applied to every bolt and aperture in order to facilitate disassembly under very difficult circumstances.

At the level of the top inner cornice the drum of the Pantheon was solid through its entire thickness, without any voids whatsoever

(Fig. 118). This enabled the cranes to be erected on a completely level, uncluttered surface twenty Roman feet thick around the entire circuit. This platform was probably raised slightly above cornice level in order to embed the vulnerable cornice blocks deep in concrete. The first elements to be constructed were the lower frames. These would have been preassembled and tested in rehearsal. No prefabricated element could exceed the lifting capacity of a crane.

As reconstructed, the complete rib frame has cradles of about twenty-nine linear meters of timber, with a mean cross section of 0.4 ×0.7 m and roughly sixty-five linear meters of straight beams at 0.3 × 0.4 m (or pairs of 0.3 ×0.2 m). According to the 1971 British Standard Code of Practice for the Structural Use of Timber, the density of fir is 380 kg/m³;[41] thus the overall mass of the frame, not including the diagonal props at the bottom or metal hardware, would be 6,050 kg, or over six tonnes. Near the lifting capacity of a conventional midsize Roman crane,[42] and cumbersome to the extreme in its overall length, this behemoth was unlikely to have been attempted in a single hoist. Far more congenial was a bipartite design that could be joined on a horizontal line (see Fig. 116). A two-phase centering process allowed the cranes to be repositioned for the second phase on the much higher masonry drum encasing the lower frames.

As it was, the cranes were exceptionally tall in relation to their bulk. Themselves weighing several tonnes, they could be raised to the ring wall only by smaller cranes or cantilevered pulley hoists (gins). Certainly in the early stages there was enough surface area to allow assembly of cranes at cornice level, even if their long masts caused some inconvenience. In point of fact this was necessary only for the first crane: The others could be raised in partially assembled form by their neighbors and set in their upright positions onto the platform (see Fig. 118). Once a crane was in position far enough back from the inner cornice to ensure that it would not interfere with the positioning of the hoisted frame, its mast was secured with stay lines to capstans anchored in the ground outside the rotunda, probably in a radial configuration resembling the one around the Colosseum. The hoisting cables would raise the frame from the rotunda floor in the upright position that it would assume in place. The frame's foot was guided down upon wedges carefully positioned on the surface of the cornice. The diagonal props, raised with much smaller hoists, could be added at this time to stabilize the foot,

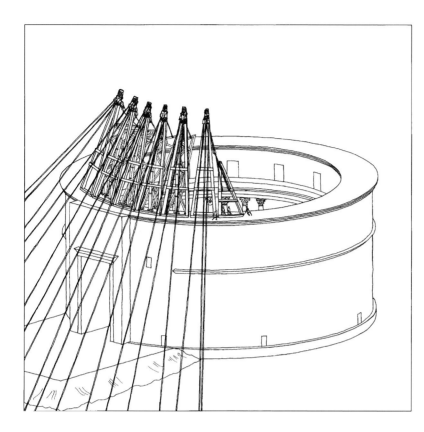

118. Rome: Panthe-
on, first construction
phase of dome.
Illustration: R. Taylor.

each with its own set of wedges. There was no need to fasten them
to the rib – only to tighten them in place by hammering the wedges
under their feet. Vertical alignment of the frame along the meridional plane could be adjusted in the same way. It remained to position the frame at precisely the correct angle in profile. This was
doubtless a time-consuming process, not because it was hard to
measure the angle – that would be established by some predetermined method of visual alignment without any need to take measurements – but because the task was accomplished with the crane's
two independent dynamic systems, the stays and the hoists. Complicating the orchestration of movements was the likelihood that,
because of the shortage of space, the treadmills were not on the
cranes but on the ground far below.

    At this point in the rationalization of the Pantheon project we ar-
rive at a sobering realization. The crane was not just a hoisting and
positioning mechanism for the frame; it was also the only means to
hold it in place until the entire ring of frames had been secured to
one another with horizontal struts. As each crane was used it be-

came anchored in place, useless for any other task – and hemmed in, perhaps, by additional rigging to secure the frames against wind. At the end of the first phase, the entire ring wall was crowned by a circle of cranes standing side by side. This scenario not only explains why the Pantheon's porch and south annex were added later – they would have obstructed the radial rigging – but it could offer a clue about the puzzling choice of twenty-eight meridians in the coffer pattern of the Pantheon dome. The engineers may have established in the experimental phase that this was the maximum number of cranes of the necessary height and base width that could fit around the rotunda; indeed, one can see in the illustrations that they are quite narrow.[43] The original intent likely was to create thirty-two, a multiple of eight and four, both important numerological components in the scheme of the lower rotunda. But the splayed shears of thirty-two cranes of the minimum base width would have overlapped, rendering them useless. Now there is no compelling reason to urge that the coffers followed the rib pattern; after all, they were separated by a continuous skin of lagging. But the patterns of application – perhaps meridional lines of nails at each rib – would have served as twenty-eight ready-made alignment guides for the coffers. Such a prosaic solution to this most-discussed problem will not satisfy everyone, but it is in character with other pragmatic compromises in the Pantheon's design and realization.[44] The first centering campaign thus presents the image of a great spray of tackle radiating from the rotunda in every direction: a logistical reality that would have profoundly influenced the sequence of construction. The buildings in the vicinity had for the most part been destroyed in the fire during the reign of Trajan. We may therefore presume that the ground had been cleared all around the site, and that the great front porch remained unbuilt at this stage – a hypothesis that is buttressed by independent evidence.[45]

Above the cornice level the disposition of the ribs would inevitably have been slightly uneven. Positioned on the cornice or on makeshift platforms laid loose across the horizontal frame tops, workers could correct these irregularities in several ways: by adjusting the wedges, pulling the ribs together with ropes tightened by twirling, or separating them by hammering temporary spacing bars between them. It is unlikely that *permanent* spacers were installed between the frames at this time, for they would obstruct the hoisting of the upper frames. Mutatis mutandis, the workers could then insert the encircling rings of struts. Beginning at the lowest tier, they set into place these relatively portable elements, which had been carefully shaped to a curve and tested in rehearsal, pounding them into the halved joints cut into the ribs and securing their own scarf joints with keys. As a ring was completed, the lagging could quickly be nailed to it; this, along with minimal scaffolding and ladders, would serve as a working surface from which to approach the next level. Each complete circuit of struts became a stabilizing cincture in the wooden structure. When about five rings had been completed all the ropes could be removed and the cranes detached. The truncated dome was completely self-supporting. The temporary platforms were removed to allow the mating of the upper and lower frame sections in the second phase.

The Pantheon's prefabricated coffer molds would have to disengage from the surface when the centering was to be eased downward. The two lowest tiers – fifty-six in all – were likely applied to the lagging surface in a single effort and held in place by pegs that could be extracted as the level of the concrete rose to encase the lower parts of the coffers. Both sets of coffers were probably set in place at once, after which the cranes could be removed entirely to make way for the brick-and-concrete crews. These had no inordinately large materials to worry about, only bricks, mortar, and stone aggregate, all of which could be raised in buckets on small pulleys.

The next seven or eight meters of elevation developed much as the lower levels of the rotunda, renewing the convoluted circuits of arched and vaulted chambers within the wall's core (Fig. 119). But while these voids and the exterior surface, all realized in traditional brick and rubbled concrete, continued to rise vertically, the inboard surface began to assume the form of the dome. Up to the second tier of coffers brick relieving arches (trimmed to conform to the stepped coffer profiles) were laid directly against the centering and surrounded with concrete. About eight meters above inner cornice level the core voids were vaulted over, and the great enclosing brick cylinder ceased its vertical ascent. The first and largest step ring commenced here; it was of solid concrete with the predominantly broken-brick aggregate that had been used throughout this level. Its upper surface, eleven meters above the inner cornice, was a perfect platform for the second centering phase (Fig. 120). And in fact a continuous bonding course of brick – a good working surface – is known to exist at this level.[46]

119. Rome: Pantheon, analytical cutaway view of vertical construction. Beltrami 1898.

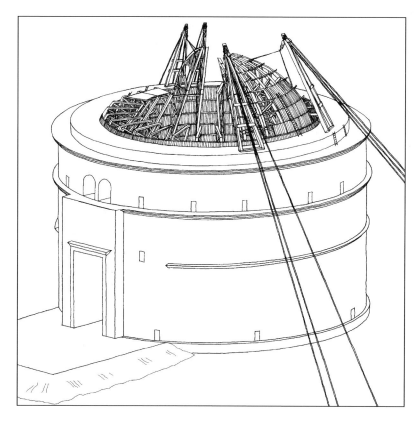

120. Rome: Pantheon, second phase of dome construction. Illustration: R. Taylor.

The centering construction now resumed in much the same manner as before but with one major difference. Now there was no need for a continuous line of cranes, for each frame could immediately be bolted to its mate below and secured to its neighbors with horizontal struts, both inboard and outboard. The initial crane may have been kept in place to provide some stability (as in Fig. 120), but only one other crane in the sequence was needed, and it could be moved for the installation of each new frame. Struts, lagging, and coffers were applied as before on the ever-relaxing gradient. A final ring of struts, perhaps somewhat stouter than the others (but also extremely short), formed the contours of the oculus. Meanwhile, in anticipation of later stages, when workmen would have to be clambering about in the centering, lightweight scaffolding platforms and ladders were being lashed to the frames already in place.

With all the lagging and coffers again in place, the second and final masonry campaign could begin. As the pitch of the dome diverged from vertical, the concrete would be applied in thinner layers and gradations of lighter aggregate to minimize the gravitational effect of each upon the centering. At midlevel the rubble of broken bricks gave way to thin alternating layers of broken brick and lightweight tufa. At the level of the fourth coffer the tufa layers began to alternate with pumicelike volcanic slag. Interspersed with these were irregularly spaced brick bonding courses penetrating the entire thickness of the dome.[47] It is not known whether the small step rings, which are made of brick, were laid down after this stage or as a part of it. They may have served as outer formwork to dam in each progressive layer of concrete on its relatively steep ascent.[48] The oculus was edged with a four-foot-thick ring of interlocking bricks laid radially on edge as if upon a perfectly horizontal surface, not to the pitch of the dome. It consequently rested upon a thin circular wedge of concrete and must have been constructed after the concrete had reached the level of its underside. Rising about five feet, the bricks eliminated any need for cylindrical wooden formwork to contain the concrete as it accumulated around the oculus. To the entire outer surface of the dome was applied a layer of bricks overlapped like scales, then a thick layer of *opus signinum* to serve as a waterproofing agent, interrupted only by the four staircases leading up to the oculus from the diagonal points of the compass.[49] The thickness of the concrete and *signinum* above the level of the step rings is consistently about 1.7 m, or six Roman feet. Precisely how the thickness was regulated without visual guides such as brick ribs is unknown. Perhaps thin graduated wooden rods were embedded in the concrete to serve as thickness gauges.

Typically Roman roofs were finished in terra-cotta tile.[50] Lead sheathing, as it appears on the Pantheon today, was not used to any great extent on Roman architecture. The Pantheon, however, was finished in more opulent materials: white marble tiles on the lower step rings, and (gilded?) bronze tiles above. A few of the marble pantiles survive, but the bronze was removed and carried off in late antiquity.[51] Tiling was a relatively simple procedure that could begin as soon as the dome's extrados had been laid and waterproofed. Tiles would have been laid circumferentially on a new bed of mortar, beginning at the lowest levels and working upward. No special attention to accuracy was needed here, and the procedure could progress speedily without measuring instruments or supervision from the architect or builder. The only concern was that the abutment of adjoining pantiles matched from tier to tier, so that the semicylindrical cover tiles laid over the joints progressed in neat radial lines up the side of the dome. Pantiles may have been manufactured in a variety of widths to accommodate the decreasing circumference of the tiers.

A couple of weeks after completion, when the dome fabric was adequately cured, the centering could be eased. Workers standing on the cornice or on adjacent flying scaffolding carefully worked the two overlapping wedges out from under each rib with sledgehammers and iron levers if necessary. This was done incrementally, a few taps at a time, around the entire circuit to ensure that the framework descended evenly. With the wedges removed, they could proceed to climb the preinstalled scaffolding and remove the lagging strips with crowbars and hammers. The coffer molds were knocked and pried to pieces in their places, and their wooden components extracted from the voids. If necessary, some of the loosened timber could have been reused on the spot to augment the scaffolding for the decorators. Finally, all that remained was the basic skeleton of the centering and the scaffolding, which was given over to the stuccoists and painters.

After decoration was complete began the difficult task of decentering. The process began at the top, relying on the autonomy of the lower structure as each successive ring of upper timbers was removed. It was aided substantially by the oculus, without which the process would have been far more difficult and dangerous. There was no need for large cranes now, for the ribs would not be removed in their assembled form as they had been erected. Small but sturdy pulley devices could be set up at the edge of the oculus for the extraction and lowering of individual timbers.

Decentering was the hardest process of all, requiring a systematic consideration of every action and counteraction generated by the disengagement of a joint. Would the members spring apart or squeeze together? Would they swing free, and in what direction? Did the disengagement of one joint endanger another? Should members be sawed apart between joints (a possibility only for tensile, not compressive, beams)? Would the release of a single strut break the whole compression ring? And where would the workers be positioned to accomplish these tasks? The sequence was so fraught with peril and difficulty that it must have been rehearsed long before – at least to the extent that rehearsal was possible without the presence of the concrete dome itself. The dome's materiality was in fact an integral part of the process; for example, many workers must have operated in harnesses suspended from the oculus and controlled either from the dome's extrados or from the floor below.

The general tendency would be to dismantle the straight timbers first, since the curved ribs would be held in place by the circumferential struts. Dismantling the trusses was a matter of removing bolts or spikes in compressive joints and bolts alone in tensile or shear joints. If bolts, many under significant shear stress, could not be pulled free, they were driven out with a hammer and a thinner bolt, or the wood around them was simply hacked apart. All but one upper bolt of a member would be removed, allowing it to swing free; then its final action, a vertical drop, could be easily predicted. Near the crown there was no need to lower these timbers by ropes. They could simply be dropped to the floor, which would have been covered with earth, scrap wood, or other materials to cushion the fall of the timbers. But as decentering progressed downward and outward, many timbers would have been tied to ropes extending from the oculus to ensure that they would swing inboard when disengaged and not damage the lower centering or the building itself.

Removing the circumferential struts was an especially delicate operation. They were jointed, not bolted, and so their disengagement was a simpler task – knocking out the little wedges in their splayed indent scarf joints – but unless the ribs were supported in some way, the initial loosening of a single joint could cause the whole compression ring to dissolve, bringing an entire tier of ribs crashing down. The problem at hand was twofold: The ribs had to remain in place while the struts were removed, and they had to be lowered individually without doing damage. Since the compound ribs of the upper frames rested on the lower frames, they presented few problems. But how did one keep the ribs of the lower frames in position as the final rings of struts were being removed? The solution is simple and intuitive. But like the operations involving the oculus, it could not have been easily rehearsed, for it depended on the centering's symbiosis with the actual dome. Today one can see metal eyelets in the dome, which are used to secure scaffolding against the inner surface. Prior to the decoration phase similar eyelets may have been driven into the concrete, perhaps at the level of the center of the second coffer, one on each side of every rib. Now, at the final phase of the decentering, ropes could be looped through these eyelets, tied to the ribs at a point slightly below eyelet level, gently tautened, and secured to the windlasses anchored in the ground. As the final ring of

struts was knocked loose, each rib remained upright and independent, cradled by its rope harness. A stay line was tied to the bottom
of each rib, and now the eyelet ropes were pulled with greater force,
lifting the rib gently from its footing on the cornice. The stay line
guided the foot of the rib out beyond the cornice, and the rib was
carefully lowered to the floor.

I have intentionally paid lavish attention to the problems of flying
centering only to come back to the initial question: Was it worth it?
Certainly Roman builders could have built centering scaffolds from
the ground up, eliminating all kinds of engineering headaches in the
process, all the while creating others. But this would have been in
a sense un-Roman. The corollary of speed is high design, and both
characteristics exemplify Roman imperial building at the center of
power. Excessive scaffolding was the enemy of speed, and in the case
of great vaulted imperial projects such as the Pantheon, the Baths
of Caracalla, and the Basilica of Maxentius – all of them, we sur-
mise, essentially complete within less than a decade of their com-
mencement – we can conclude only that no expense was spared, no
leap of daring or imagination dismissed.

6

DECORATION AND FINISHING

We think ourselves poor and mean if our walls are not resplen-
dent with large and costly mirrors; if our marbles from Alexandria are not set off by mosaics of Numidian stone; if their
borders are not faced over on all sides with difficult patterns,
arranged in many colours like paintings; if our vaulted ceilings
are not buried in glass; if our swimming-pools are not lined
with Thasian marble, once a rare and wonderful sight in any
temple – pools into which we let down our bodies after they
have been drained weak by abundant perspiration; and finally,
if the water has not poured from silver spigots. I have so far
been speaking of the ordinary bathing-establishments; what
shall I say when I come to those of the freedmen? What a vast
number of statues, of columns that support nothing, but are
built for decoration, merely in order to spend money! And what
masses of water that fall crashing from level to level!
– Seneca *Ep.* 86.6–7

Roman architects, like all others, envisioned buildings
not only as forms but also as vehicles of color, pattern,
sound, and movement.[1] Plastering, painting, tessellating,
furnishing – these were the peroration of the architectural argument,
its grand rhetorical summing up. And like any final exhortation,
they held an influence out of all proportion to the effort that went
before. But even if a building emerged in a single campaign, it was
rarely left alone thereafter. With every remodeling, refurnishing, or

121. Barcelona: nave of Antoni Gaudí's church of the Sagrada Familia. Photo: R. Taylor.

redecoration, the argument in stone changed its tenor. If, as Pierre Gros suggests, Roman architecture cannot be reduced to autonomous units in space, if there is a continuity and connectivity between volumetric entities that blurs their identity, the same can be said of any building's existence *over time*. A building could emerge dramatically from the ashes with former identity intact. Or it could evolve in fits and starts over centuries. Either way, its demeanor changed. This book has to some degree isolated structures artificially from their context in space; it must do the same with time. Although the present chapter treats finishing as if it were just that – the completion of a unified initiative – we must not presume that it was the final word in an architectural process. Indeed, as I suggested at the beginning, process has its own aesthetic that is a desirable adjunct to the building, adorning it with the allure of potentiality and contingency: the marriage of what came before to what is to become. If Gaudí's church of the Sagrada Familia in Barcelona is ever finished (Fig. 121), will it have the same appeal that it has now, when one can gape in amazement at the act of its weird and vertiginous emergence? The prolongation, continuation, or renewal of a temporal aesthetic is in some ways desirable. Its ideological and economic appeal competes with an attendant desire for contractual closure.

Roman decoration, whether it subverted form or served it, or evolved to serve new tastes, was openly functional. This is true even in a structural sense, thanks to the columnar order, which is both decoration and structure at once. Adapted from Hellenism, the Roman tradition encompasses structural colonnades that support porches, porticoes, and canopies of various sorts; it also embraces colonnaded confections that support nothing but other colonnades (Fig. 122).[2] More fundamentally, decoration served a social purpose. To every visible or tangible architectural element there is a component both of constancy and of signification. As a constant, form is an array of physical relationships. As a signifier, it is the principle that activates mental correlatives to those relationships, from visceral aesthetic reactions to the form's identification as an architectural type. As a constant, a wall is an orderly matrix of matter and energy, solid and void. As a signifier, a wall may be a barrier (e.g., to human vision or locomotion) or a sign (e.g., of iconographic content or of directionality). It may be beautiful or ugly; it may help you scratch your back in those hard-to-reach places. It may even be a paradox (e.g., if it is covered with mirrors).

Form reigns supreme in the hierarchy of architectural signifiers. It is often the earliest and most elemental catalyst of our faculty of recognition: One distinctive form instantly denotes a temple, another an amphitheater. But in Roman society the richest potential for signification resided in decoration. Despite a strong current of Stoicism running through the intellectual tradition, exemplified by the epistolary rebukes of Seneca, one rarely sees the Stoic ideal of severity and restraint exercised in imperial architecture. Like laws repeatedly enacted and transgressed, such complaints, by taking sharp exception to a trend, confirm its general acceptance by society at large. Floors, walls, and vaults of Roman buildings were strewn liberally with the fruit of signification. It was the visitor's privilege to stop and taste, to pass by heedlessly, or to hold his nose (Seneca's literary posture). But almost everyone understood the basic visual vocabulary of imperial ideology and the broader cultural signs embedded in the ubiquitous Greek myths, or fragments of them, played out

122. Miletos: reconstructed view of terminal aqueduct distribution tank and nymphaeum. Ward-Perkins 1981. By permission of Yale University Press.

on floors, walls, and ceilings. Where broad cultural signs were not enough, inscriptions could warn and instruct. Theaters, amphitheaters, circuses, and other venues of spectacle carried their rigidly hierarchical seating designations on inscriptions.

As Bettina Bergmann has observed, from the beginning of the imperial period architectural *ornamenta* – imported paintings, fresco, inlay, and so on – were legally assimilated to the buildings they adorned.[3] The visual arts became attached to physical space as never before in Roman society. While preserving an abstract function as cultural reinforcements of general values they acquired site-specific meaning as dividers and definers of spatial function and hierarchy. Divisions often emerged within a single medium, as when elaborate figural wall frescoes in atria or peristyles gave way to simpler patterns in service corridors, or when floor mosaics clearly delineated the placement of furniture.[4] But there were also social and contextual distinctions among various media. Simply decorated with stone tesserae, *opus signinum* was considered an elegant flooring material during the Republic.[5] In the empire its primacy gave way to mosaic and *opus sectile* (discussed below in the section "Wall and Floor Veneers"), yet it remained important as a utilitarian material for waterproofing surfaces. All three flooring techniques, as well as the increasingly popular herringbone brick pavement of *opus spicatum*,[6] are sometimes seen in a single building of the imperial era, the choice determined by the status or function of the immediate space. Mosaics, it is noted, appear most frequently in private houses and baths, less often in commercial spaces and tombs, and rarely in temples of the state cult or civic buildings such as basilicas and council houses.[7] Mosaics and affairs of state did not inhabit the same psychological sphere.

The architect and patron would not have worked out every detail of the decoration; that was left to the specialists. But they would certainly have envisioned the types of decoration they wanted and the ways in which each enhanced the form and responded to light. Borderlines, as moments of transition, were especially important. Cornices and entablatures formed strong continuous horizontal lines that helped to define large spaces and the boundaries between formats, such as the zones where marble wall sheathing gave way to plaster or mosaic. Coffers, which were inherited from the flat ceilings of the Greek tradition, were adapted to vaults, helping to define their geometric forms against a cage of crisp lines and voids. Column sizes and positions were extremely important too. Poorly placed columns might obstruct lines of passage or of sight, and a wrongly sized colonnade could spoil the sense of proportion. Many of these elements, part decoration and part structure, had to be selected before construction began and incorporated into overall design and work plan.

COORDINATING VARIOUS DECORATIVE SCHEMES

Finishing can be the most expensive and time-consuming part of the building process. If we marvel at the sheer scale and efficiency of the Roman labor force in construction, we owe equal attention to the legion of artisans who covered acres of surface area with stucco and elaborate and often opulent works of art. As a general rule, noncolumnar surface decoration tends to be applied from the top downward. Scaffolding erected for the construction phase could be used by the decorators and then dismantled level by level as they completed their tasks. At least on the exterior, where there was no concern about installing a floor under the supports, the original putlog scaffolding must often have been left in place over much of the surface. The expenditure of timber was well worth the return in time saved. On the interior, cantilevered putlogs could have been used at the upper levels and movable trestles at the lower levels. In both cases the fixed scaffolding was dismantled permanently as the workers descended, for the decorative process closed off the putlog holes once and for all.

This approach, combined with a strict division of labor among specialists, may explain why Roman wall and ceiling art is not grandly gestural. While our impressions are inevitably biased by the lack of decorative remains far above ground, it would seem that most scene paintings appeared at relatively low levels where they could be appreciated as if in an art gallery, and they remained on a human scale. Narrative friezes in stucco sometimes appear just below the haunches of vaults,[8] but overhead the decoration tends to become more schematic, relinquishing heavy "content." Human and animal figures are often abstracted from a narrative context and float in the ground of the decoration. Overall, wall and ceiling schemes seem to have been designed with the gridlike division of labor units in mind. If they reveal any lapses in logic or continuity, these tend to follow vertical or horizontal seams corresponding to workspace boundaries. Consider the tendency in all four Pompeian styles to organize the wall into three zones: the socle at the bottom, a broad central band, and an often unrelated decorative zone above. Columns or pillars in the foreground serve as hard breaks in the horizontal continuity of the background (Fig. 123, and see Fig. 6).

123. Boscoreale: decorated bedroom from the Roman luxury villa. The Metropolitan Museum of Art, New York. Bedroom (03.14.13): Rogers Fund, 1903. Couch (17.190.2076): gift of J. Pierpont Morgan, 1917; mosaic (45.16.2): anonymous gift, 1945.

Such divisions are only natural for workers operating in fairly confined spaces using techniques that require speed of application.

SURFACE RENDERINGS

Rendering is the artistic finishing of floor, wall, and ceiling surfaces by the layered application of semiliquid compounds. The commonest Roman decorative renderings were frescoed plaster, stucco (frequently frescoed or painted), mosaic, and *opus signinum*. During application their materials were in constant supply, often in small quantities at a time. Mortars, plasters, and colors all were mixed in small batches and used up before they dried. Especially if the artisans worked in color, they required a continuous supply of carefully sorted tesserae or dyes and pigments, as well as assistants to sort, mix, or procure colors on demand.

In all its manifestations rendering followed a common pattern of labor: the application of a series of compounds in layers, the drawing of outlines or patterns in the penultimate phase to guide the decorative design, and the manual application of the final layers – the surface treatments – in conformity to the design. Sometimes this was followed by a finishing step, such as polishing the surface or the application of a protective layer of wax. With plaster and stucco, at least, and perhaps mosaic as well, speed and sequence of application was a problem not merely of two dimensions but of three. To ensure the proper bonding of mortar or plaster layers, each new layer was applied before the previous one had completely dried. The plasterer or fresco artist thus had to be aware not only of the speed of his own progress, but also of the amount of time since the layer under which he was working had been applied.[9]

In large buildings rendering tasks were undertaken by a workforce operating in many areas simultaneously. But even the emperor did not have an unlimited supply of skilled labor. The most efficient labor models, for builders and decorators both, would have groups of rooms in a building constructed in succession, allowing the crews to complete some areas as others became ready to receive them. Working in stone and faced concrete simultaneously, builders and planners had some deep thinking to do. Stone surfaces can receive scaffolding at any time, but rendered surfaces cannot. Once the stuccowork, frescoing, or mosaic has been completed, it must not be subjected to the pressure and friction of wood or rope. Wher-

ever stonework shared a scaffolding regime with rendering, the
stone took precedence, because rendering required the permanent
removal of the timbers. This consideration was most essential outdoors, where all but the lowest scaffolds would have been secured
to the wall against the wind.

I have already suggested that in some imperial projects the flying vault centering itself was used as scaffolding. By allowing work
to continue below without impediment, this method could trim
months or years off the project's duration. But the job was difficult
and hazardous. Probably for that very reason Diocletian's Price
Edict of 301 A.D. mandated that the *musaearius*, or ceiling-and-wall
mosaicist, should earn higher maximum wages than the *tessellarius*,
or floor mosaicist. An epitaph from Beneventum makes the distinction all too clear: It laments Hermas, a ceiling-and-wall mosaicist,
who fell from the scaffolding to his death.[10]

As far as we know, there was no Roman Michelangelo working
the ancient equivalent of the Sistine Chapel ceiling for years in succession. His nearest known equivalent in antiquity, Famulus or Fa-
bullus, the painter of Nero's Golden House, must have entrusted
much of the actual painting, and even certain aspects of design, to
assistants and copyists. No single artist could have hoped to realize
more than a small fraction of the overall program, which proceeded
at a breakneck pace. The assignment of tasks was highly distribu-
tive; a single creative impulse was blurred in the act of its diffuse
realization. Highly skilled and dedicated craftsmen plied the decorative trades, but even the best could ill afford to nurse outsize
ambitions or egos. Artistic temperament gave way to a mandate of
speed.[11]

Decorative schemes must have been worked out on the drawing
board or even, in the case of vaulting, on three-dimensional models.
Perhaps negative castings of wax or unfired clay were used for this
purpose. In clay or wax, the erasable surface could be repeatedly
worked with a stylus and burnishing tool until the desired pattern
was achieved. Execution of the design had two principal stages:
first, the laying out of the geometric framework with flexible wood-
en rulers, plumb lines, compasses, and the like; and second, the filling in of the enframing devices with figural or genre scenes (Figs.
124, 125). Often different specialists handled each task.

Roman architectural decoration is well suited to defining space
by outline. Floor mosaics, no matter how organic in effect, are

124. Rome: tomb of Arruntii near Porta Maggiore. G.-B. Piranesi, *Le antichità romane* (Rome 1756).

grounded almost exclusively in orthogonal grids, diagonal lines, and arcs of circles.[12] The implicit grid behind a floor or wall design is a visual aid to scale and distance as well as a reminder of the solid materiality of a barrier even as its intervals fall away into pictorial scenes. Wall and ceiling mosaics are also subjected to schemes of subdivision. The forced proximity of the scaffold-bound artists engendered a preference for compartmentalized designs. Square, octagonal, or diamond-shaped coffer patterns of Greek tradition were pushed up into a third dimension, crisply defining curvature with its smoothly modulating cellular catenaries. Countless elaborations emerged in stucco, all founded on simple grids. A barrel-vaulted ceiling at the Fondo Caiazzo at Pozzuoli, for example, combines elements of a grid of rectangles with circles and circle segments (Fig. 125). Or at the Stabian Baths in Pompeii, in the anteroom of the apodyterium of the men's baths, straight lines have been avoided altogether, but they remain implicit in the double helices connecting the circles, which are centered on a simple grid (Fig. 126).

125. Pozzuoli: stuc-
coed vault at Fondo
Caiazzo. Deutsches
Archäologisches
Institut, neg. 72.1674.
Photo: Singer.

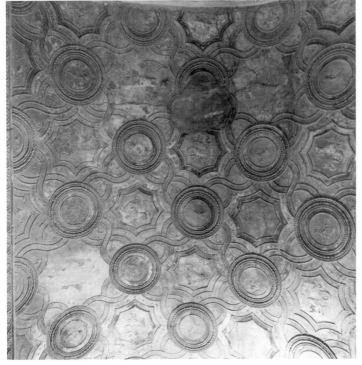

126. Pompeii: stuc-
coed vault in ante-
room of apodyterium
of men's baths, Sta-
bian Baths. Deutsches
Archäologisches
Institut, neg. 72.1708.
Photo: Singer.

On walls and floors, straight lines and circles could easily be incised or painted with rulers or sweeping lines (Fig. 127).[13] On vaults the maintenance of a strict geometry was less straightforward. In small rooms with shallow vaults, such as most surviving examples in Pompeii, workers could operate from trestles of a uniform elevation just below the vault haunches and make grid measurements directly on the vault surface. Certain elements – such as straight lines – can be transmitted to a barrel vault by means of a horizontal string grid stretched across the base of the vault and traced on the surface with the help of a plumb line and a marking tool. Evenly spaced lines laid out in this way will retain their uniform spacing when transferred to the cylindrical surface on a transverse axis, but not on the main axis or a diagonal. Axial lines must therefore be measured out on the surface of the barrel vault itself. On a dome surface, evenly spaced radial lines can be faithfully transferred from horizontal strings, but not parallel lines; these latter too must be measured out on the surface of curvature.

Few Roman frescoes represent figures larger than life, or present single narrative scenes on a truly mural scale.[14] Instead they rely on rich but often repetitive ornamentation and small motifs such as simple human or animal figures or conventional objects like shields, musical instruments, or sacral objects. If a ceiling does feature narrative scenes, as in Nero's Golden House, they are quite small in relation to the whole.[15] Walls are a somewhat different matter. In the first century B.C. central-Italian artists mastered the megalographic fresco format, a sometimes elaborate perspective view of colonnaded enclosures (see Figs. 6, 123). But these are often smaller than advertised and are confined mostly to domestic contexts where the scaffolding was minimal and the artists could easily assess their work from across the room. They are schematized within an organizing grid of uprights and distinct vertical zones, which could be conveniently subdivided and allotted to different artists or work phases. The traditional modern medium for transferring onto walls images that are too large to assess from close range is the paper or parchment cartoon. We have no evidence that decorative artists in antiquity worked from cartoons; however, the Greek term *prokentêma*, "first-pricking," to mean a diagram or model (it is the term inscribed on the Niha temple model; see Fig. 7), suggests that such templates, transferred by pinpricks to the wet plaster, were used at least for architectural renditions in fresco.

127. Workers incising lines in plaster. Adam 1994. By permission of Chrysalis Books.

PLASTER AND FRESCO

This genre has received the most attention of any rendering technique, but mostly in domestic contexts.[16] Roman wall paintings are frescoes; that is, the colors were applied to the final coat of rendering while it was moist, just as Vitruvius recommends.[17] Roman plaster was a compound of slaked lime mixed with aggregate – fine gravel in the underlayers and powdered marble or volcanic sand in the surface layer, sometimes laced with kaolin to add sheen to the final polished surface.[18] Plaster shrinks as it dries; to minimize cracking in the final design, workers usually applied the material in fairly small, discrete zones on any large wall or ceiling. Some separation was inevitable at the borders of these zones. To mask any disruption of the design the borders were made to correspond to the edges of painted features. Thus a framing motif was plastered separately from the scene within it. The House of the Iliadic Shrine in Pompeii, which was in the process of being redecorated when the town met its end, reveals the sequence of steps in the process. In any room destined to be painted, no layer of plaster was applied to an entire wall at one time. Instead, each discrete zone was built up in all its layers and painted before work began on the next. A zone is called a *giornata di lavoro*, or "day's work," but this term is not strictly correct. The application of several layers of plaster, often with different formulas and varying times between applications, took days, whereas the plastering or painting of a discrete zone would not necessarily have required an entire day's work. Only the figural scene paintings, usually no larger than an easel painting, are likely to have been done in a day. If numerous rooms or zones were

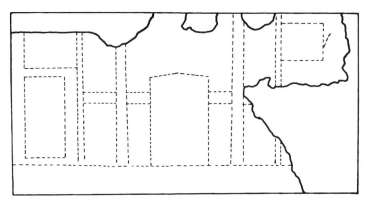

128. Rome: plaster-
ing divisions of a wall
in House of Livia.
Ling 1991. By per-
mission of Cambridge
University Press.

planned, plasterers might have applied a single layer to several
zones in a day just so long as no two zones abutted one another. Such would appear to be the technique used in the House of
Livia in Rome, where the zones are of varying size and complexity (Fig. 128). But the sequence was carefully planned, for any zones
built up simultaneously would have to be painted simultaneously.
In this house a number of painters and plasterers worked together
on the six rooms that were undergoing redecoration. They divided
the walls into horizontal zones, corresponding to divisions in the
planned design, and worked from the top down. Since no design
had been laid down for the plasterers they simply took measurements to establish the limits of the zone, ensuring some overlapping
of excess plaster into the next zone. After the plastering and painting was complete the workers neatly trimmed off the excess with
knives or chisels and began to plaster the abutting zone.[19] String
was used to serve as visual guides dividing the zones, but the final
layer was often incised with guidelines for the painters. The geometry of these lines is rather approximate; the painter would have had
to compensate visually for its inaccuracies, as can be seen on a
"wallpaper" pattern in the Villa Ariana at Stabiae (Fig. 129).

The complexity of the wall-painting process, not to mention the
number of contingent tasks involved, presumes some kind of preliminary planning. Workshops probably had a repertoire of stock
framing designs on parchment, but even these were necessarily
adapted to the dimensions of every wall. Scene paintings – the figural narratives upon which the fame of Pompeian painting largely
rests – were entrusted to a specialist known later as the *pictor imaginarius,* who in the Price Edict of 301 earned twice as much as the
pictor parietarius, painter of the framing designs. A few *imaginarii*

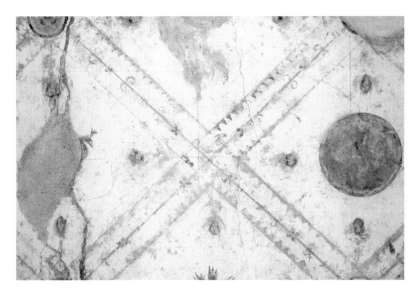

129. Stabiae: Villa Ariana, close-up of decoration and incised guidelines in *diaeta* 9. Photo: K. Coleman.

were artists of the highest originality and standing. But artists of all abilities seem to have relied on a repertoire of gestural figures and groups drawn from memory or from pattern books, which would have been equally important in helping the client choose a program of paintings. A stone relief in Sens shows a man in toga and boots – either patron or *imaginarius* – consulting a pattern book while the plasterer, *parietarius*, and an assistant work on the upper zone of a wall (Fig. 130).[20]

130. Sens: Roman relief depicting frescoists at work. Adam 1994. By permission of Chrysalis Books.

STUCCO

Writing in the early third century, Tertullian attributed to the *albarius tector*, or wall finisher, a large array of skills, from plastering to stuccowork to painting figural images.[21] Whether or not we can take the author at his word (he is preparing the way for a spiritual analogy), it is true that wall- and vault-finishing teams had to operate with a single will and intelligence. But just as with painters, there must often have been a division of labor between the *imaginarius* and the *parietarius*.

Almost by definition, stucco is a compound applied in relief. This fact, along with differences in the compound itself, distinguishes it from plaster, which tends to be applied smooth. Roman stucco was commonly made of water, marble dust, and lime (despite Vitruvius' warnings against the latter) applied in relief to undercoats of mortar (water, lime, and sand).[22] The surface of a wall or vault may have been prepared initially by notching to give purchase to the mortar, a not-inconsiderable task that took six weeks in Michelangelo's Medici Chapel.[23] As Vitruvius suggests, the stucco was applied directly upon the still-moist underlayer, which had been roughened to receive it. At Pompeii wall and ceiling moldings were constructed around iron pins projecting from the wall and overlaid transversely with reeds. All steps were carefully timed and sequenced. For effects in high relief, sometimes a layer of mortar was laid down on the surface with a mold or template and then the final coat of stucco applied over it with a slightly larger mold. In other cases all the work was hand-modeled with a trowel or other tools.[24] If color was desired, it was applied shortly thereafter, as soon as the moist surface had developed a skin resistant to the brush. Certainly the same frescoists working on the flat plaster surfaces would have been enlisted to paint the stuccoes.

Because of its high decorative value at relatively low expense and weather-resistant properties that are superior to pure plaster, stucco is by far the most common exterior treatment for Roman buildings.[25] Outer walls may often have been among the first surfaces to receive attention from the stuccoists. Here the sequence of application caused few problems, and the decorative patterns – usually replicas of drafted stone masonry – were simple enough to be applied by apprentices. On interiors stucco usually appeared in conjunction with flat fresco work and was itself often richly painted. Although applied to walls in imitation of marble blocks or pilasters, it was

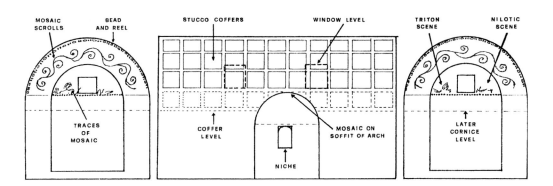

131. Lepcis Magna:
Hunting Baths,
schematic drawing of
mosaic decoration.
Sear 1977. By
permission of F. Sear.

favored in the upper zones of enclosed architectural spaces, particularly vaults and lunettes under vaults. Decorative cornices around interior walls were often made of it as well.

WALL AND CEILING MOSAICS

Mural and vault mosaic, with its thousands of glass and stone tesserae (accompanied periodically by seashells and chunks of a silicate known as Egyptian Blue or *lomentum*) set into a mortar or plaster bedding, was a more time-consuming and expensive medium than stucco or painting. Yet it is attested in over three hundred sites around the empire, and its legacy lives on in churches and mausolea from the fourth century to the present (see Fig. 25).[26] Many Roman wall and vault mosaics adorned small, precious structures such as domestic nymphaea. But many large interior vaults are thought to have been decorated with colored mosaics, including those of the frigidaria (and many other halls) at the Baths of Caracalla and of Diocletian at Rome; at the Hadrianic Baths at Lepcis Magna; the Antonine Baths at Carthage; most of the largest vaulted spaces at the thermal spa of Baiae; and the Scenic Triclinium (Serapeum-Canopus) at Hadrian's villa.[27] The method of transferring and applying the designs is not certain. The Odyssey mosaic in the Golden House of Nero indicates that an outline was applied in light blue paint to the wet bedding plaster to guide the hand of the mosaicist.[28] It seems likely that only small patches of the design were sketched out at once, enough to occupy the mosaicists for the day without allowing mortar beds to dry fully between applications.

The Hunting Baths at Lepcis Magna have what is perhaps the best-preserved mosaic program on walls and vaults (Fig. 131). The coffered ceiling of the barrel-vaulted frigidarium, typically, was stuccoed; too troublesome for the application of mosaics, coffers were deemed ideal vehicles for elaborate stuccoed moldings.[29] Also typically, the more favored sites for mosaics were the vaults of small apsidal spaces and the faces and soffits of arches, all of which preserve traces of mosaics in this room.

FLOOR MOSAICS

The floor mosaicist operated without the constraints of scaffolding but confronted an equally harsh, if different, logic formulated by the presence of his own bulk, and of much unwanted activity, on the work surface.[30] Archaeological evidence suggests that floor mosaics of the Roman imperial era were laid entirely at the site, not prefabricated in sections.[31] The implications for building logistics are profound. To a greater or lesser degree, wall and ceiling decorators could avoid hampering the processes of storage and transport that characterize every building site. But the artistic domain of floor decorators was encumbered by heavy traffic and temporary depots of materials, which could seriously compromise the desired sequences of the generative process. It may be no coincidence, then, that in large, multiroom Roman bath buildings with a single dominant construction phase, mosaics are often confined to the peripheral rooms, where traffic patterns were lighter.

Floor mosaic is perhaps unique in that it is intended to be viewed obliquely. The artists could rarely withdraw to view their creations from directly above. The restraint on distance influenced composition and style, and therefore the process of designing and creating the whole. Framing devices, which orient the viewer to the room's boundaries, are an important element of the design. The attendant interest in border geometry tends to outweigh the kind of pictorial virtuosity and stage-set clutter often seen in wall decoration. Geometric patterning, which required meticulous measurements, was dictated by the dimensions of the room, so the design would start at the periphery and work inward. Borders often served as a buffer between irregular room plans and the more precise interior pattern; the Insula of the Muses at Ostia is a typical example, demonstrating how one technique (patterned mosaic) adapts to another technique with a lower precision standard (planimetric layout) (Fig. 132). Sometimes, however, the mosaic departed from its rigid regime and embraced the room's asymmetry. At a house in Saint-Romain-en-Gal the organizing grid follows the orientation of the walls, which

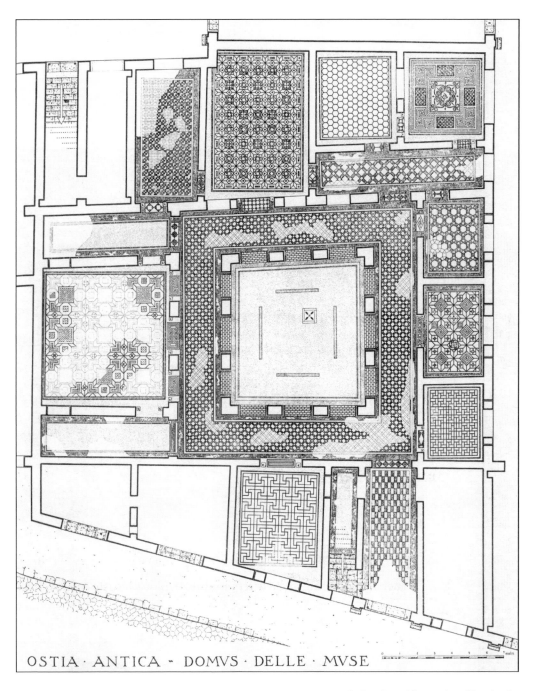

OSTIA · ANTICA · DOMVS · DELLE · MVSE

132. Ostia: plan with mosaics of Insula of
the Muses. *Scavi di Ostia* 4. By permission
of Soprintendenza Archeologica di Ostia.

133. Vienne, Saint-Romain-en-Gal: hexagon mosaic from House of the Five Mosaics. *Recueil general des mosaïques de la Gaule* III.2. By permission of J. Lancha.

form a parallelogram. The result is that the whole design is slightly skewed (Fig. 133).

Certain rules limit the freedom to resize a mosaic pattern. For example, patterns (as opposed to complex modeling) tend to comprise tesserae of roughly a standard size. Many band motifs were two or three tesserae wide, and so the extent to which they could be modified depended on the skilled mosaicist's ability to "cheat" perfection by crowding or loosening tesserae. Sometimes, even if borders were perfectly precise, the patterns within were not drawn in advance, compelling the mosaicist to solve emerging problems of ir-

134. Verulamium: portion of a geometric mosaic illustrating flaws in guilloche borders. Verulamium Museum, St. Albans. Illustration: R. Taylor.

regularity as best he could. The guilloche pattern on a mosaic from Verulamium shows a variety of ways in which the mosaicist wove his strands together at awkward intersections (Fig. 134). Indeed the incising of every detail before tessellation was a prohibitively cumbersome process. The whole design could not be incised into the final bedding layer all at once; this would have required an elaborate suspension system to keep the artist off the wet mortar. It was done in patches or strips, no more at a time than could be tessellated in a session. The principal guiding elements of the grid could be set out with string and nails, but lesser details often emerged only with the mosaic itself. A room in the Villa Arianna at Stabiae preserves large tracts of the inscribed underlayer of a geometric mosaic. Not only are the string marks and nail holes clearly visible, but the entire pattern preserves traces of paint that provided a complete color guide for the *tessellarii,* the workmen applying the tesserae.[32]

On mosaics with complex content, the borders and other peripheral patterns were established before the figural specialists generated pictorial scenes or floating figures to conform to the geometry. Scale drawings laid out on a grid were probably consulted for the figural elements. Decoration did not proceed evenly across a floor. While master mosaicists were creating the figural work, which required the highest skill in colorism, modeling, and impressionistic techniques, less skilled artisans laid the border patterns and apprentices filled in the monochrome backgrounds.[33] A leveling square was constantly on hand to ensure that all work was evenly horizontal or slightly pitched for drainage. If "islands" of thematic material developed, their relative thickness would be monitored to ensure ultimate uniformity.

Since the design of floor mosaics was defined by, and thus began at, the periphery, scaffolding was unwelcome. Wall decoration in the room should either have been complete, or not yet begun, when the mosaic work commenced. It is possible to imagine cantilevered scaffolding in such a context, but when one peoples the scene with busy assistants constantly walking about with fresh buckets of plaster or pots of paint, and a hail of stone chips, dripping paint, or mortar from the workers aloft, it is easy to see that the overlapping of these tasks was undesirable.

WALL AND FLOOR VENEERS

Veneer in expensive stone plaques or inlay (*opus sectile*) was a luxury.[34] Most places in which it appeared have been thoroughly plundered of their plaques and the cramps that held them in place, leaving only the patterns of holes in the walls. Even Pompeii's marble-clad public buildings were stripped of their decoration by ancient salvagers. Marble veneer was never used on vaults; it was strictly a medium for floors and upright surfaces. Much of the design and preparation of *opus sectile*, such as cutting and testing the fit of the thin slabs of colored marble – or occasionally glass[35] – could have been done off site. In addition to being set into a bed of mortar the larger and heavier components were affixed to the wall with metal cramps.

Roman veneer was usually abstract and geometric.[36] Figural decoration evidently was a rarity reserved for private residences of the ultrarich, like the mid-fourth-century Basilica of Junius Bassus in Rome or the late-fourth-century house outside the Porta Marina at Ostia. This latter example offers strong evidence that some *opus sectile* artists worked from the top down. Excavations revealed that the wall decoration had never been completed: Though the upper eight meters of the wall had received their facing, the lower two and a half meters had not (Fig. 135).[37] But this was work of unusual subtlety, a veritable jigsaw puzzle of figural components. In simpler projects gravity could be used to better effect working in horizontal zones from the bottom up. Each band of slabs could be rested upon the preceding one during the setting phase. Most revetment panels, which were rarely more than a couple of centimeters thick, were light enough to be positioned by hand but heavy enough to require metal fasteners (Fig. 136). Before mortar was applied to the zone

receiving a large panel, it was moved into place and used as a template for marking the cramp hole spots on the wall around three edges. The panel was removed, holes gouged into the masonry, and bronze cramps wedged into them with small pieces of stone; then the holes were packed with mortar. Often longitudinal fragments of amphorae were used as shims or spacers between the panels and the masonry. (They are visible on the walls in Fig. 137.) Hooked at both ends, the cramps on the two disengaged sides of each panel would have been splayed slightly to receive it before being pushed or bent laterally into the waiting slots in its edges.[38] The surface and edges were checked with plumb lines and levels, then the procedure was repeated on the adjacent panel. Skillful artisans could have positioned an entire row of slabs before the mortar in the cramp holes had set, manipulating the cramps by hand and relying on the lower zone (or the floor, if it was the first zone) to hold the slabs in balance. Only when the cramps were firmly set was mortar poured into the gap between the masonry and the slab.

On floors as on walls, *opus sectile* was the richest of all decorative techniques, reserved for the most opulent spaces. Its materials were more expensive than any other, and the labor involved in producing and installing its close-fitting elements the most exacting.

135. Ostia: reconstruction of *opus sectile* wall decoration of house outside Porta Marina. *Scavi di Ostia* 6. By permission of Soprintendenza Archeologica di Ostia.

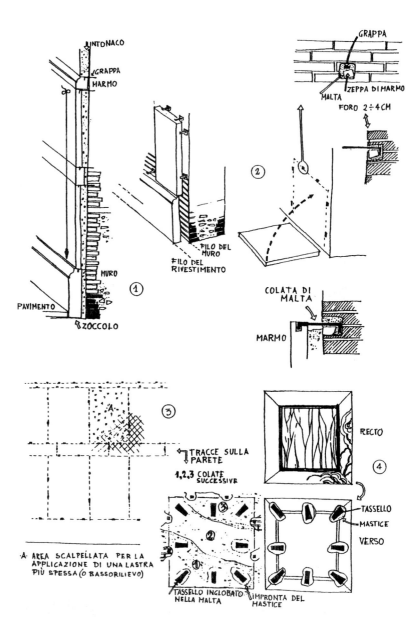

136. Method for applying revetments to walls. Giuliani 1990.

Opus sectile floors follow modular, repetitive patterns; the House of Cupid and Psyche at Ostia offers a brilliant example (Fig. 137). In many cases the modules were prefabricated and their elements cemented together on a terra-cotta backing before transport to the site (Fig. 138, 139; and see Fig. 136). One obvious benefit of this technique is that the pavement, so laboriously shaped and fitted in the yard or workshop, could be assembled rapidly on the floor. In most cases the modules were small enough to be applied by hand.

137. Ostia: House of
Cupid and Psyche,
opus sectile walls
and floor. Photo:
R. Taylor.

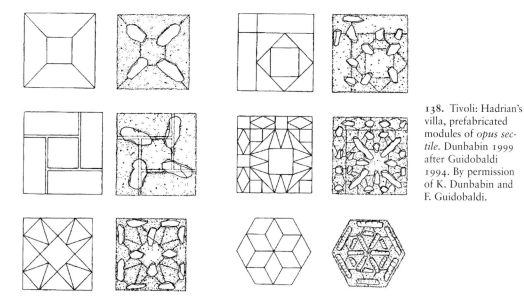

138. Tivoli: Hadrian's
villa, prefabricated
modules of *opus sec-
tile*. Dunbabin 1999
after Guidobaldi
1994. By permission
of K. Dunbabin and
F. Guidobaldi.

139. Rome: inscribed marble slab depicting assembly of an *opus sectile* pattern unit on a temporary table. The worker appears to be filing down the edge of a component slab. Museo Nazionale Romano. Illustration: R. Taylor.

Like tiles, they simply had to be abutted against one another on a bed of mortar and tamped to a uniform level with the aid of stone shims (potsherds, typically) set into the mortar. On the floor no metal cramps were necessary.

It is likely, then, that the decision to pave some of the grand central spaces of Roman imperial buildings with *opus sectile* – which could be prepared off-site – rather than mosaic – which could not – was not an entirely aesthetic one. These crossroads of building activity remained unfinished while their floor decorators produced and shaped the paving material in the workshop. Meanwhile the less heavily trafficked peripheral rooms were given over to the patient work of the mosaicists. Its time-efficiency and linear mode of assembly made *opus sectile* especially suited to the final phases of the decorating process in the largest and grandest halls. These rooms, whose walls and vaults required the greatest concentration of artisan labor, retained their scaffolding and centering longer than most other zones of construction. Decentering could easily damage existing floor decoration. Moreover, as I have already suggested, these large vaulted spaces continued to serve as thoroughfares or materials depots for as long as possible. It is no surprise, then, that their paving waited until the carpentry had been dismantled and the majority of building activity completed.

STONEWORKING

Because of their special status as both an aesthetic and a structural material, worked stone blocks transgress many general

rules of the decorative process. Most decoration is in some sense applied to a surface or introduced into a waiting void; it is therefore an additive process, and to some degree reversible. But the carving of stonework is purely subtractive and therein uniquely dangerous.[39] And yet it could be done on a massive scale with supreme confidence. We must not forget that in a few regions of the Roman Empire, the most impressive works of architecture are pure sculpture, carved as monolithic units out of the faces of cliffs (Fig. 140).

It is generally presumed that among the many tasks involved in more conventional architectural stonework, sculpture – either in relief (as on friezes) or in the round (as on column capitals) – required the greatest expenditure of time. But that is not necessarily the case. One authority argues that the most critical and time-consuming phases of ancient stonework were quarrying, transport, and the smoothing and jointing of the blocks.[40] The geometry of unmortared joints is less forgiving than that of the plastic arts, for while slight incongruencies in repeated or symmetrical sculptural elements can be artfully muted by the more powerful argument of the overall form, the joint is utterly deaf to rhetoric. It insists upon straight lines and flat surfaces. In most styles of dry masonry favored by the Romans, the task remained the same: bringing together perfectly even

140. Petra: landscape with rock-cut tombs. D. Roberts, *The Holy Land* (1843). By permission of Duke University Museum of Art.

surfaces, each a perfect profile of the other in mirror image, into a perfectly compatible seal. And this was necessarily achieved during construction of the building – though occasionally a stone element, if it wasn't too large, could be slotted into position later.

How close to completion was the surface decoration when dressing was complete? The answer, it seems, depended on a combination of circumstances and the preferences of the stonemasons. If a building was to receive much cut and carved stone, then the distinct but interconnected strategies of dressing and carving must have been among the most challenging problems faced by the planners. The pool of skilled laborers was always limited. Some characteristics of the decoration had to be known even to the quarrymen, who could deliver stone blocks in a roughed-out version of the final form to minimize the weight for transport. But carving the decoration was accomplished in multiple stages, many of which could be done before or after the block became part of the building. When was early finishing preferable to late? Peter Rockwell declares, in essence, never:

It is always easier to move a carver than it is to move a carving. Human beings do not weigh 2.7 tons per cubic meter and can move by themselves; they are generally less fragile than finely carved details in stone. . . . In terms of the economy of time and motion, the best choice has often been to have the carver climb the scaffolding to finish his carving rather than to move the finished work after carving.[41]

The point is well taken. But the stone must be moved anyway, and it may take less energy to move a completely finished piece very carefully with little scaffolding than to do so with less care and then erect full scaffolding. And what of the economy of time? Work on the ground could continue through the winter under shelters while construction was at a halt: Can any other model be conceivable for such vast but efficient enterprises as the Forum of Trajan in Rome (Fig. 141)?[42] Other considerations are at stake too, such as the method and angle of carving the craftsmen preferred, or the effect of scaffolding on other tasks.

But we must also consider an operational question confined to the stoneworking process itself: Can a continuous portion of the stonework be fitted together experimentally on the ground? As in the weaving of a tapestry, alignment is achieved more naturally in one dimension than the other. It is no coincidence that most of the evi-

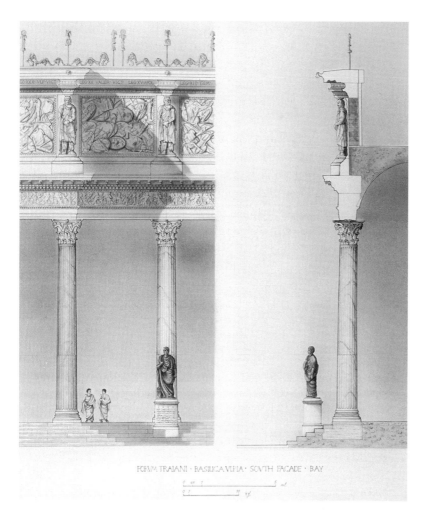

141. Rome: Forum of Trajan, Basilica Ulpia facade; restored elevation of bay of south facade. Packer 1997. By permission of J. Packer.

FORVM TRAIANI · BASILICA VLPIA · SOVTH FACADE · BAY

dence for full-sized templates of architectural stonework is confined to horizontal features such as cornices and pediments.[43] These can be fully assembled before erection, either on the ground or flat against a wall. Because the workers may presume that the surface upon which the feature will eventually be installed is perfectly horizontal, they can lay their test rows accordingly, like lines of movable type spring-loaded in the chase. Once this has been done, they can complete the carving, transmitting even the most delicate details across vertical joints, confident that these will match after installation. But vertical carved elements such as pilasters have no analogous guide except at corners, where the sharp return of the wall governs alignment. Of course the typesetter can justify columns of type

vertically, but only with continuous vertical joints separating each
column. Stone masonry almost never has continuous vertical joints;
in fact, most relief elements carved vertically onto walls do not conform to the jointing at all. Thus there is no vertical baseline by
which to ensure perfect alignment. The unfinished southern tower
of the great propylaea at Baalbek offers an instructive example of
compensations made for anticipated misalignment (Fig. 142). Each
roughly shaped tier of the pilasters was given enough extra breadth
to compensate for the inevitable joggling of the vertical edge, which
would have been trimmed down to an elegant line in the final stage.
This measure is a fine example of preemptive inaccuracy, though it
was never given its final form.

Some craftsmen must have preferred to complete their carving on
the ground, where they could work in relative safety at the angle
they preferred. In an age before protective goggles, a carver never wanted to be looking up at his work. Better to carve a capital
upside-down, or an overhanging entablature on its back.[44] The two-
part architrave soffits of the Temple of Mars Ultor in Rome are instructive in this respect: They plainly were carved on the ground,
not from below, for their decoration is misaligned and mismeasured
across the longitudinal joints.[45] And the monumental capitals on the
same site had lewis holes both at top and bottom – clear evidence
that they were carved in an inverted position.[46] Other advantages
accrued to the earthbound stonemason. Blocks spoiled inadvertent-
ly could be cut down or even discarded, whereas those lodged in
place required patching. As for the completed work, the delicate
carved surface theoretically could go untouched throughout the lifting, levering, and clamping process. Most blocks of dry masonry
were hoisted by lewises or forceps, levered into their final position,
and clamped across the top of the joint. All of these techniques required nothing more than small holes cut into the joining surfaces,
which would be invisible to the viewer after completion.

Nonetheless, the risk of subsequent damage or of misalignment
often trumped the advantages of precarving. Uncompleted buildings
around the empire indicate that finishing had been left for last, only
to be neglected altogether or in part. Some things simply demanded
to be finished in place. The most obvious of these were columns.[47]
Column scaffolding, it must be noted, is easier to construct and dismantle than wall scaffolding, having equal purchase on all sides of

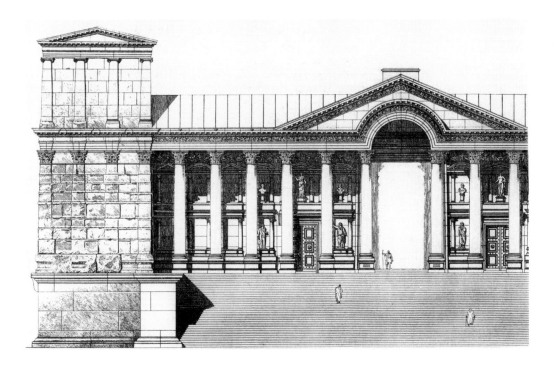

its host structure. The stacked drums of fluted columns could not be perfectly aligned to one another before assembly, nor could they be set in profile against a template. And fluting, being prone to damage from transport of materials through the building, must often have been left unfinished – at least at lower levels – until construction was complete. Various drawings in stone indicate that even the entasis, or tapered curvature, of columns could have been established after erection. These drawings were not outlines to be traced literally but references for determining the precise thickness of columns at regular height intervals. An especially illuminating Greek example, from the Temple of Apollo at Didyma, represents the lower elements of a column in life-size profile but compresses the shaft by a factor of 16 so that each interval between horizontal lines, a *daktylos* or finger-width on the diagram, represents a foot of height (Fig. 143).[48] The carvers could set their calipers to the length of each line and transfer the measurements to the shaft in its "decompressed" mode. This method of encoding information distills subtlety of line and surface (what architects sometimes call *refinement* or *temperament*), making it easier to control in the design process and more intelligible to the stoneworkers.

142. Baalbek: Sanctuary of Jupiter Heliopolitanus, restored elevation of propylaea. Wiegand 1921–5.

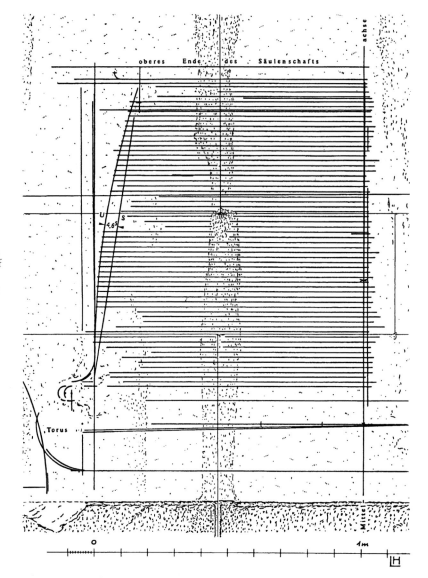

143. Didyma:
Sanctuary of Apollo,
inscribed template of
column compressed
vertically by a factor
of 16. Haselberger
and Seybold 1991.
By permission of
L. Haselberger.

FREESTANDING SCULPTURE

Monumental sculpture is the most discussed and least con-
textualized of all ancient artistic genres.[49] Most of it was
fixed in place and thus embedded in a built environment. Was not
all sculpture therefore "architectural sculpture"? The question, it
seems, has never been carefully parsed in a Roman context.

In no other decorative genre except for the columnar orders were
Roman buildings apt to be so promiscuous. Sculpture could be
made to fit almost every surface of a structure, and in the case of

many triumphal and honorific arches, it did. These and a few other building types, such as the great "Asiatic" nymphaea of the East, tiered like wedding cakes with aedicules and statuary, were little more than displays for their surface decoration (see Fig. 122).[50] Pitched roofs, floors, stairs, and pools, the only surface expanses that functionally did not admit continuous sculpture, could nevertheless bear a great deal of it intermittently.

Yet we would be mistaken to presume that most of this sculpture was an organic component of architecture. More expansive, linear decorative genres such as rendering and *opus sectile* genuinely help to characterize space by reflecting light and defining form. But rarely was a building designed with individual sculptures or even a special sculptural program in mind. After all, figural sculpture introduces complexity, not unity: It is a loose confederation of individuals. To the extent that architects paid heed to freestanding sculpture, they seem to have been concerned not with singular forms but with genres. The most important genres are figural reliefs and freestanding niche statuary. Freestanding pedimental sculpture, so prominent in the Greek period, was only incidental to the Roman repertoire.

The realization of these two genres follows quite different paths. Relief sculpture was an extension of stonemasonry and was carved by teams of specialists working seriatim on architectural blocks, usually at or near the site.[51] As I suggested in the preceding section the design, if not the realization, of reliefwork was essentially complete by the time the blocks were installed into the building's fabric. But statuary, which frequently was produced off site or even recycled from another context, did not have the same architectural integrity. Intercolumniations, wall niches, and exedras, so fundamental to the Roman aesthetic, were more important in organizing and punctuating space than the sculptures installed in them.[52] Figural statuary simulates the users and beneficiaries of buildings (i.e., people and gods), not buildings themselves; and while the relationship of figure and ground may be harmonious, it is nevertheless predicated upon a functional dialectic. Niches are the shelter, statues the sheltered. Even human figures used as structural supports, like the telamones in the Forum of Trajan (see Fig. 141), do not dissuade us of that fundamental distinction.

Architectural need drove the development of certain sculptural types and styles. For instance, the dimensions of the enframing device could influence the sculptural form. By the second century

architectural statuary, like column components, was being manufactured in standard sizes to conform to a quasi-canonical system-
atization of design principles.[53] If necessary, statues were given a
rigid, attenuated form to accommodate narrow frames.[54] And because enframement is such an important principle, much Roman
niche sculpture is only frontally resolved; it is not meant to be seen
from the sides or the rear, where its volumetric logic and even its
finish dissipates. In exceptional cases statues may make sense from
both front and rear but are less persuasive when seen from the sides.
Such seems to be the case for two great Hercules statues found in
the frigidarium of the Baths of Caracalla. Miranda Marvin contends
that their poor lateral resolution made them ideal candidates to
stand in a pair of intercolumniations at one open end of the great
hall, where one could admire them coming and going yet not while
passing them by.[55]

Such measures do not make statuary "architectural." Instead, the
very process of subordinating one genre to the other emphasizes
their functional differences. Most statuary was therefore governed
by, and did not govern, its environment. Its influence was semantic,
not architectonic. The principal practical task of the sculptor was
to create variety within a confined spatial framework. Patron, architect, and sculptor may have discussed the size, content, placement,
and desired effects of statues, especially the most prominent ones
at lower levels. Particularly fine statues or groups may have been
placed in unobstructed areas where they would be seen to best advantage and allow room to draw the viewer in a circle around
them.[56] But all this was incidental to the originary impulse that created their environment.

Of course the task of erecting statues could not be ignored in the
planning process. The final positioning of all heavy statuary await-
ed cranes. Cast bronze was favored for large and complicated sculptural groups atop buildings, partly because it was far lighter than
stone and allowed the group to be hoisted *tout court* in a single procedure. The offset position of niches meant that statues could not
be lowered directly onto their bases from above. Instead they were
suspended directly before the niche and levered onto their bases with
wooden beams or tilted sledges. Indoor statuary was often painted,
probably after it was in place. The wax-based pigments were vulnerable to high temperatures; it is for this reason, Marvin concludes,
that the hot rooms of Roman imperial baths often lacked statues.[57]

LANDSCAPING

Landscaping consists principally of two things: the manipulation of the site's vertical topography and the horizontal articulation of its surface. Having dealt with earthworks earlier, I focus here on surface effects. Views, sightlines, and physical presence in the environment were fundamental elements in the design of Roman luxury villas, hilltop sanctuaries, and other privileged domains. But open plots of land on a construction site have always been apt to serve as workyards until construction and even decoration are complete. To what extent were the images of trees, lawns, and gardens woven into the generative process of buildings?

Vitruvius seems uninterested in gardens himself; he merely suggests in passing that they should be planted in peristyles for reasons of health.[58] But he offers unusual (and archaeologically unexampled) attention to the drainage system under the garden area of a peristyle: it should be excavated, filled with charcoal and a layer of sand, presumably topped with soil, and conjoined with a drains in the portico subfloors and walls. From a functional standpoint, then, if not an aesthetic one, the garden space and its enclosure are a single design unit. Indeed the excavations of the Water Court (Piazza d'Oro) at Hadrian's villa reveal a complex drainage system all of a piece with the planting beds and the surrounding peristyle, sans charcoal (Fig. 144).[59] The Stadium Garden at the same villa and the sunken courts at Domitian's palace in Rome, each arrayed with complex waterworks, show the impressive degree of integration to which natural and man-made elements could be taken.[60] Roman landscaping contributed to high design at least to the extent that it relied on waterworks and drainage systems.

But only in a few rare cases when the architecture evoked a natural formation – such as a villa grotto or a tumulus tomb – was the built structure not given prior consideration over its landscaping.[61] Of all Roman architectural genres only houses, villas, palaces, and tombs had a robust landscaping tradition.[62] Excavated Roman house and villa gardens seem to suggest that on a small scale, at least, their design was incidental to the built environment. They conformed to the shape, sightlines, and proportions of the enclosure after the fact.[63] Some public peristyles and fora were landscaped, perhaps most famously the great portico of the Theater of Pompey in Rome.[64] Certainly temples could be adorned with gardens and

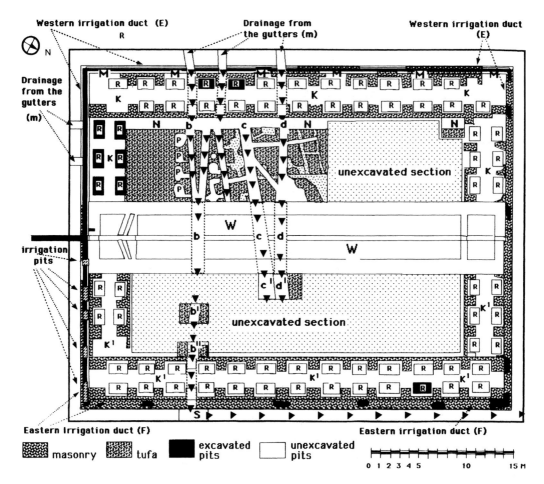

144. Tivoli: Hadrian's villa, Water Court, plan of excavations with planting pits and drains. Jashemski and Salza Prina Ricotti 1992. By permission of E. Salza Prina Ricotti.

groves; Pseudo-Lucian vividly describes the gardens adjoining the famous Temple of Aphrodite at Knidos, and recent excavations in the Vigna Barberini on the Palatine Hill in Rome have suggested that formal gardens surrounded the Temple of Heliogabalus.[65] But of the extent to which garden and structure were integrated in such places, either in space or in time, we know little. Many urban structures had no green space at all.

Formal landscaping is a modular art. Most species of domesticated trees, shrubs, crops, or plants come with a recommended spacing distance. These modules can be adjusted if necessary; and more important, the larger design elements comprising them can be reshaped. Most of the gardens documented by Jashemski were made to conform to built enclosures dictated by circumstance. As with mosaics, their principal organizing elements of the design were intentionally elastic. Let us briefly consider the only surviving Roman

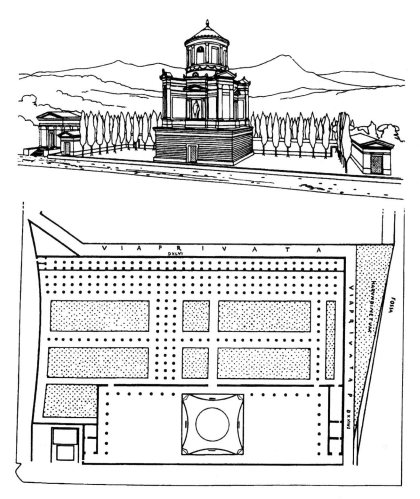

145. Urbino: inscribed plan of a tomb and garden, with hypothetical reconstruction of site. Wilson-Jones 2000. By permission of Yale University Press.

ground plan of a building and its garden, etched on a slab of marble found outside Rome. It depicts the plot of a lavish tomb (Fig. 145). In relation to the tomb and its court (which must have faced the road at the bottom of the plan) the garden is asymmetrical. But the trees have been planted according to a module carefully calculated from the available space, and the planting beds have been made to conform to it. Both the module and the rectangular beds acknowledge the tomb's priority by means of a modulewide path directly on axis with it.[66] The larger trees planted in the tomb courtyard stop at the tomb's corners, allowing a magnificent view of the structure down this corridor, which also is thinned of its trees for the sake of the axial view.

The completed Roman building normally takes precedence over its environment for at least two reasons: It is the principal source and object of the view; and it is the only fully realized element of a newly minted landscape. The building is an anchor for imagined sightlines over, between, and under the mature trees that exist only on papyrus or in the mind of the landscaper. Perhaps the Tour Magne, a Roman tower-tomb overlooking the Jardins de la Fontaine at Nîmes, was once given a similar priority over its surrounding gardens (Fig. 146).

DYNAMIC MEDIA

Two other artistic media, light and water, I leave for last. They stand apart in their infinite mutability and dynamism.[67] During the daytime, when most nonprivate structures were in use, they were in constant flux; but they had an undeniably profound effect upon the visitor, and deserve to be called media despite a somewhat unusual property shared by both: their intended effect is largely absent during the creative process.

LIGHT. Though not in itself a decorative material, natural light was subject to manipulation and exploitation at the decorative phase, when consideration was given both to the transmission of light (through glazing) and its reflection (through surface treatment of walls and floors). Direct and reflected sunlight, powerful elements in psychological structure, brushed across hard and liquid surfaces, continuously molding and remolding volumes afresh with their unique capacity to foreshorten or dilate perceived depth of field. Against inner vaulted surfaces lunette windows emulated the sky, brightening the periphery of the vault. In the Pantheon the wand of light penetrating the oculus probes the textured perimeter like a finger in a honey pot. Details leap into relief on the receptive surface and then subside in shadow as the ray passes.

Techniques in natural lighting followed structural innovations but may also have driven them. While we need not assert, as one author does, that "without glass windows the great bath buildings would never have existed,"[68] it is nevertheless true that their nature and form would have been altogether different. Seneca reports on the gloom permeating the old-fashioned baths of Scipio, but by his own time the development of pane glass, along with the exploitation of the lighting potential of the cross vault, was helping to revolutionize architectural form.[69] He goes on to remark that "people regard

146. Nîmes: Tour
Magne. Photo:
R. Taylor.

baths as fit only for moths if they have not been so arranged that
they receive the sun all day long through the widest of windows,
if men cannot bathe and get a coat of tan at the same time, and if
they cannot look out from their bath-tubs over stretches of land and
sea." Until the first century, natural lighting – whether with colonnades, windows, clerestories, or oculi – could only be admitted *al
fresco*. The new cross vaults now allowed skylighting without the
wind and chill. Great expanses of semitransparent or translucent
glass punctuated the heated side of bath buildings, generating radiant heat to supplement the hypocaust heating. Even colonnades
could be fitted with glass partitions, which were simply mortared
to the columns on either side.[70]

In antiquity windows were built in place. The great thermal windows of Roman imperial baths were typically supported by a grid
of stone or metal. The arched window of the sweat room in the
Baths of Faustina at Miletos, for example, had a tripartite skeleton
of slim marble mullions reinforcing a web of smaller marble muntins framing square or rectangular panes (Fig. 147).[71] The hot rooms
at the much smaller Suburban Baths of Herculaneum show evidence

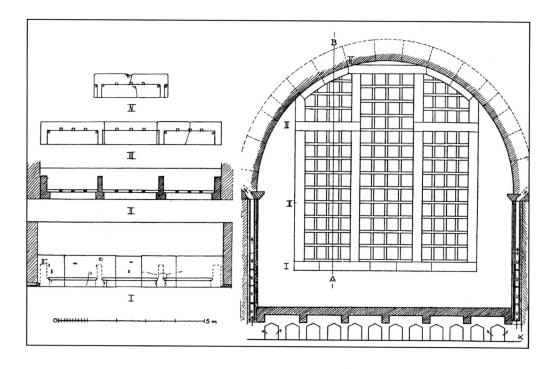

147. Miletos: Baths of Faustina, reconstruction of thermal window. Von Gerkan and Krischen 1928.

of double glazing, but here the muntins were made of wood and the added insulation helped to preserve this more perishable material from condensation.[72] In most large baths there is no evidence of double glazing. Whatever the material of their muntins, they had to retain enough rigidity to hold the fragile panes in place without imposing their weight on the panes below. In especially large windows this was not always easy. At Miletos each row of four panes was structurally isolated from those above and below by the use of continuous horizontal muntins anchored to the pillars. To ensure that no pressure at all was placed on the panes, the muntins would have been erected first and then each pane custom-cut and fitted into place with room to spare. In many cross-vaulted spaces this was achieved most easily from scaffolding on the exterior, but it could also have been done from the centering.

WATER. Water was exploited in numerous ways to augment the architectural experience.[73] Under the sky it was laid out in great reflective sheets, as if to extend the Roman taste for bilateral symmetry from the horizontal plane to the vertical. In a few places, vertical and arcing water jets were used to architectural effect, emulating columns and vaults.[74] But the most distinctively Roman wa-

148. Tivoli: Hadrian's villa, view of Scenic Canal and Triclinium from north end. Photo: R. Taylor.

ter effect was to animate solid, unmoving masses through the mediation of sculpture or miniaturized architecture. The variation of the water's movement was minuscule and its textures exceedingly fine. Its applications in architectural programs could be whimsical or stately, even hieratic.

As an artistic medium, water is unusual in a number of ways. It is penetrable by both eye and body. It can produce sound and subtly alter the immediate climatic conditions. And because it is the least coherent of tectonic substances, it is absent during the design and construction of the elements meant to enchamber and display it. Until the final adjustments are made in the hydraulic system, it is shaped and manipulated by proxy. Where water is to be collected, it is initially defined and envisioned by means of the collecting vessel. Where water is to move, its movement must be imagined against stationary surfaces and backgrounds. Under such circumstances design is not an easy task. If a pool is meant to reflect a focal structure, then it must be of the right shape and dimensions to do so from the desired human perspectives. The far rounded end of the Scenic Canal (Serapeum/Canopus) at Hadrian's villa, with its alternating straight and arched entablatures, may have been a mere touch of whimsy, but it also enframed and reinforced the curvature of the domed Scenic Triclinium reflected in it (Fig. 148). Just below the diners, in the couch's embrace, was a lunette-shaped pool to re-bound the mosaic-encrusted canopy and colonnade above and be-fore them (Fig. 149). Because refinements of this kind work so well, they are not at all obvious. Yet a skilled landscape architect who un-derstood the optics and psychology of reflected light could envision the pool and its enframed picture on site, staking out the measure-ments in the process and calculating its hydraulic needs. Because the volume of water moving through pools was rarely a critical issue, the architect could work with almost any volume available.[75]

More common than reflecting pools were the cascades or jets of engaged or freestanding fountains. These were integral to the archi-tecture, for their effects depended heavily on correct volumes drawn from the water supply soon to be coursing through the infrastruc-ture. A dribbling jug under a Cupid's arm, a crocodile spewing an arc of water into a pool, a purling water stair – each desired effect was a collaborative effort between artist and technician. Sculpture often did without metal pipes, relying only on a channel drilled through it. But where the statue joined a base or back wall, a wait-ing pipe emerged from the masonry, the product of a much earlier process in which the entire hydraulic network of the building had been mapped out. These little details merely remind us that water-works, though often manipulated at a late phase, were hardly an afterthought.

BUILDINGS AND PEOPLE

It could be said that a great Roman building was not genuine-ly initiated into its cultural life until its halls and byways first echoed with the sound of water. When water broke loose into the expectant pools and receptacles, beginning its errant course through the building's bowels, construction was definitively in its conclusive phase. With this inaugural gush the final and most important pro-cess could begin in earnest: the building's socialization, a process for which water, the humor of life, itself is an apt metaphor. Even in the open air Roman architecture is often an interiorization of space, an enveloping of human movement in colonnaded courts, plazas, vault-ed halls, streets, and corridors. Where many great premodern archi-tectures (e.g., Mayan, Egyptian, Khmer) are most successful when monumentalizing solid geometric forms, Roman architects were of-ten at their best when sculpting negative space. Their finest architec-

149. Tivoli: Hadrian's villa, view from Scenic Triclinium. Photo: R. Taylor.

ture is participatory and highly kinetic. People flow easily along its narrow ways, then relax and mingle in its broadenings – but ever within a larger scheme of containment – not unlike the Romans' beloved waterworks, which alternated swiftly flowing channels with placid settling tanks. Buildings of spectacle are veritable reservoirs of humans: They well up inside it from below and then subside again. One wonders whether such considerations inspired the radial cascades that animated the *cavea* of Hadrian's fantastic Stadium Garden, or the marble model of a stadium found nearby that may have served as a fountain basin.[76] Is it such a coincidence that the stairway, which in earlier times had been a form designed exclusively for human locomotion, became under the Romans a favorite *topos* of water play?

We tend to think of the users of a building as purely subjective participants in it – its "clients," as it were. But people are an important component of architecture too – not, perhaps, as a constant but as a received phenomenon. We are a part of its dimensional fabric and ornament; we realize a building's semiotic, kinesthetic, and acoustic properties, which in turn guide our distribution, speech, movements, and reactions. Human figures – along with architectural elements standardized to human proportions, such as stairs and railings – are primary indices of scale. Doorways, columns, statues, stories can be made in many sizes and may deceive. The grand stairway as an intentional scaling of Roman buildings is principally an exterior feature, and like temples themselves is one of the few exteriorizing forms in the Roman architectural canon (Fig. 150). Except occasionally in temple cellas, stairways never serve as a major visual component of Roman indoor architecture; they are habitually tucked away in stairwells. Often the only means of comprehending the scope of an interior space is by reference to our own bodies and those of other people – whether by size, rate of movement, or projection of voice. The drama of a seemingly endless vista down the long axis of an imperial bath block would have been enhanced by human silhouettes diminishing almost to nothingness in its distances. Movement and gesture inform the unfolding drama of place: Other people's reactions inevitably guide our own. A casual visitor may follow the crowd, seeking its assistance in the experience of a building. Our gazes may follow theirs, or fix upon bodies as referents for the space around them. We are all both viewers and viewed in the built environment; we frame and fashion architectural vistas and pose within them.

Everywhere Roman designers, builders, and decorators served as agents for the channeling and retention of humanity; but could they control or even anticipate the dynamic of reception? The social reciprocity (Bettina Bergmann's term) between buildings and pedestrians is a complex phenomenon to which each individual brings a unique personal conditioning, whether within the culture of origin or not. Design, construction, and decoration are thus in one sense a latent creation – the ovum, if you will, englobing the swimming seed of a million different approaches, impressions, reactions. The Roman building is a body that we inseminate and forever transform by our presence. The offspring of these unions are potentially in-

150. Lepcis Magna:
reconstructed view of
Temple of Jupiter.
Ward-Perkins 1981.
By permission of Yale
University Press.

finite but far from random, ineluctable but never predictable. If
Roman builders and their patrons sired a great architecture now in
ruins, we, who wander through the ruins with open ears and eyes,
are parents to its refashioning.

NOTES

INTRODUCTION

1 Donderer 1996: A8. My translation.
2 Cited in Rivoira 1925: 89 n. 2.
3 Pliny *HN* 16.201–2, 36.69–70. All English translations from the Latin and Greek in this book are from the Loeb Classical Library except where specified. References to weight/mass are metric; a tonne, or metric ton, is equivalent to 1.1 U.S. tons.
4 Lancaster 1999; DeLaine 1997: 99–100.
5 Ragette 1980: 33; Jidejian 1975: 22.
6 Wattenbach 1896; Burford 1972: 76–7.
7 On another document possibly dealing with the columns of Diocletian's baths, a letter calling for more column transport ships at Aswan, see Ward-Perkins 1992b: 73.
8 The translation of Vitruvius used throughout is Rowland and Howe, eds., 1999.
9 Wilson-Jones 2000: 38. Pages 33–46 offer an excellent overview of Vitruvian scholarship and theory. See also Callebat 1994; 1989; Gros 1994. See Hodge 1992: 13–16 for an indictment of Vitruvius' hydraulics.
10 Wilson-Jones 2000: 59–63.
11 Vitr. 5.1.6–10.
12 Gros 1989.
13 Theater of Marcellus: Suet. *Aug.* 43.5. Fidenae: Suet. *Tib.* 40; Tac. *Ann.* 4.62–3. See also Suet. *Calig.* 31 and Oros. 7, 4, 11.
14 Coulton 1977: 15–29; Ward-Perkins 1992b: 61–3. Lack of a contractual budget was of course not universal.
15 Vitr. 1.2.8–9; 2.8.7.
16 Anderson 1997: 83–5, 98–9.

17 *Dig.* 45.1.124.

18 *MA*; *MA2*; Pensabene 1994; Fant 1993; Ward-Perkins 1992a–c; Baccini Leotardi 1989.

19 MacDonald 1982: 1.153–4. See Lechtman and Hobbs 1986.

20 The presumption of the patron's involvement in his commissions may underlie the hierarchy of gestures in a well-known relief from Terracina (illustrated in Wilson-Jones 2000: 28; Adam 1994: 45). The patron, large and seated, grasps a scroll (the plans?) in his left hand; with his right he points vigorously at a building project under way. The intermediary role of his architects or master builders (medium-sized, in tunics) is evident in their less emphatic replication of the patron's gesture.

21 Donderer 1996. On Roman architects and their careers see Wilson-Jones 2000: 19–30; Anderson 1997: 3–67; and bibliographies.

22 Donderer 1996: A38, A43–51, A53, A56, A59, A61, A66–9, A74–9, A81–4, A93, A95, A103–4, A117–18, A123, A127, A131, A134–5, A138, A145, A152, A154, A157–9, C3–5, C11, C13–14. The inscription on the amphitheater of Nîmes, "T. Crispius Reburrus fecit" (*CIL* 12.3315), probably refers to the patron (*pace* Donderer 1996: 218–19) for the simple reason that architects almost never appear alone on signature inscriptions; or when they do, as on the theater of Pompeii, the signature is in close conjunction with inscription plaques naming the patron(s) (Donderer 1996: A95, 197). The "godlike Aristainetos" reported to have been inscribed prominently on the great Hadrianic temple in Cyzicus (*IG Rom.* 4.140) was not necessarily the architect; he may have been the local patron. According to SHA *Hadr.* 19.9, Hadrian did not as a rule construct buildings in his own name, and he rededicated buildings in the names of their original sponsors. Following J. Colin, Donderer (287–8) considers the inscription spurious. See also Burford 1972: 21, 86, 132, 212–16, and bibliography.

23 Donderer 1996: 37–9.

24 *CIL* 2.760.

25 *CIL* 2.761; Donderer 1996: A121. My translation.

26 E.g., see Ward-Perkins 1992b: 103.

27 Jouffroy 1986.

28 The patron also bore responsibility for a building's failure. Hence an Atilius who sponsored the amphitheater at Fidenae was exiled after its collapse; see Tac. *Ann.* 4.63. The grounds for his exile seems to have been his failure to meet the expense of an adequate structure; but the legal liability probably stems from the *probatio*, the magistrate's official approval of a mostly completed project.

29 On sculpture see Ridgway 1984; Neudecker 1998; on furniture, see Moss 1988; on painting, see Ling 1999, 1991; and bibliographies.

30 MacDonald 1982: 2.271 notes that triumphal and honorary arches are an exception. But even the putatively rigid and regimented architecture of military camps and fortifications was not uniform; see Evans 1994. Houses sometimes are built uniformly, but exclusively within a single building program in a very localized spot. For Cosa, see Brown 1980. Recent excavations there suggest that even these houses were not so uniform as once thought. Temples occasionally were built in serial. The Area Sacra di S. Omobono in Rome is an early and famous example of twins. Series of virtually identical temples on a continuous podium are known at Ostia and Brescia. An especially clear example of triplets is at Belo in Spain; see Gros

1996: 154. Sbeïtla in Tunisia has twins on either side of a slightly larger central temple; see Gros 1996: 227.

31 Coulton 1977: 53–5 and passim; Troyes: Murray 1987; Florence: Wallace 1994; Goldthwaite 1980; Rome: Scavizzi 1983.

32 Burford 1972: 62–3 and bibliography; Burford 1969.

33 CIL 1.698; trans. Humphrey, Oleson, and Sherwood 1998: 269–70.

34 Vitr. 1.1.10.

35 Anderson 1997: 91–2, 112–13; Martin 1989: 60–2. Meanwhile, production industries such as brickworks, mines, and quarries came increasingly under central imperial control. On the *opera publica* see Daguet-Gagey 1997; Kolb 1993; Strong 1968. There is some doubt that any imperial bureau oversaw new construction; see Lancaster 1996: 241–2; Pearse 1974: 38. The *curatores* plainly had the duty to approve building sites (Kolb 1993). In the Severan period, at least, they could also dedicate a building; see *CIL* 6.1352 (Daguet-Gagey 1997: 415–16; Kolb 1993: no. 1.57). In some cases it is clear that the projects approved were financed by independent sponsors; see *CIL* 6.1585, *AE* 1971: 28 (Kolb 1993: nos. 1.51, 54). But the staff of *tabularii* and *dispensatores* shows that the department was responsible for a great deal of financial activity (Kolb 1993: nos. 111.1–7). In the Severan period an *exsactor operum dominorum nostrorum duorum et publicorum* (as Kolb reconstructs the title) is involved in procuring materials for the construction of a dwelling for a special procurator of the Column of Marcus Aurelius; see *CIL* 6.1585, 8480; Daguet-Gagey 1997: 104–5, 206–7, 487–91; Kolb 1993: 311–14.

36 Pliny *Ep.* 10.17.

37 On the social status of architects and divisions of labor in Roman architectural projects see Anderson 1997: 3–118 and bibliography; Gros 1978; Pearse 1974; and various articles in *AES*, especially Gros 1983.

38 Vitr. 1.2.8.

39 Martin 1989: 62–72.

40 Daguet-Gagey 1997: 195–230; Kolb 1993: 131–6.

41 DeLaine 1997; Shirley 2001, which is modeled after the fortress at Inchtuthil, Scotland. Burford 1969 is a worthy predecessor of these studies. Naturally the organization of a legionary fortress project at the edges of the empire would have a significantly different look from that of a great trophy building in the capital city, beginning with its ready-made source of semiskilled labor: the legion itself.

42 Donderer 1996: A32, A35, A47, A61, A74–8.

43 Lancaster 1996: 32, 231–2 offers an instructive example of the way in which planning may have influenced the sequence of construction in the Golden House.

44 Mark 1990: 3.

45 Cato 14. See Anderson 1997: 73–4. See also *lex Tarentina* 1.28 (Crawford 1996: 1.301–12). In large imperial Roman projects, it is unlikely that estimates of cost were done simply on the basis of floor space, as proposed by Thornton and Thornton 1989: 21.

46 Deadlines certainly could be set in a *stipulatio*; see *Dig.* 45.1.124; Martin 1989: 27.

47 Col. 5.1.3. See *Dig.* 11.6.1; Martin 1989: 49. On Byzantine formulas see Ousterhout 2000: 72–4.

48 Martin 1989: 74–88.

49 *CIL* 1.698; trans. Humphrey et al. 1998: 269.

50 Anderson 1997: 74–5 and bibliography.

51 The *dies operis*, November 1, is a deadline, not a beginning date as presumed by the translators. See Frontin. *Aq.* 123; *Dig.* 50.16.5.1; Cic. 2 *Verr.* 1.148; Martin 1989: 36–7, 74–8.

52 *Mor.* 498 E.

53 Gell. 10.10.2 relates an instance when bidders for a bath offered an overall cost, but a dishonestly low one.

54 Ousterhout 2000: 74.

55 Col. 5.1–2. See Dilke 1971: 52–6.

56 Duncan-Jones 1974: 75–80, 89–99. Riders: Martin 1989: 32–3.

57 Duncan-Jones 1974: 126, 164 no. 513.

58 See ibid.: 124–5.

59 DeLaine 1997: 101.

60 Davies, Hemsoll, and Wilson-Jones 1987.

1. PLANNING AND DESIGN

1 Lucian *Hipp.* 8; trans. Humphrey, Oleson, and Sherwood 1998: 326.

2 MacDonald 1982: vol. 1 passim.

3 Wallace-Hadrill 1994.

4 For examples in private architecture see ibid.: 38–63, 143–74; Anderson 1997: 298–304; MacDonald and Pinto 1995 (e.g., Service Quarters, Water Court, Southern Hall).

5 Vitr. 1.2. See Frézouls 1985 and illustrations and notes in Rowland and Howe 1999.

6 Wilson-Jones 2000: 38–45 and bibliography.

7 The global use of modules in both plan and elevation may be a Roman invention; Coulton 1989 argues that Greek temples are fully modular only in plan.

8 Geertman 1994.

9 But the term has a range of meanings; see Wilson-Jones 2000: 40–3.

10 *R.* 3.399e–401a.

11 Wilson-Jones 1997.

12 Wilson-Jones 2000: 58–63 lays out four Vitruvian stages of design, each of which relies on one or more of the principles of *symmetria, eurythmia,* and *decor.* The model is ingenious, but it does not unravel the semantic tangle of Vitruvius' vocabulary.

13 Vitr. 1.2.5–7.

14 *Plt.* 259e–260a.

15 Anderson 1997: 68–118.

16 Coulton 1977: 26–9.

17 MacDonald 1982: 2.271–2.

18 Wilson-Jones 2000: 11–14.

19 Nohlen 1985.

20 Dio 69.4.

21 Wilson-Jones 2000: 49–56; Lancaster 2000: 760–2; Haselberger 1997; *CDA*; Heisel 1993; Sear 1989: 69–70; Hesberg 1984; Conticello De' Spagnolis 1984; Coulton 1977: 51–3; Kalayan 1971. On a fragment of an unfinished plan found recently in Rome, see Rizzo 1999.

22 *Dig.* 19.2.24.pr; Martin 1989: 30–1.

23 Conticello De' Spagnolis 1984.

24 Wilson-Jones 1993: 431–2.

25 Adam 1997; Heisel 1993: 131–5.

26 Coulton 1983; 1977: 51–73; Jeppesen 1958. The term *paradeigma* is also used of a master mosaic pattern in a Hellenistic contract of the third century B.C.; see Bruneau 1980.

27 Wilson-Jones 2000: 56–8 and bibliography; Haselberger 1997 and bibliography; Heisel 1993: 210–13; Krause 1985a; Kalayan 1971; 1969.

28 Lancaster 1996: 228–9.

29 Wilkinson 1991.

30 Greek: Coulton 1977; Byzantine: Ousterhout 2000; Gothic: Bucher 1968; Branner 1963.

31 Kuttner 1998; Tybout 1989.

32 Anderson 1997: 11 and n. 21; Pearse 1974: 100–1. See especially Gell. 10.10.2; Plut. *Mor.* 498 E.

33 Gros 1985. See also Krause 1985b.

34 *Mor.* 498 E.

35 Wallace 1994: 88–9. For Alberti, the principal purpose of models was "to estimate the likely trouble and expense" of the undertaking. On the motivation for elaborate models in the Italian Renaissance see Goldthwaite 1980: 372–80.

36 *Leg.* 643b–c.

37 Votive models of buildings, on the other hand, tend to be made of fired clay. For a good sampling and bibliography, see *CDA.*

38 Wilson-Jones 2000: 50–6; 1997; Haselberger 1997: 79–82; Pensabene 1997; Will 1985; Kalayan 1971. See also *CDA* 232–5.

39 Kalayan 1971: 272–3 and figs. 12–13.

40 Collart and Coupel 1977; 1951.

41 Gell. 10.10.2.

42 The bibliography on Greek and Roman planning and metrology is extensive. For specifically Roman planning see, among others, Sperling 1999; Wilson-Jones 2000: 87–106, 120–30; 1993; Jacobson 1986; Geertman 1980; and various articles in DeLaine and Johnston 1999: vol. 2; *MNI; BBA;* and *DASA.*

43 Wilson-Jones 2000: 120–2.

44 Wilson-Jones 2000: 60–1; 1993. For a quick reference on Greek and Roman measures, see Rowland and Howe 1999: 148.

45 Vitr. 6.3.

46 DeLaine 1997: fig. 39.

47 De Jong 1989; Hellström 1985.

48 Certainly the theories of proportion in three dimensions developed by Polykleitos and subsequent sculptors could have influenced architecture; see Burford 1972: 131–3; 1969: 145. Coulton 1989, however, is skeptical of elaborate altimetric schemes.

49 For example, see Sperling 1999: 80–104; Jacobson 1986.

50 Compass and ruler, along with other tools of the trade, are frequently depicted on the grave reliefs of architects and master builders; see Zimmer 1984.

51 Vitr. 9.pr.6–8.

52 Congès 1996: 370–2.
53 DeLaine 1997: 45–53.
54 Coulton 1985; see also Coulton 1977: 65–7. The thesis, though sensible, is still controversial.
55 Wilson-Jones 1993.
56 Ibid.; Wilson-Jones 2000: 58–63.
57 Wilson-Jones 1993; Golvin 1988.
58 Wilson-Jones 1993.
59 On structural design see Mainstone 1998; Mark 1990; MacDonald 1982: 1.161–83.
60 DeLaine 1997: 56.
61 Vitr. 3.3.11.
62 Ibid. 3.5.13.
63 MacDonald 1982: 1.177–8.
64 Smith 1991.
65 Taylor 1996.
66 Heyman 1995: 27–41; Lechtman and Hobbs 1986: 119–20.
67 Personal discussion with Ahmet Çakmak.
68 *BG* 4.17–18; trans. Humphrey et al. 1998: 421.
69 O'Connor 1993: 140.
70 For reconstructions of pile drivers see Galliazzo 1994: 1.300–1.
71 Mark 1990: 32.
72 Mainstone 1998: 31–46.
73 O'Connor 1993: 176–7; Fitchen 1986: 72; 1961: 81.
74 On the Roman use of iron tie rods see Hoffmann 1991.
75 The idea may have been borrowed from the half-circular annular barrel vaults at the Temple of Fortuna at Palestrina, which were built around 110 B.C. But these prototypes, not being full circles, do not make use of the compression-ring principle.
76 Mainstone 1998: 118; Lancaster 1996: 157. Rakob 1988 argues that the dome deformed dramatically during construction.
77 Heyman 1995: 41–2.

2. LAYING THE GROUNDWORK

1 Bergmann 1991.
2 Davies 2000, esp. 136–71.
3 Kleiner 1992: 230–2 and bibliography.
4 *Att.* 12.19–52, passim.
5 Vitr. 6.4.
6 Vitr. 4.5.
7 Greek temples, however, seem to have been subject to mystical alignments. For two interesting hypotheses see Doxiades 1972 and Scully 1979.
8 Pliny *Ep.* 2.17.5, 21, 27; Stat. *Silv.* 1.3, 2.2. Cf. Philostr. *Im.* 295.
9 I thank Pieter Broucke for his ideas on this topic.
10 Betancourt Serna 2000.
11 Taylor 2000: 93–127.
12 Livy 1.55.
13 Tac. *Ann.* 15.43.
14 Vitr. 6.2.1; Wilson-Jones 2000: 58–63.

15 Vitr. 1.4–7, 8.1–4.
16 Galliazzo 1994: 1.289–90, 298–9; O'Connor 1993: 193–201.
17 On Roman land surveying techniques see Congès 1996.
18 *Hipp.* 4; trans. Humphrey, Oleson, and Sherwood 1998: 325.
19 On terracing in the Republican period, see Gullini 1983.
20 Ibid.
21 MacDonald and Pinto 1995: 28.
22 Shirley 2001: 41, 66; DeLaine 1997: 175–6. Shirley includes in her calculations the felling of trees and grubbing out of roots. DeLaine's estimate
   of 174,000 man-days for terracing the Baths of Caracalla seems to exclude
   the labor of actual removal from the site, which would have been fully as
   intensive as work on the site itself.
23 For a good discussion of the tools for setting out see Evans 1994: 149–51.
24 Ibid.: 152–3.
25 Dilke 1971: 58–9.
26 However, simpler structures laid out on principles of quadrature, such as
   military installations, dispensed with such refinements; see Evans 1994:
   152–3.
27 Lynne Lancaster, personal correspondence.
28 *CIL* 8.2728.
29 Hodge 1992: 184–91.
30 As one of many examples, Cozzo 1928 noted that the travertine ashlar
   foundations under the piers of the Colosseum, although laid out with the
   same stonecutting precision as the piers themselves, are not always in perfect alignment with them.
31 See DeLaine 1997: 138–9. Vitruvius seems to suggest the construction of
   foundations, drains, and substructures on a completely excavated and
   cleared portico site (5.9.7). But his prescription to fill the site with charcoal
   and sand layers for good drainage would place the whole scheme more in
   the realm of theory than of practice.
32 Many areas of the substructures have putlog holes, while the outer maintenance corridor wall on the south side does not. Most of the substructures,
   then, were built with scaffolding, though DeLaine seems to imply that it
   was never more than one or two stages high before being dismantled and
   raised on a layer of fill.
33 DeLaine 1997: 133–5.
34 Ibid.: 64–5. See also 133–5.
35 Obviously, if the margin of error is projected to exceed 3 : 10,000, and the
   terminus cannot be lowered further, the enterprise must be abandoned. For
   an excellent discussion of the logistics of aqueduct surveying see Hodge
   1992: 171–214.
36 Judson and Kahane 1963: 86.
37 As at Bologna: Hodge 1992: fig. 148. On ancient tunnel planning and technique see Grewe 1998: 18–32, 58–69, 156–73.
38 The loosest earth, wrote the fourth-century architectural writer Palladius,
   required the deepest foundations; but his prescription, a mere quarter the
   height of the walls, has been challenged. Vitruvius is ambiguous, recom-
   mending only that foundations be sunk down "as much as seems reason-
   able for the size of the work" (3.4.1). See DeLaine 1997: 65–6 and n. 27;
   Schwartz 1968.

39 Rowland and Howe 1999: 193; Mainstone 1998: 187.

40 *HN* 36.95; see Humphrey et al. 263. Pliny's presumption is false; marshy ground tends to magnify earthquake loads.

41 For example, see Adam 1994: 125 for practices in Gaul, which do not reflect the monumental approach in central Italy and the East. Giuliani 1990: 121 suggests the Romans followed a tradition used until quite recently: At the corners of the anticipated structure, shafts were dug down to a point where a rock of at least 10 kg dropped from above bounced off the bottom with a dry sound. Foundation trenches should then follow the stratum from corner to corner.

42 I thank A. Trevor Hodge for this information.

43 *Ep.* 10.39; trans. Humphrey et al. 257.

44 Mocchegiani Carpano 1977. Cozzo 1971: 20–3 presumed travertine substructures extending uniformly to the depth of the underground axial entrances, but it now appears that the travertine beds for the piers are less than a meter deep; everything below it is concrete. For a good illustration see Lamprecht 1993: Bild 176.

45 Mainstone 1998: 188–9. The courtyard of this unique structure actually spans the Selinus River on vaults over twelve meters wide; see O'Connor 1993: 125.

46 Giuliani 1990: 121–35.

47 DeLaine 1997: 135–6; MacDonald 1982: 1.154–6; Lugli 1957: 385–7.

48 Lancaster 1996: 148–58; Lamprecht 1993: 11–87; Lechtman and Hobbs 1986.

49 Adam 1994: 73–6.

50 Lechtman and Hobbs 1986: 89–93; Waddell 1984: 234–7.

51 In Italy and many other regions, they were often of brick or stone and mortar and roofed with pairs of pitched tiles.

52 Because of the drainage connection, substructures could begin at a very low level: At the Baths of Caracalla the brick-faced concrete begins a full eight meters below grade, the secondary drains at five and a half meters. See DeLaine 1997: fig. 3.

53 As at the Baths of Caracalla; see Lombardi and Corazza 1995.

54 See DeLaine 1997: 137–8.

55 Lombardi and Corazza 1995; Manderscheid 1991.

56 Lombardi and Corazza 1995: 76–8.

57 Maiuri 1955: 35–42. The Colosseum has recently been shown to have a similar multilevel drainage system; see Mocchegiani Carpano and Luciani 1981: 11–13.

58 MacDonald and Pinto 1995: 80.

59 Yegül 1992: 192–6.

60 Lombardi and Corazza 1995: 50–6.

61 Ibid.: 112–20.

62 Vitr. 7.1.

63 Giuliani 1990: 139–40 notes a few later examples of the technique, but acknowledges that most Roman buildings do not conform exactly to Vitruvius' prescriptions.

64 Vitr. 5.10.2.

65 Yegül 1992: 357.

66 Lynne Lancaster, personal correspondence.

3. WALLS, PIERS, AND COLUMNS

1　MacDonald 1982: 1.157.
2　Wheeler 1962: 8.
3　DeLaine 1997; Lombardi and Corazza 1995.
4　DeLaine 1997: 15–16, 183.
5　For example, see ibid.: 154–5, 172–3; Lombardi and Corazza 1995: fig. 85.
6　Packer 1971. Light party walls may be added in upper stories, but the structural walls are retained; see Giuliani 1990: 106–8. This author's clear-cut distinction between the armature and connective walls of outer structures, however, is not germane to most Roman concrete construction. Lancaster 2000: 762–5 has drawn attention to noncongruent floor patterns in the Markets of Trajan in Rome, where various measures were taken to "relieve" the weight of structural walls that were laid over vaults.
7　DeLaine 1997: sheet 1.
8　It can be argued that in the case of hot rooms, putlog holes too had to be carefully positioned to allow for the continuity of vertical columns of box tiles.
9　Lombardi and Corazza 1995: 76–8.
10　Ibid.: 78; DeLaine 1997: 153 and fig. 69.
11　Lugli 1957: 574–5; Blake 1947: 294–5.
12　Vitr. 1.5.8; 2.3–8; 5.10.3.
13　Wright 2000: 115–17, 120.
14　This is probably why *opus reticulatum* was laid diagonally. Even so, Vitruvius complains that it tends to crack along its seams (2.8.1).
15　Lugli 1957: 583–5. For a succinct summary of the methods, see Adam 1994: 147–8; Sear 1989: 77.
16　Lugli 1957: 612.
17　Wood grain can sometimes be detected in the mortar of putlogs, strongly suggesting this sequence of construction. I thank Lynne Lancaster for this information. The sequence may also explain why putlog holes tend to be spaced quite irregularly: They are responding to the irregularities of the scaffolding.
18　Lancaster 1998a: 290–3, 306–7.
19　MacDonald 1982: 1.150.
20　DeLaine 1997: 170–1. The Aurelianic wall of Rome has visible seams in its curtain walls every fifteen to twenty horizontal feet. The wall was built without putlogs, probably because the facing pairs of scaffolding were secured to each other with cross-braces at a level just above the work; see Richmond 1930: 60.
21　Lancaster 1998a: 290–3.
22　DeLaine 1997: 143–5. See also Blake 1959: 104–41; Lugli 1957: 570–2.
23　Lancaster 1998a: 284–5.
24　Lugli 1957: 571–2, 600–1 greatly exaggerates the Trajanic anomaly, as Lancaster has observed to me. Lancaster 1998a notes that the bonding courses in the Markets of Trajan are indeed Trajanic, not Domitianic as Lugli suggests.
25　DeLaine 1997: 143–5.
26　*Ep.* 10.39; trans. Humphrey, Oleson, and Sherwood 1998: 257.

27 MacDonald 1982: 1.162–3. This may actually help to preserve a building, just as it helps to arrest vertical cracks; see Lechtmann and Hobbs 1986: 108.

28 Waddell 1984: 4; Sear 1989: 73–4.

29 Fitchen 1986: 82–3.

30 DeLaine 1997: 152.

31 Ibid.: 144.

32 Lancaster 1998a: 290–1.

33 DeLaine 1997: 152–3.

34 I am grateful to Betsey Robinson and Lynne Lancaster for this information.

35 Besides the rather muted examples in the Golden House, a few are featured in the last phase of bath architecture at Pompeii, dating between 62 and 79 A.D.; e.g., see Broise 1991: fig. 17. They also appear in later baths at Ostia. On bowed arches in or under domes or semidomes see Pelliccioni 1986: 35–8.

36 DeLaine 1997: 151–3.

37 Mainstone 1998: 104–5; Giuliani 1990: 78–85.

38 On the techniques of stone masonry see Adam 1994: 102–18, 158–65; Rockwell 1993; Hueber 1989; Coulton 1977; 1974; Lugli 1957: 167–359; Blake 1947; 1959; 1973.

39 DeLaine 1997: 169 and fig. 85.

40 Ibid.: 240. In the frigidarium this proportional relationship exists among three orders: the plunge-pool screens, the screens at the east and west ends of the room, and the colossal orders.

41 Landels 1978: 84–98; Coulton 1974.

42 On the marble, granite, and porphyry trades see *MA; MA2; MIA;* Fant 2001; 1993; Pensabene 1994; Dodge 1991; Baccini Leotardi 1989; Klein 1988; Gnoli 1971; Ward-Perkins 1951.

43 Barbet and Miniero 1999: fig. 389; Adam 1994: 36–40.

44 Haselberger 1997.

45 Adam 1994: 20–43 and bibliography; Rockwell 1993.

46 Hero *Mech.* 3.7; see Landels 1978: 89–90; Drachmann 1963: 104–5.

47 See Orlandos 1966–8: 2.figs. 93, 97.2; Martin 1965: 209 and fig. 86. For Roman painted depictions see Ling 1991: figs. 21, 27; pl. IIIB. J. J. Coulton contends that almost all Greek bosses are of the wrong shape and position for rope hoisting, but are intended rather for levering the stone block into position after it has been set down. The same can be said for existing Roman bosses on squared blocks; see Coulton 1974: 4–7; Martin 1965: pls. XVII and XVIII. (Adam 1994: 47–51 is mistaken in suggesting a lifting purpose for bosses. Many are far off center and often below the centers of gravity of the blocks.) But column drums cannot be levered horizontally: They must be lowered directly onto the dowels projecting from the underlying drum or base. Drum bosses, then, were true lifting bosses, and would have provided secure resistance against ropes wound circumferentially below or looped around them.

48 Ward-Perkins 1992c: 25–6.

49 Wilson-Jones 2000: 155; Ward-Perkins 1992a; Davies, Hemsoll, and Wilson-Jones 1987: 140–6.

50 Ward-Perkins 1992b is noncommittal about the degree of finish on capitals

in transit, but he is quite firm in his belief that many Proconnesian marbles were worked by craftsmen from Asia Minor who had traveled with the stone to the destination site.

51 Ward-Perkins 1992c: 25 n. 18.

52 Ward-Perkins 1993: 39, 52, 98–9; 1992b–c; Walker 1979: 264.

53 DeLaine 1997: 120.

54 Lancaster 1999 suggests that the upper limit of a single lewis is six to eight tonnes; however, the much heavier capitals of the Temple of Mars Ultor in Rome have single central lewis holes.

55 Coulton 1974: 13 and n. 73 suggests that a treadmill crane with a compound pulley could lift twenty to thirty tonnes, but his calculations exclude friction and characteristics of the rope. For applicable formulas see Cotterell and Kamminga 1990: 89–96. Fleury 1993: 107–8 estimates a capacity of eleven tonnes with a triple-sheaf pulley, and twenty with five sheaves. However, O'Connor 1993: 49 estimates 6.2 tonnes.

56 Wiegand 1921–5: 2.Abb. 92. If a compound crane was used, it may have been a refinement on the crane described by Vitr. 10.2.6–7, which has two sets of pulleys hanging from its mast. Weight estimate: Coulton 1974: 16, 19.

57 Wiegand 1921–5: 1.66–7. Hero *Mech.* 2.3 describes a compound system with horizontal rows of pulleys attached to the load and a cross beam with a rope snaked between them; see Drachmann 1963: 53–5; Fleury 1993: 116–19. A crane could use a similar arrangement with a standard vertical compound pulley at the mast.

58 DeLaine 1997: 120. For a brief discussion of the greatest lifting feats see Wilson-Jones 2000: 170–3. See Lancaster 1999 for an unusual solution to the problem of lifting the fifty- to fifty-five-tonne sections of the Column of Trajan in Rome.

59 Wiegand 1921–5: 1.65–6.

60 DeLaine 1997: 171. No similar breaks have been seen in the natatio, but DeLaine herself acknowledges that the majority of breaks are no longer visible. My personal inspection of the natatio (heavily restored, unfortunately) suggests that on the northeast side with the theatrical facade the wall may have been built as separate panels divided by vertical gaps for the columns. Operating through the plane of the wall rather than alongside it, the pulling teams were able to tilt the column shafts into place transversely; then the gaps could be filled in behind the columns.

61 The visible presence of putlog holes in the portions of the spur walls crowded by the corner columns need not give us pause. Before the decoration phase, several inches of clearance between the column shafts and walls ensured that the brickmasons working on the inboard sides of the spur walls could secure their scaffolding to them, even if they could not stand comfortably in the narrow intervals.

62 Fitchen 1986: 53–5, as suggested by Viollet-le-Duc; DeLaine 1997: 156. DeLaine's estimate of mass is on p. 120.

63 It is probably for this reason that the engineers of Sixtus V wreaked such devastation on the entablature of the Basilica of Maxentius when dislodging one of its remaining columns to be reerected in the piazza of S. Maria Maggiore.

64 Wilson-Jones 2000: 199–212; Davies et al. 1987.

4. COMPLEX ARMATURES

1 Brown 1961: 28.
2 Ward-Perkins 1981: 67–8.
3 For an overelaborate sequence of construction see Von Gerkan 1925.
4 According to the chronographer Domitian finished the building "as far as the shields" (*usque ad clypea*) – presumably the decorative disks that coin representations (actually beginning under Titus) indicate were hung high up on the outer facade of the building, where cramp holes can still be seen. This could either be taken literally to mean that Domitian completed the construction of the building to its final height, or it may simply mean that he completed the decoration of an essentially finished building, "even to the extent of adding the shields." For a fuller discussion of the evidence see Lancaster 1996: 41–2 and bibliography.
5 But perhaps floor levels, not seating sections, are meant; see Von Gerkan 1925: 40–1.
6 *CIL* 6.2059; Rea 1988: 11–13.
7 Dio 1.16.25.
8 Sear 1989: 141.
9 Cozzo 1971: 33.
10 Luciani 1993: 103.
11 On skilled and unskilled labor see DeLaine 1997: 103–205. Burford 1972 discusses evidence of the multiple tasking of Greek labor; see esp. 99–102.
12 Rockwell 1993: 89–100; but see Chapter 6 below.
13 Wilson-Jones 1993.
14 Ibid.: 398.
15 Rea 1988: 16; 1996: 75–6. On the misinterpretation of the outboard wall of this ambulatory as the podium of the arena, see Beste 2000: 80–1.
16 Rea 1988: 16–18 and fig. 8.
17 Mocchegiani Carpano 1977.
18 Picozzi 1974; Ghini 1988.
19 Gabucci 1999: 234–40; Luciani 1993: 100–1 and caption.
20 Cozzo 1971: 34–5; 1928: 216–20. But see Von Gerkan 1925: 19–23.
21 Lancaster 1996: 58–61. Level 2 is altogether different, since the piers are straight and the fill is made of brick-faced concrete, which certainly was added after the piers had been built.
22 The high friction would have precluded levering.
23 The travertine blocks averaged about 1.5–1.7 m^3 at 2,360 kg/m^3. See Cozzo 1971: 26, 29–30. Lewis holes: Adam 1994: 49.
24 Blake 1959: 93 sees no particular ingenuity at work here. For her, these are traditional Flavian relieving arches.
25 On this technique see Hodge 1992: 130–42 and figs. 97–8.
26 Templates in medieval construction: Shelby 1971. Rockwell 1993: 98–103 dismisses the ancient use of templates too quickly.
27 O'Connor 1993: 49.
28 Landels 1978: 87–8.
29 More precisely, the Colosseum plan is a many-sided polygon. Some of the arches are completely straight in plan, but others turn slightly at the keystone. Roughly one out of every three surviving keystones has a slightly trapezoidal shape on its underside in order to effect the turn.
30 Gabucci 1999: 238–40.

31 Lancaster 1996: 55–6.
32 Blake 1959: 94. For a detailed discussion of the ribs and their reconstructions see Lancaster 1998b; 1996: 46–9. Many of the ribs visible today are from a Severan reconstruction.
33 Luciani 1993: 106.
34 Ibid.: 105–6. His only evidence for this is some ill-fitting stonework at the boundaries of these supposed zones. The notion that single teams of workers were responsible for large but entirely segregated areas is widespread. On the basis of stylistic differences and a clear north–south divide between the use of two mason's marks, Kalayan 1969 and Jidejian 1975: 25 suggest that each side of the courtyard of the Temple of Jupiter at Baalbek was assigned to an independent contractor. However, the mark used on the stones of the southern side, the letters MER, may simply designate *meridionalis,* "south." They say nothing about division of labor.
35 Lancaster 1996: 62–3, 240–2.
36 DeLaine 1997: 103–205 draws a vivid picture of the quantities of men and materials needed for such work.
37 Compare Von Gerkan 1925: fig. 9 to Cozzo 1923: tav. LXXVI. See especially Lancaster 1998b; 1996: 38–63.
38 Luciani 1993: 105–6; Cozzo 1971: 45–9; 1928: 220–3. *Contra* see Blake 1959: 93; Von Gerkan 1925: 20–1.
39 Lancaster 1998b; 1996: 61–2;Von Gerkan 1925: 20–1.
40 Most notably, Von Gerkan 1925 accepts 3a as Flavian, but attributes the stairway design of 3b and 4 and the vault between them to a later restoration; he would have the Flavian versions made entirely of wood. His argument is that the stairways and broad arches over them at Level 3b are not symmetrically placed around the building. But their landings rest on the travertine corbels, which appear to be embedded deep in the wall – a strong argument for their Flavian origin, since the northeastern quadrant of the Colosseum facade was never dismantled down to this level in any restoration.
41 See the previous note.
42 On the bases and capitals see Pensabene 1988.

5. ROOFING AND VAULTING

1 *SEG* 4.439; Donderer 1996: no. A61. My translation.
2 Mark and Çakmak 1992; Mark 1990; and bibliographies.
3 On the techniques of Roman concrete vaulting see Lancaster 2000; 1998a; 1998b; 1996; Adam 1994: 158–95; Rasch 1991; 1984; Giuliani 1990: 88–104; 1975; Mark 1990: 49–89; Rakob 1988; Sanpaolesi 1971; Lugli 1957: 663–93; De Angelis d'Ossat 1940; Giovannoni 1929–30; Choisy 1873: 31–101.
4 Waddell 1984: 4.
5 Lechtmann and Hobbs 1986: 99.
6 The situation is quite different with stone voussoir barrel vaulting. The gravitational load on the centering increases incrementally as the voussoirs are added. Then the load is relieved by the insertion of the keystone(s). Giuliani 1990: 99 estimates that Roman vaults' profiles typically flattened by a factor of about 0.005–0.0125, but he does not elaborate.
7 Rasch 1991.

8 The House of the Painted Vaults at Ostia offers another example of this phenomenon, but with cross rather than barrel vaults. See Packer 1971: 166–9 and plans 20–21.

9 O'Connor 1993: 173–4.

10 Mainstone 1998: 120–1; see Heyman 1995: 28–9, 40–1.

11 Mark 1990: 63–5.

12 This may be one reason why the stones customarily used in vaults were larger than in the concrete cores of walls. See De Fine Licht 1968: 135.

13 Rasch 1991.

14 *Mech.* 3.5. See Drachmann 1963: 97–102.

15 Coarelli 2001: 47 and fig. 3. On trusses see Mainstone 1998: 160; O'Connor 1993: 136–7; De Fine Licht 1968: 48–58. See also Hodge 1960: 21–4, 38–44.

16 Adam 1994: 175–6; Fitchen 1961: 9–13. See also O'Connor 1993: 173–5.

17 Fitchen 1961: fig. 2.

18 Choisy 1873: 62–7. His notion that two layers of bricks could be mortared together and the scaffolding then removed before pouring the concrete must be rejected; see Lancaster 1998a: 300–2; 1996: 178–83. On the use of metal cramps see DeLaine 1997: 238; Giuliani 1975.

19 On the use of reeds see Lancaster 1998a: 302–3; Blake 1947: 346 n. 41. The Flavian formwork of the Colosseum shows no evidence of wood grain, though the impressions left by later repairs show heavy grain; see Lancaster 1996: 55.

20 DeLaine 1997: 166–9.

21 O'Connor 1993: 142–5 argues that Apollodorus' bridge over the Danube used very thin timbers to good effect if the compressive elements forming the arches were braced with trusses.

22 Lancaster 1996: 170–1.

23 Mainstone 1998: 119; Rasch 1991.

24 Rasch 1991: 364–70.

25 On the question of authorship see Blyth 1992.

26 Lancaster 1996: 176.

27 Alberti 1452: 5.5, 7.11. See Lucchini 1996: 88 n. 3; Saalman 1980: 90–7. Such a system could not have been adequately rehearsed without the creation of the dome itself. Even Brunelleschi, Alberti's great inspiration, constructed a masonry model of his dome without centering before he attempted this audacious technique on the cathedral; see King 2000: 39–42; Saalman 1980: 66–9, 74, 92.

28 Rakob 1988: 282–3 and Abb. 17.

29 Lancaster 1999.

30 Rasch 1991: 369–70.

31 Viollet-le-Duc 1875: 9.465–88. See Adam 1994: 175–6.

32 Terenzio 1933 and pl. XXVI.

33 De Fine Licht 1968: fig. 143.

34 Ibid.: fig. 199.

35 Mark 1990: 59–67; Lechtman and Hobbs 1986: 114–20.

36 Such joinery is known to have existed in Republican times; see Lancaster 1996: 166–7.

37 O'Connor 1993: 58. See also Lancaster 1996: 160–9. On the constructional use of timber in ancient Rome see Meiggs 1982: 218–59.

38 Diocletian's Price Edict indicates that fir was available in a variety of stan-

dard sizes, from fifty cubits by four cubits to twenty cubits by four feet; see Meiggs 1982: 365–9; Lauffer 1971: §12.1–8. The term for thickness, *in quadrum*, refers to the perimeter of the cross section. One cubit per side of a fifty-cubit beam seems too thin for anything but a truss tie.

39 Viollet-le-Duc 1875: 9.474. The effectiveness of these trusses has recently been confirmed by O'Connor 1993: 132–9, 142–5. He suggests that the rods might have been riveted, but this would greatly complicate their extraction in the decentering process. On the possible use of cotter bolts in Roman timber engineering, see Rasch 1991: 367–8 and n. 166.

40 Coarelli 1999: tav. 5, 14, 52; De Fine Licht 1968: figs. 52–3.

41 O'Connor 1993: 58.

42 Ibid.: 49 calculates that a crane with a five-pulley hoist and a six-meter-diameter treadmill operated by five men could lift loads of 6.2 tonnes.

43 Vitruvius describes a kind of crane with a mast consisting of a single post that could be rotated as well as raised and lowered (10.2.8–10), but it was very difficult to manage. No such crane would have been risked on the windy heights of the Pantheon's drum.

44 Davies, Hemsoll, and Wilson-Jones 1987.

45 Ibid.

46 De Fine Licht 1968: 134 and fig. 99.

47 Ibid.: 131–6 and fig. 148; De Angelis d'Ossat 1940: 231–4, 244–5, and fig. 3. Rasch 1991: 373 n. 188 proposes that each of the bonding courses marked the end of an incremental centering phase. But the irregularity of the courses militates against this.

48 Most step buttresses on Roman buildings seem to have been laid as integral horizontal units through the entire thickness of the dome, each step separated from its predecessor by a horizontal layer of bricks; see Rasch 1991.

49 Terenzio 1933: 54.

50 On roof tiles see Lancaster 1996: 220–4; Brodribb 1987: 5–33 and bibliographies.

51 Cozza 1983; De Fine Licht 1968: 136.

6. DECORATION AND FINISHING

1 On Roman architectural decoration in general see especially the bibliography of McNally 1996.

2 MacDonald 1982: 2.183–203.

3 Bergmann 1995: 99–100.

4 On defining and ranking space by means of decoration, see Dunbabin 1999: 304–16; Wallace-Hadrill 1994; Bergmann 1994; Moorman 1993; Clarke 1991; and their repective bibliographies.

5 A particularly fine example of the virtuosic use of *opus signinum* and *opus figlinum* (a related technique that employs ceramic tesserae in lieu of a continuous matrix of cement containing sporadic marble tesserae) is the second-century-B.C. Villa Prato at Sperlonga; see Lafon 1991.

6 On *opus spicatum* see Brodribb 1987: 50–4.

7 Dunbabin 1999: 304–5. Certain genres of religious spaces, however, were frequently decorated with mosaics – most notably Mithraea, probably because of their grottolike form. See Sear 1977: 28, 116–22.

8 For example, at the House of the Iliadic Shrine in Pompeii; see Mielsch 1975: K75.

9 Vitr. 7.3.3–7; Häfner 1997; Ling 1991: 200.
10 *CIL* 9.6281; Sear 1977: 17–18; Lauffer 1971: §§7.6–7.7 and 234–5; *contra*, see Dunbabin 1999: 274–5.
11 E.g., see Dunbabin 1999: 270–2.
12 Ibid.: 282 and bibliography.
13 A few patterns of floor mosaics survive incised or painted onto the underlayer or setting bed. See ibid.: 281–6.
14 In Pompeii, occasionally figures exceed the standard size, like the reclining Venus at the House of Venus Marina.
15 See Ling 1991: 85–91.
16 On Roman painting techniques and patronage see Ling 1999; 1991: 198–220; Adam 1994: 216–24; Barbet 1985; Davey and Ling 1981: 51–62.
17 7.2–4, 6–14. See Ling 1991: 198–211.
18 On wall preparations see the following articles in *RWP*: Dubois 1997; Häfner 1997; Ramjoue 1997; Varone and Béarat 1997.
19 Ling 1991: 201–2, 215–16; Klinkert 1957; Cagiano d'Azevedo 1949. See also Varone and Béarat 1997; Varone 1995.
20 Adam 1994: 222–4 and fig. 522; Ling 1991: 215–16 and bibliography.
21 *Idol.* 8.
22 Vitr. 7.3.3; *contra*, Pliny *HN* 37.59. See Adam 1994: 225–6; Frizot 1977: 6–11, 34–50. The principal secondary sources on Roman stucco are Ling 1999; 1991; 1976; Frizot 1977; Mielsch 1975.
23 Wallace 1994: 90.
24 Laidlaw 1985: 21–4; Frizot 1977: 50–1; Martin 1965: 428–9 and fig. 188.
25 For discussions of the common technique of *faux* drafted masonry, used both indoors and outdoors, see Martin 1965: 435–9; Ling 1991: 12–22; and especially Laidlaw 1985. The emphasis is invariably on the interiors.
26 Dunbabin 1999: 236–53; Lavagne 1988; Sear 1977; and bibliographies. Egyptian blue was also referred to as *kyanos skeuastos*.
27 Sear 1977: passim.
28 Ibid.: 90.
29 Ibid.: 149–50. On mosaic coffers, real and illusional, see ibid.: 27, 45–7, 97–8.
30 On the technique of laying mosaics see Dunbabin 1999: 279–99 and bibliography.
31 E.g., Robotti 1973. Rare exceptions merely confirm this rule. See Dunbabin 1999: 288–90 and bibliography. I exclude *emblemata*, which are not a major feature of high-imperial architecture.
32 Robotti 1973. For an example in France see Fouet 1979.
33 On the use of apprentices in the trades, including mosaic, see Burford 1972: 87–91.
34 On *opus sectile* and the methods of its application see A. G. Guidobaldi 2001; Dunbabin 1999: 254–68; F. Guidobaldi 1994; 1985; and Adam 1994: 227–8; with bibliographies. On its reuse in churches, see Ousterhout 2000: 235–9.
35 Ibrahim, Scranton, and Brill 1976.
36 Guidobaldi 1985.
37 Becatti 1969: 49–71, 181–215.
38 Giuliani 1990: 143–5. See also Packer 1997: 257; MacDonald 1982: 1.146. Remarkably, the base moldings at the Forum of Trajan seem to have been installed as the walls were being constructed.

39 On working stone see Korres 2000; 1995; Rockwell 1993 and bibliography.

40 Korres 2000: 7.

41 Rockwell 1993: 98.

42 Packer 1997. Certainly some of the carving was done in place, e.g., on the Column of Trajan; see Rockwell 1993: 181–2.

43 Haselberger 1997 and bibliography; Heisel 1993: 158–70, 211–14. Arches can be included here too; they are assembled in sequence like horizontal courses.

44 See Packer 1997: 253–7 and bibliography. Some capitals of the Forum of Trajan seem to have been completed on the ground, others in place; see n. 42.

45 Ganzert 2000: 57–60.

46 Precisely how the top and bottom lewises were used remains a mystery. Perhaps after carving was complete the inverted capital was suspended in the air with one lewis while a second lewis suspended from a separate crane was attached to the opposite hole. Then, by a process of tightening one rope and loosening the other, the capital was inverted in the air. But this process must have generated dangerous shear or torsion on the lewis holes, for the capitals are enormous.

47 Wilson-Jones 2000: 127–32; Packer 1997: 250–2 and bibliography; Rockwell 1993: 93–6.

48 Rowland and Howe 1999: 199; Heisel 1993: 170–3, 208–10; Haselberger and Seybold 1991; Haselberger 1983. For a similar technique used to lay out the curved foundations, see Haselberger 1999. On Roman entasis see Wilson-Jones 1999.

49 On Roman sculpture in general see Kleiner 1992; Ridgway 1984; and bibliographies. On sculpture in context see Neudecker 1988; Fuchs 1987; Raeder 1983; Manderscheid 1981; Bejor 1979; and excavation series for major Roman archaeological sites. I am grateful to Natalie Taback for her insights on sculpture and its architectural context.

50 See Walker 1979, esp. 290–306 and bibliography.

51 Rockwell 1993: 178–86.

52 On the typology and development of niche architecture see Hornbostel-Hüttner 1979.

53 Wilson-Jones 1993; Davies, Hemsoll, and Wilson-Jones 1987; Walker 1979: passim.

54 Pensabene 1989: 65.

55 Marvin 1983: 355–7.

56 DeLaine 1997: 75–6.

57 Marvin 1983: 352–3. But see Manderscheid 1981 for numerous exceptions.

58 Vitr. 5.9.5–7.

59 Jashemski and Salza Prina Ricotti 1992.

60 Grimal 1984: 252–5; Hoffmann 1980.

61 Grottoes: Lavagne 1988. Mausoleum of Augustus: Strabo 5.3.8.

62 Jashemski 1979–93.

63 Ibid. The many wall paintings of garden scenes almost never depict architecture at all, except in the form of latticed enclosures.

64 Grimal 1984: 173–8.

65 Lucian Am. 12. The Palatine excavations, under the auspices of the École

Française de Rome and the Soprintendenza Archeologica di Roma, were the subject of a recent exhibit at the Museo alle Terme. A late-first- or early-second-century peristyle garden underlying this one was also partially recovered. See Villedieu 2001.

66 Landscape paintings confirm a taste for the formal arrayed in rigid symmetry, at least on the facade side of buildings. An especially precious document of a formal garden in Rome is the fragment of the Severan marble plan recording a large rectangular planted space labeled the Adonaea (?). See the entries in Steinby 1993–2000 (vol. 1, 1993); Richardson 1992.

67 MacDonald 1982: 178.

68 Baatz 1991: 12.

69 *Ep.* 86.4, 8; 90.25.

70 Broise 1991; Baatz 1991.

71 Von Gerkan and Krischen 1928: 76–80 and Abb. 99.

72 Baatz 1991: 10–11.

73 See especially MacDonald and Pinto 1995: 170–82.

74 De Alarcão and Étienne 1981.

75 Whatever the amount of movement, all pools would have required maintenance, including the skimming of algae.

76 Hoffmann 1980. Marble fountain: see caption.

GLOSSARY

abutment: The solid masonry that bears the weight or pressure at the haunch of an arch or vault.

addorse: To place with the back against a surface or object.

aedicule: A miniature representation of a pedimented facade, often serving as a framing element.

altimetry: The measurement of altitudes or heights, as for elevations.

amphitheater: An oval or elliptical arena for blood sports.

annular: Ring-shaped.

antae: A pair of symmetrical walls projecting from the facade of a building or room to extend its length.

apodyterium: The changing room of a Roman bath.

apse: A covered, roomlike recess forming a circular or polygonal segment in plan.

arch: Any masonry element spanning two supports that comprises discrete smaller components.

  clear-span arch: An arch positioned directly over a void.

  relieving arch: An arch embedded in a wall with the purpose of deflecting weight to either side of a vulnerable feature further down.

ashlar: A carefully shaped block of building stone.

atrium: The rectangular open area in the center of a Roman house.

attic: The horizontal upper level of an unpedimented colonnaded facade, often consisting of a relatively solid wall of masonry. On an amphitheater facade the attic is the upper zone above the arcades.

bay: Any relatively coherent space demarcated on either side by a column or pier.

bessalis: A square brick measuring two-thirds of a Roman foot to a side.

bipedalis: A square brick measuring two Roman feet to a side.

caldarium: The hot-water room in a Roman bath.

cantilever: A freely projecting horizontal element engaged to a vertical element at one end.

cavea: The curved seating area of a theater, amphitheater, circus, or stadium.

cella: The inner structure of a Roman temple, housing the image of the divinity; usually a single room with a single opening in front.

centering: The wooden formwork upon which arches and vaults are built.

  flying centering: Centering that begins not at the floor but near the haunches of the arch or vault.

chorobates: A long leveling table, incorporating plumb lines and a water trough.

clapboard: A board designed for siding that, when applied horizontally, overlaps the one below it, creating a serrated effect in profile.

clerestory: A row of windows or openings in the upper zone of a large hall.

coffer: A decorative geometric recess in a ceiling.

colonnade: A series of columns forming a unified pattern.

column: A support that is circular in cross section. Usually it conforms to one of the columnar orders.

columnar order: One of several traditional architectural categories (Doric, Ionic, Corinthian, Composite, Tuscan, etc.) governing the shape and proportions of column bases, shafts, capitals, entablatures, and moldings.

corbel: An element that projects horizontally from a vertical or near-vertical surface; often it serves as a support for an element above it.

cornice: A horizontal molding that projects from a wall or a vertical face to form a narrow shelf.

crown: The top part of an arch, including the keystone.

cryptoportico: A covered corridor that lies mostly underground, but is lit by windows above ground level.

dado: A pedestal for a column or pilaster.

drafting: The careful preparation of the margins (edges) of stone blocks to ensure precise joints with their neighbors.

dropshaft: A vertical channel used to control the flow of and/or aerate water.

drum: A cylindrical element such as a segment of a column shaft or a continuous wall underlying a dome.

emblema: A small mosaic panel composed of miniature tesserae and inset into a floor.

entablature: A horizontal band of decoration at the top of a columnar order. This usually comprises three distinct bands: the ARCHITRAVE (directly above the capitals), the FRIEZE (in the middle), and the CORNICE (uppermost).

entasis: The tapering curvature that characterizes the shape of a classical column shaft.

exedra: Any large recess, roofed or unroofed, opening off a larger space.

extrados: The upper surface of an arch or vault.

flutes/fluting: The vertical hollows carved into the shaft of a column
drum.

frigidarium: The cold-water room in a Roman bath.

gantry: An overarching framework or scaffold that straddles the work
zone for which it is intended.

guilloche: An ornamental border comprising two or more interlacing
curved bands that repeat a circular design.

haunches: The lowest parts of an arch or vault.

hypocaust: In a heated building, the hollow space beneath a floor for
the circulation of hot gases.

impost: Any visibly distinguishable element, other than a column capital, which serves as the support for the springing of an arch.

insula: A multistory apartment house or tenement block, often vaulted
throughout its lower stories with concrete construction.

intercolumniation: The space between two columns.

intrados: The lower surface of an arch or vault.

keying: The roughening of a surface to improve its bond with plaster,
mortar, brick, or concrete. Brick keying can be achieved either by
gouging the completed surface or by recessing and projecting alternate courses of bricks.

lewis: An expanding key which, when fitted into a flared hole at the
top of an object, serves as a grip for lifting.

lunette: A half circle, usually with the straight side toward the bottom.

molding: A decorative band projecting in relief from a surface.

natatio: The outdoor swimming pool in a Roman bath.

nymphaeum: A fountain, often in the form of an elaborate facade with
water displays.

oculus: A circular hole at the crown of a dome.

odeum: A small, roofed theater for concerts and lectures.

opus incertum: A facing for concrete walls that uses irregularly sized
stones in an irregular pattern.

opus latericium: Brick-faced concrete.

opus reticulatum: A facing for concrete walls that comprises small
shaped stones forming a diagonal grid pattern.

opus sectile: A covering for floor or wall consisting of carefully interlocked slabs of inlaid marble.

opus signinum: A waterproof cement made with crushed brick or pottery often inset with decorative marble tesserae.

opus spicatum: A floor made of quite small, elongated tiles, laid in a
herringbone pattern.

order: See columnar order.

palaestra: In Roman baths, an open-air exercise court.

pantile: A large rectangular roofing tile with raised edges on opposing sides.

party wall: A small, nonstructural wall dividing up a larger room.

pediment: The triangular gable on either end of a temple or similar monumental building.

peristyle: A continuous colonnade around a courtyard.

pier: A large vertical support with a rectangular or complex cross section.

pilaster: A false pillar set in low relief against a wall.

pillar: Any support smaller than a pier that has a rectangular cross section.

planimetry: The measurement or disposition of horizontal, planar areas.

podium: a) In a *cavea*: A wall forming a vertical divide between two seating tiers. b) On a building: A high base or platform with vertical sides upon which a building stands.

porphyry: A hard, purplish or green stone quarried in Egypt and favored for column shafts.

portico: *See* peristyle.

pozzolana: A volcanic sand used in making concrete.

putlog: One of the short pieces of wood supporting the floor of a scaffold; one end rests on the scaffold's ledger, the other in a hole in the wall.

quadriga: A two-wheeled chariot drawn by four horses abreast.

reentrant: An angle formed by two surfaces creating an inner corner.

relieving arch: *See* arch, relieving.

revetment: A sheathing of decorative stone applied to a wall or floor.

riser: The front (vertical) surface of a step.

Roman foot (*pes*): A unit of measure equal to 0.296 m.

sesquipedalis: A square brick measuring one and a half Roman feet to a side.

sestertius: A monetary unit equivalent to two and a half *asses*, or one-quarter of a *denarius*.

shuttering: An often movable wooden mold for constructing walls in a semiliquid material.

socle: A plain face or plinth forming a low pedestal or the lower part of a wall.

soffit: The underside of an arch, lintel, or architrave.

span: The distance between two supports, as of an arch.

spandrel: The triangular zone between two adjacent arches.

springing: The emergence of an arch or vault from its supports.

stadia rod: A graduated rod used for determining topographical elevations.

stereotomy: The cutting, dressing, and carving of building stone.

strut: Any oblong rod or beam holding two other members apart.

tegulae mammatae: "Nippled" (i.e., footed) tiles attached to a wall by nails either through the footings or in notches at the edges.

telamon: A structural support in the form of a sculpted male figure.

tepidarium: The warm-water room in a Roman bath.

terminus ante quem: The latest possible date ("time before which") of an event or an object.

terminus post quem: The earliest possible date ("time after which") of an event or an object.

terra cotta: Clay fired in a kiln. Used more commonly of architectural elements than of pottery.

tessellate: To install the tesserae of a mosaic.

tessera: A small cube of stone or glass in a mosaic.

thermae: A Roman bath complex, often large and splendid, generally containing various rooms for bathing and perhaps exercise rooms, swimming pools, lavatories, and/or libraries.

tonne: One metric ton (1,000 kg), equivalent to 1.1 U.S. tons.

tubuli: Interlocking terra-cotta tubes set vertically into a wall to allow the heated air from a hypocaust to be drawn upward.

tufa: Any of a variety of yellow or brown volcanic stones used for building.

trabeate: Having horizontal beams or lintels rather than arches.

travertine: A distinctive pitted limestone used widely in central Italy.

tread: The upper (horizontal) surface of a step.

vault: Any traditional roofing method that is concave below and convex above.

  barrel vault: A vault in the form of a segment of a cylinder.

  cross vault (groin vault): The intersection of two barrel vaults of equal heights.

voussoir: A component of a stone arch or vault, usually of roughly trapezoidal shape.

REFERENCES

Collections cited more than once are given an abbreviation, by which they are alphabetized. All other abbreviations are those of the *American Journal of Archaeology* 104 (2000) 10–24.

Adam, J.-P. 1997. "Dibujos y maquetas: La concepción arquitectónica antigua." In *CDA* 25–33.

Adam, J.-P. 1994. *Roman Building: Materials and Techniques.* Trans. A. Mathews. Bloomington and Indianapolis: Indiana University Press.

AAE. 1999. L. Haselberger, ed. *Appearance and Essence: Refinements of Classical Architecture – Curvature.* Philadelphia: University Museum, University of Pennsylvania.

AES. 1983. *Architecture et société: de l'archaïsme grec à la fin de la République romaine: Actes du colloque international organisé par le Centre national de la recherche scientifique et l'École française de Rome, Rome 2–4 décembre 1980.* Paris: Centre nationale de la recherche scientifique; and Rome: École française de Rome.

AF. 1988. A. M. Reggiani. *Anfiteatro Flavio: Immagine, testimonianze, spettacoli.* Rome: Quasar.

Alberti, L. B. 1987 [1452]. *The Ten Books of Architecture (De re aedificatoria).* New York: Dover (reprint of 1775 Leoni edition).

Anderson, J. C. 1997. *Roman Architecture and Society.* Baltimore and London: Johns Hopkins University Press.

Baatz, D. 1991. "Fensterglastypen, Glasfenster und Architektur." In *BDA* 4–13.

Baccini Leotardi, P. 1989. *Nuove testimonianze sul commercio dei marmi in età imperiale.* Rome: Istituto italiano per la storia antica.

Barbet, A. 1985. *La Peinture murale romaine: Les Stiles décoratifs pompéiens.* Paris: Picard.

Barbet, A., and P. Miniero, eds. 1999. *La Villa San Marco a Stabia.* 3 vols. Naples: Centre Jean Bérard; and Rome: École française de Rome.

BBA. 1984. *Bauplanung und Bautheorie der Antike*. Berlin: Deutsches Ar-chäologisches Institut.

BDA. 1991. A. Hoffmann, E.-L. Schwandner, W. Hoepfner, and G. Brands, eds. *Bautechnik der Antike: Internationales Kolloquium in Berlin vom 15.–17. Februar 1990*. Mainz: Zabern.

Becatti, G. 1969. *Edificio con opus sectile fuori Porta Marina*. Scavi di Ostia 6. Rome: Istituto poligrafico dello Stato, Libreria dello Stato.

Bejor, G. 1979. "La decorazione scultorea dei teatri romani nelle province africane." *Prospettiva* 17, 37–46.

Beltrami, L. 1898. *Il Pantheon*. Milan: Tipografia U. Allegretti.

Bergmann, B. 1995. "Greek Masterpieces and Roman Recreative Fictions." *HSCP* 97, 79–120.

Bergmann, B. 1994. "The Roman House as Memory Theater: The House of the Tragic Poet in Pompeii." *ArtB* 76, 225–55.

Bergmann, B. 1991. "Painted Perspectives of a Villa Visit: Landscape as Status and Metaphor." In *Roman Art in the Private Sphere*, ed. E. Gazda, 49–70. Ann Arbor: University of Michigan Press.

Beste, H.-J. 2000. "The Construction and Phases of Development of the Wood-en Arena Flooring of the Colosseum." *JRA* 13, 79–92.

Betancourt Serna, F. 2000. "Normativa y legislación constructiva en la antigüe-dad y en la alta edad media." In *La técnica de la arquitectura medieval*, ed. A. Graciani, 75–96. Seville: Universidad de Sevilla.

Blake, M. E. 1973. *Roman Construction in Italy from Nerva through the An-tonines*. D. T. Bishop, ed. Philadelphia: American Philosophical Society.

Blake, M. E. 1959. *Roman Construction in Italy from Tiberius through the Flavians*. Washington, D.C.: Carnegie Institution of Washington.

Blake, M. E. 1947. *Ancient Roman Construction in Italy from the Prehistoric Period to Augustus*. Washington, D.C.: Carnegie Institution of Washing-ton.

Blyth, P. H. 1992. "Apollodorus of Damascus and the *Poliorketika*." *GRBS* 33, 127–58.

Branner, R. 1963. "Villard de Honnecourt, Reims and the Origin of Gothic Architectural Drawing." *Gazette des beaux-arts, 6e sér.* 61, 129–46.

Brodribb, G. 1987. *Roman Brick and Tile: An Analytical Survey and Corpus of Surviving Examples*. Gloucester: A. Sutton.

Broise, H. 1991. "Vitrages et volets des fenêtres thermales à l'époque impéri-ale." In *TR* 61–78.

Brown, F. 1980. *Cosa: The Making of a Roman Town*. Ann Arbor: University of Michigan Press.

Brown, F. 1961. *Roman Architecture*. New York: George Braziller.

Bruneau, P. 1980. "Un Devis de pose de mosaïques: Le Papyrus Cairo Zen. 59665." In *Stêlê: Tomos eis mnêmên Nikolaou Kontoleontos*, 139–43. Athens: Somateion tôn Philôn tou Nikolaou Kontoleontos.

Bucher, F. 1968. "Design in Gothic Architecture: A Preliminary Assessment." *JSAH* 27, 49–71.

Burford, A. 1972. *Craftsmen in Greek and Roman Society*. London: Thames & Hudson.

Burford, A. 1969. *The Greek Temple Builders at Epidauros: A Social and Eco-nomic Study of Building in the Asklepian Sanctuary during the Fourth and Early Third Centuries B.C.* Liverpool: Liverpool University Press.

Cagiano d'Azevedo, M. 1949. "Il restauro degli affreschi della Casa di Livia." *BdA* 34, 145–9.

Callebat, L. 1994. "Rhétorique et architecture dans le *De architectura* de Vitruve." In *PDV* 31–46.

Callebat, L. 1989. "Organisation et structures du *De architectura* de Vitruve." In *MNI* 34–7.

CDA. 1997. *Las casas del Alma: Maquetas arquitectónicas de la antigüedad (5500 a.C./300 d.C.)*. Barcelona: Fundación Caja de Arquitectos.

Choisy, A. 1873. *L'Art de bâtir chez les romains*. Paris: Ducher & Cie.

Clarke, J. 1991. *The Houses of Roman Italy, 100 B.C.–A.D. 250: Ritual, Space, and Decoration*. Berkeley: University of California Press.

Coarelli, F. 2001. "Gli anfiteatri a Roma prima del Colosseo." In *Sangue e arena*, ed. A. La Regina, 43–7. Milan: Electa.

Coarelli, F., ed. 1999. *La Colonna Traiana*. Rome: C. Colombo, in collaboration with Deutsches Archäologisches Institut.

Collart, P., and P. Coupel. 1977. *Le Petit Autel de Baalbek*. Paris: P. Geuthner.

Collart, P., and P. Coupel. 1951. *L'Autel monumental de Baalbek*. Paris: P. Geuthner.

Congès, A. R. 1996. "Modalités pratiques d'implantation des cadastres romains: quelques aspects." *MEFRA* 108, 299–422.

Conticello De' Spagnolis, M. 1984. *Il Tempio dei Dioscuri nel Circo Flaminio*. *LSA* 4. Rome: De Luca.

Cotterell, B., and J. Kamminga. 1990. *Mechanics of Pre-Industrial Technology*. Cambridge and New York: Cambridge University Press.

Coulton, J. J. 1989. "Modules and Measurements in Ancient Design and Modern Scholarship." In *MNI* 85–9.

Coulton, J. J. 1985. "Incomplete Preliminary Planning in Greek Architecture: Some New Evidence." In *DASA* 103–21.

Coulton, J. J. 1983. "Greek Architects and the Transmission of Design." In *AES* 453–70.

Coulton, J. J. 1977. *Ancient Greek Architects at Work: Problems of Structure and Design*. Ithaca, N.Y.: Cornell University Press.

Coulton, J. J. 1974. "Lifting in Early Greek Architecture." *JHS* 94, 1–19.

Cozza, L. 1983. "Le tegole di marmo del Pantheon." In *Città e architettura nella Roma imperiale*, ed. K. de Fine Licht, 109–18. Odense: Odense University Press (*AnalRom – Supplementa* 10).

Cozzo, G. 1971. *Il Colosseo: L'anfiteatro flavio nella tecnica edilizia, nella storia delle strutture, nel concetto esecutivo dei lavori*. Rome: Fratelli - Palombi.

Cozzo, G. 1928. *Ingegneria romana: Maestranze romane, strutture preromane, strutture romane, le costruzioni dell'anfiteatro Flavio, del Pantheon, dell'emissario del Fucino*. Rome: Libreria Editrice Mantegazza di P. Cremonese.

Crawford, M. H., ed. 1996. *Roman Statutes*. 2 vols. London: Institute of Classical Studies, School of Advanced Study, University of London.

Daguet-Gagey, A. 1997. *Les Opera pvblica à Rome (180–305 ap. J.-C.)*. Paris: Institut d'études augustiniennes.

DASA. 1985. *Le Dessin d'architecture dans les sociétés antiques. Actes du Colloque de Strasbourg 26–28 janvier 1984*. Leiden: Brill.

Davey, N., and R. Ling. 1982. *Wall Painting in Roman Britain*. Gloucester: A. Sutton.

Davies, P. 2000. *Death and the Emperor: Roman Imperial Funerary Monuments from Augustus to Marcus Aurelius*. Cambridge and New York: Cambridge University Press.

Davies, P., D. Hemsoll, and M. Wilson-Jones. 1987. "The Pantheon: Triumph of Rome or Triumph of Compromise?" *Art History* 10, 133–53.

De Alarcão, J., and R. Étienne. 1981. "Les Jardins à Conimbriga (Portugal)." In *Ancient Roman Villa Gardens,* ed. E. MacDougall and W. Jashemski, 67–80. Washington, D.C.: Dumbarton Oaks.

De Angelis d'Ossat, G. 1940. "La forma e la costruzione delle cupole nell'architettura romana." In *Atti del III Convegno nazionale di storia dell'architettura,* 223–50. Rome: C. Colombo.

De Fine Licht, K. 1968. *The Rotunda in Rome: A Study of Hadrian's Pantheon.* Copenhagen: Gyldendal.

De Jong, J. J. 1989. "Greek Mathematics, Hellenistic Architecture and Vitruvius' *De architectura.*" In *MNI* 100–13.

DeLaine, J. 1997. *The Baths of Caracalla: A Study in the Design, Construction, and Economics of Large-Scale Building Projects in Imperial Rome.* Portsmouth, R.I.: Journal of Roman Archaeology.

DeLaine, J., and D. E. Johnston, eds. 1999. *Roman Baths and Bathing: Proceedings of the First International Conference on Roman Baths held at Bath, England, 30 March–4 April 1992.* 2 vols. Portsmouth, R.I.: Journal of Roman Archaeology.

Dilke, O. A. W. 1971. *The Roman Land Surveyors: An Introduction to the Agrimensores.* New York: Barnes & Noble.

Dodge, H. 1991. "Ancient Marble Studies: Recent Research." *JRA* 4, 28–50.

Donderer, M. 1996. *Die Architekten der späten römischen Republik und der Kaiserzeit: Epigraphische Zeugnisse.* Erlangen: Universitätsbund Erlangen.

Doxiades, K. A. 1972. *Architectural Space in Ancient Greece.* Cambridge, Mass.: MIT Press.

Drachmann, A. G. 1963. *The Mechanical Technology of Greek and Roman Antiquity.* Copenhagen: Munksgaard; and Madison: University of Wisconsin Press.

Dubois, Y. 1997. "Les Villae gallo-romaines d'Orbe-Boscéaz et d'Yvonand-Mordagne: Observations sur les techniques de réparation et de réalisation des parois peintes." In *RWP* 153–66.

Dunbabin, K. 1999. *Mosaics of the Greek and Roman World.* Cambridge and New York: Cambridge University Press.

Duncan-Jones, R. 1974. *The Economy of the Roman Empire.* Cambridge: Cambridge University Press.

Evans, E. 1994. "Military Architects and Building Design in Roman Britain." *Britannia* 25, 143–64.

Fant, J. C. 2001. "Rome's Marble Yards." *JRA* 14, 167–98.

Fant, J. C. 1993. "Ideology, Gift and Trade: A Distribution Model for Roman Imperial Marbles." In *The Inscribed Economy: Production and Distribution in the Roman Empire in the Light of Instrumentum Domesticum,* ed. W. V. Harris, 145–70. Ann Arbor: Journal of Roman Archaeology.

Fitchen, J. 1986. *Building Construction before Mechanization.* Cambridge, Mass.: MIT Press.

Fitchen, J. 1961. *The Construction of the Gothic Cathedrals: A Study of Medieval Vault Erection.* Oxford: Oxford University Press.

Fleury, P. 1993. *La Mécanique de Vitruve.* Caen: Université de Caen, Centre d'études et de recherche sur l'antiquité.

Fouet, G. 1979. "Sauvetage d'une mosaïque dans la villa de Valentine." *Revue de Comminges* 92, 3–13.

Frézouls, E. 1985. "Vitruve et le dessin d'architecture." In *DASA* 213–29.

Frizot, M. 1977. *Stucs de Gaule et des provinces romaines: Motifs et techniques.* Dijon: Faculté des sciences humaines, Centre de recherches sur les techniques gréco-romaines.

Fuchs, M. 1987. *Untersuchungen zur Ausstattung römischer Theater in Italien und den Westprovinzen des Imperium Romanum.* Mainz: Zabern.

Gabucci, A., ed. 1999. *Il Colosseo.* Milan: Electa.

Galliazzo, V. 1994. *I ponti romani.* 2 vols. Treviso: Canova.

Ganzert, J. 2000. *Im Allerheiligsten des Augustusforums.* Mainz: Zabern.

Geertman, H. 1994. "Teoria e attualità della progettistica architettonica di Vitruvio." In *PDV* 7–30.

Geertman, H. 1980. "Aedificium celeberrimum: Studio sulla geometria del Pantheon." In *BABesch* 55, 203–29.

Ghini, G. 1988. "Prime indagini archeologiche." In *AF* 101–5.

Giovannoni, G. 1929–30. "La tecnica delle costruzioni romani a volta." *Atti della Società italiana per il progresso delle scienze* 8, 229–51.

Giovannoni, G. 1925. *La tecnica della costruzione presso I romani.* Rome: Società editrice d'arte illustrata.

Giuliani, C. F. 1990. *L'edilizia nell'antichità.* Rome: La Nuova Italia scientifica.

Giuliani, C. F. 1975. "Volte e cupole a doppia calotta in età adrianea." *RM* 82, 329–42.

Gnoli, R. 1971. *Marmora romana.* Rome: Edizioni dell'Elefante.

Goldthwaite, R. A. 1980. *The Building of Renaissance Florence.* Baltimore and London: Johns Hopkins University Press.

Golvin, J.-C. 1988. *L'amphithéâtre romain: Essai sur la théorisation de sa forme et de ses fonctions.* Paris: De Boccard.

Grewe, K. 1998. *Licht am Ende des Tunnels: Planung und Trassierung im antiken Tunnelbau.* Mainz: Zabern.

Grimal, P. 1984. *Les Jardins romains: La Fin de la république aux deux premiers siècles de l'empire.* Paris: Fayard.

Gros, P. 1996. *L'Architecture romaine du début du IIIᵉ siècle av. J.-C. à la fin du Haut-Empire,* vol. 1: *Les Monuments publics.* Paris: Picard.

Gros, P. 1994. *"Munus non ingratum:* Le Traité vitruvien et la notion de service." In *PDV* 75–90.

Gros, P. 1989. "L'*Auctoritas* chez Vitruve: Contribution à l'étude de la sémantique des ordres dans le *De architectura.*" In *MNI* 126–33.

Gros, P. 1985. "Le rôle de la *scaenographia* dans les projets architecturaux du début de l'empire romain." In *DASA* 231–53.

Gros, P. 1983. "Statut social et rôle culturel des architectes (période hellénistique et augustéenne)." In *AES* 425–52.

Gros, P. 1978. *Architecture et société à Rome et en Italie centro-méridionale aux deux derniers siècles de la République.* Brussels: Latomus.

Guidobaldi, A. G. 2001. "Pavimenti marmorei a Roma e nel suburbio nei secoli IV–VII." In *MT* 191–202.

Guidobaldi, F. 1994. *Sectilia pavimenta di Villa Adriana.* Rome: Istituto poligrafico e Zecca dello Stato; Libreria dello Stato.

Guidobaldi, F. 1985. "Pavimenti in *opus sectile* di Roma e dell'area romana: Proposte per una classificazione e criteri di datazione." In *MA* 171–233.

Gullini, G. 1983. "Terrazza, edifizio, uso dello spazio: Note su architettura e società nel periodo medio e tardo repubblicano." In *AES* 119–89.

Häfner, K. 1997. "Experiments on the Reconstruction of the Roman Wall Painting Technique." In *RWP* 143–52.

Haselberger, L. 1999. "Curvature: The Evidence of Didyma." In *AAE* 173–84.

Haselberger, L. 1997. "Architectural Likenesses: Models and Plans of Architecture in Classical Antiquity." *JRA* 10, 77–94.

Haselberger, L. 1983. "Bericht über die Arbeit am Jüngeren Apollontempel von Didyma." *IstMitt* 33, 92–123.

Haselberger, L., and H. Seybold. 1991. "Seilkurve oder Ellipse? Zur Herstellung antiker Kurvaturen nach dem Zeugnis der didymeischen Kurvenkonstruktion." *AA* 165–88.

Heisel, J. P. 1993. *Antike Bauzeichnungen*. Darmstadt: Wissenschaftliche Buchgesellschaft.

Hellström, P. 1985. "Dessin d'architecture hécatomnide à Labraunda." In *DASA* 153–65.

Hesberg, H. von. 1984. Römische Grundrißplänne auf Marmor. In *BBA* 120–33.

Heyman, J. 1995. *The Stone Skeleton: Structural Engineering of Masonry Architecture*. Cambridge and New York: Cambridge University Press.

HHA. 1990. W. Hoepfner and E.-L. Schwandner, eds. *Hermogenes und die hochhellenistische Architektur: Akten des XIII. Internationalen Kongresses für Klassische Archäologie, Berlin 1988*. Mainz: Zabern.

Hodge, A. T. 1992. *Roman Aqueducts and Water Supply*. London: Duckworth.

Hodge, A. T. 1960. *The Woodwork of Greek Roofs*. Cambridge: Cambridge University Press.

Hoffmann, A. 1991. "Konstruieren mit Eisen." In *BDA* 99–106.

Hoffmann, A. 1980. *Das Gartenstadion in der Villa Hadriana*. Mainz: Zabern.

Hornbostel-Hüttner, G. 1979. *Studien zur römischen Nischenarchitektur*. Leiden: Brill.

Hueber, F. 1989. "Gestaltungsfeinheiten und Quaderbautechnik an Bauten der frühen Kaiserzeit." In *MNI* 217–29.

Humphrey, J. W., J. P. Oleson, and A. N. Sherwood, eds. 1998. *Greek and Roman Technology: A Sourcebook*. London and New York: Routledge.

Ibrahim, L., R. Scranton, and R. Brill. 1976. *Kenchreai, Eastern Port of Corinth II: The Panels of Opus Sectile in Glass*. Leiden: Brill.

Jacobson, D. M. 1986. "Hadrian's Architecture and Geometry." *AJA* 90, 69–85.

Jashemski, W. F. 1979–93. *The Gardens of Pompeii, Herculaneum and the Villas Destroyed by Vesuvius*. 2 vols. New Rochelle, N.Y.: Caratzas.

Jashemski, W. F., and E. Salza Prina Ricotti. 1992. "Preliminary Excavations in the Gardens of Hadrian's Villa: The Canopus Area and the Piazza d'Oro." *AJA* 96, 579–97.

Jeppesen, K. 1958. *Paradeigmata: Three Mid-Fourth Century Main Works of Hellenic Architecture, Reconsidered*. Aarhus: Aarhus University Press.

Jidejian, N. 1975. *Baalbek, Heliopolis: "City of the Sun."* Beirut: Dar el-Machreq.

Jouffroy, H. 1986. *La Construction publique en Italie et dans l'Afrique romaine*. Strasbourg: AECR.

Judson, S., and A. Kahane. 1963. "Underground Drainageways in Southern Etruria and Northern Latium." *PBSR* 31, 74–99.

Kalayan, H. 1971. "Notes on Assembly Marks, Drawings and Models Concerning the Roman Period Monuments in Lebanon." *AAS* 21, 269–73.

Kalayan, H. 1969. "The Engraved Drawing on the Trilithon and the Related Problems about the Constructional History of Baalbek Temples." *BMus-Beyr* 22, 151–5.

King, R. 2000. *Brunelleschi's Dome: The Story of the Great Cathedral in Florence.* London: Walker.

Klein, M. J. 1988. *Untersuchungen zu den kaiserlichen Steinbruchen an Mons Porphyrites und Mons Claudianus in der östlichen Wuste Ägyptens.* Bonn: Habelt.

Kleiner, D. E. E. 1992. *Roman Sculpture.* New Haven: Yale University Press.

Klinkert, W. 1957. "Bemerkungen zur Technik der pompejanischen Wand-dekoration." *RM* 64, 111–48.

Kolb, A. 1993. *Die kaiserliche Bauverwaltung in der Stadt Rom: Geschichte und Aufbau der cura operum publicorum unter dem Prinzipat.* Stuttgart: Steiner.

Korres, M. 2000. *The Stones of the Parthenon.* Malibu: J. Paul Getty Museum.

Korres, M. 1995. *From Pentelicon to Parthenon: The Ancient Quarries and the Story of a Half-Worked Column Capital of the First Marble Parthenon.* Athens: Melissa.

Krause, C. 1985a. "Das graffito in Terracina." In *LPP* 131–3.

Krause, C. 1985b. "Skenographie, Architektur und perspektivisches Sehen." In *LPP* 43–77.

Krencker, 1929. *Die Trierer Kaiserthermen.* Augsburg: Filser.

Kuttner, A. 1998. "Prospects of Patronage: Realism and *Romanitas* in the Architectural Vista of the 2nd Style." In *RV* 93–107.

Lafon, X. 1991. "Les Bains privés dans l'Italie romaine au IIᵉ siècle av. J.-C." In *TR* 97–114.

Laidlaw, A. 1985. *The First Style in Pompeii: Painting and Architecture.* Rome: Giorgio Bretschneider.

Lamprecht, H.-O. 1993. *Opus caementitium: Bautechnik der Römer.* 4th ed. Düsseldorf: Beton-Verlag.

Lancaster, L. 2000. "Building Trajan's Markets 2: The Construction Process." *AJA* 104, 755–85.

Lancaster, L. 1999. "Building Trajan's Column." *AJA* 103, 419–39.

Lancaster, L. 1998a. "Building Trajan's Markets." *AJA* 102, 283–308.

Lancaster, L. 1998b. "Reconstructing the Restorations of the Colosseum after the Fire of 217." *JRA* 11, 146–74.

Lancaster, L. 1996. "Concrete Vaulted Construction: Developments in Rome from Nero to Trajan." Ph.D. thesis, Wolfson College, Oxford University.

Landels, J-G. 1978. *Engineering in the Ancient World.* London: Constable.

Lauffer, S. 1971. *Diokletians Preisedikt.* Berlin: De Gruyter.

Lavagne, H. 1988. *Operosa antra: Recherches sur la grotte à Rome de Sylla à Hadrien.* Rome: École française de Rome.

Lechtman, H. N., and L. W. Hobbs. 1986. "Roman Concrete and the Roman Architectural Revolution." In *High-Technology Ceramics: Past, Present, and Future,* ed. W. D. Kingery, 81–128. Westerville, Ohio: American Ceramic Society.

Ling, R. 1999. *Stuccowork and Painting in Roman Italy.* Aldershot: Variorum; and Brookfield, Vt.: Ashgate.

Ling, R. 1991. *Roman Painting.* Cambridge and New York: Cambridge University Press.

Ling, R. 1976. "Stuccowork." In *RC* 209–21.

Lombardi, L., and A. Corazza 1995. *Le terme di Caracalla.* Rome: Fratelli Palombi.

LPP. 1985. C. Krause, ed. *La prospettiva pittorica: Un convegno.* Rome: Istituto svizzero di Roma.

Lucchini, F. 1996. *Pantheon.* Rome: La Nuova Italia scientifica.

Luciani, R. 1993. *Il Colosseo.* Milan: Fenice 2000; and Novara: Istituto geografico De Agostini.

Lugli, G. 1957. *La tecnica edilizia romana con particolare riguardo a Roma e Lazio.* 2 vols. Rome: Bardi.

MA. 1985. P. Pensabene, ed. *Marmi antichi: problemi d'impiego, di restauro e d'identificazione.* Rome: "L'Erma" di Bretschneider.

MA2. 1998. P. Pensabene, ed. *Marmi antichi II: cave e tecnica di lavorazione, provenienze e distribuzione.* Rome: "L'Erma" di Bretschneider.

MacDonald, W. L. 1982. *The Architecture of the Roman Empire.* 2 vols. New Haven: Yale University Press.

MacDonald, W. L., and J. Pinto. 1995. *Hadrian's Villa and Its Legacy.* New Haven: Yale University Press.

McNally, S. 1996. *The Architectural Ornament of Diocletian's Palace at Split.* Oxford: Tempus Reparatum.

Mainstone, R. J. 1998. *Developments in Structural Form.* 2d ed. Oxford and Woburn, Mass.: Architectural Press.

Maiuri, A. 1955. *Studi e richerche sull'Anfiteatro Flavio puteolano.* Naples: Macchiaroli.

Manderscheid, H. 1991. "La gestione idrica delle Terme di Caracalla: Alcune osservazioni." In *TR* 49–60.

Manderscheid, H. 1981. *Die Skulpturenausstattung der kaiserzeitlichen Thermenanlagen.* Berlin: Mann.

Mark, R. L. 1990. *Light, Wind and Structure: The Mystery of the Master Builders.* Cambridge, Mass.: MIT Press.

Mark, R. L., and A. S. Çakmak, eds. 1992. *Hagia Sophia from the Age of Justinian to the Present.* Cambridge and New York: Cambridge University Press.

Martin, R. 1965. *Manuel d'architecture grecque,* vol. 1: *Matériaux et techniques.* Paris: Picard.

Martin, S. 1989. *The Roman Jurists and the Organization of Private Building in the Late Republic and Early Empire.* Brussels: Latomus.

Marvin, M. 1983. "Freestanding Sculptures from the Baths of Caracalla." *AJA* 87, 347–84.

Meiggs, R. 1982. *Trees and Timber in the Ancient Mediterranean World.* Oxford: Oxford University Press.

MIA. 1992. J. B. Ward-Perkins. *Marble in Antiquity: Collected Papers of J. B. Ward-Perkins.* Ed. H. Dodge and B. Ward-Perkins. London: British School at Rome.

Mielsch, H. 1975. *Römische Stuckreliefs.* Heidelberg: Kerle.

MNI. H. Geertman and J. J. de Jong, eds. 1989. *Munus non ingratum: Proceedings of the International Symposium on Vitruvius' De architectura and the Hellenistic and Republican Architecture, Leiden, 20–23 January 1987.* Leiden: Stichting Bulletin Antieke Beschaving.

Mocchegiani Carpano, C. 1977. "Nuovi dati sulle fondazioni dell'anfiteatro Flavio." *Antiqua* (Capua) 7, 10–16.

Mocchegiani Carpano, C., and R. Luciani. 1981. "I restauri dell'anfiteatro Flavio." In *RivIstArch* ser. 3, 4, 9–69.

Moss, C. F. 1988. "Roman Marble Tables." 4 vols. Ph.D. thesis, Department of Fine Arts, Princeton University.

Moorman, E. M., ed. 1993. *Functional and Spatial Analysis of Wall Painting: Proceedings of the Fifth International Congress on Ancient Wall Painting, Amsterdam, 8–12 September 1992*. Leiden: Stichting Bulletin Antieke Beschaving.

MT. 2001. M. Cecchelli, ed. *Materiali e tecniche dell'edilizia paleocristiana a Roma*. Rome: De Luca.

Murray, S. 1987. *Building Troyes Cathedral: The Late Gothic Campaigns*. Bloomington and Indianapolis: Indiana University Press.

Neudecker, R. 1998. "The Roman Villa as a Locus of Art Collections." In *RV* 77–91.

Neudecker, R. 1988. *Die Skulpturenausstattung römischer Villen in Italien*. Mainz: Zabern.

Nohlen, K. 1985. "La Conception d'un projêt et son évolution: L'Exemple du Trajaneum de Pergame." In *DASA* 277–81.

O'Connor, C. 1993. *Roman Bridges*. Cambridge and New York: Cambridge University Press.

Orlandos, A. 1966–8. *Les Matériaux de construction et la téchnique architecturale des anciens Grecs*. Paris: Boccard.

Ousterhout, R. 2000. *Master Builders of Byzantium*. Princeton: Princeton University Press.

Packer, J. E. 1997. *The Forum of Trajan in Rome: A Study of the Monuments*. 3 vols. Berkeley: University of California Press.

Packer, J. E. 1971. *The Insulae of Imperial Ostia*. Rome: American Academy in Rome.

PDV. 1994. *Le Projêt de Vitruve: Objet, destinataires et réception du "De architectura."* Rome: École française de Rome.

Pearse, J. L. D. 1974. "The Organization of Roman Building during the Late Republic and Early Empire." Ph.D. thesis, Trinity College, Cambridge University.

Pelliccioni, G. 1986. *Le cupole romane: La stabilità*. Rome: Paleani.

Pensabene, P. 1997. "Maqueta de templo en marmol de Luna." In *CDA* 129–32, 232.

Pensabene, P. 1994. *Le vie del marmo. I blocchi di cava di Roma e di Ostia: Il fenomeno del marmo nella Roma antica*. Rome: Ministero per i beni culturali e ambientali; Soprintendenza archeologica di Ostia.

Pensabene, P. 1989. *Il teatro romano di Ferento: Architettura e decorazione scultorea*. Rome: "L'Erma" di Bretschneider.

Pensabene, P. 1988. "Elementi architettonici in marmo." In *AF* 53–82.

Picozzi, S. 1974. "Il collettore del Colosseo." *Capitolium* 49.12, 13–23.

Raeder, J. 1983. *Die statuarische Ausstattung der Villa Hadriana bei Tivoli*. Frankfurt: Lang.

Ragette, F. 1980. *Baalbek*. Park Ridge, N.J.: Noyes.

Rakob, F. 1988. "Römische Kuppelbauten in Baiae." *RM* 95, 257–301.

Ramjoue, E. 1997. "Quelques particularités techniques des fresques romaines de Vandoeuvres dans le canton de Genève." In *RWP* 167–79.

Rasch, J. J. 1991. "Zur Konstruktion spätantiker Kuppeln vom 3. bis 6. Jahrhundert." *JdI* 106, 311–83.

Rasch, J. J. 1984. "Metrologie und Planung des Maxentius-Mausoleums." In *BBA* 250–62.

RC. 1976. D. Strong and D. Brown, eds. *Roman Crafts*. London: Duckworth.

Rea, R. 1996. *Anfiteatro flavio*. Rome: Istituto poligrafico e Zecca dello Stato; Libreria dello Stato.

Rea, R. 1988. "Recenti osservazioni sulla struttura dell'Anfiteatro Flavio." In *AF* 9–22.

Richardson, L., Jr. 1992. *A New Topographical Dictionary of Ancient Rome*. Baltimore and London: Johns Hopkins University Press.

Richmond, I. A. 1930. *The City Wall of Imperial Rome: An Account of Its Architectural Development from Aurelian to Narses*. Oxford: Oxford University Press.

Ridgway, B. 1984. *Roman Copies of Greek Sculpture: The Problem of the Originals*. Ann Arbor: University of Michigan Press.

Rivoira, G. T. 1925. *Roman Architecture and Its Principles of Construction under the Empire*. Oxford: Oxford University Press.

Rizzo, S. 1999. "Un frammento revelatore." *Archeo* 15.6 (June), 10–11.

Robotti, C. 1973. "Una sinopia musiva pavimentale a Stabia." *Bollettino d'arte* 58, 42–4.

Rockwell, P. 1993. *The Art of Stoneworking: A Reference Guide*. Cambridge and New York: Cambridge University Press.

Rowland, I., and T. Howe, eds. 1999. *Vitruvius: The Ten Books on Architecture*. Cambridge and New York: Cambridge University Press.

RV. 1998. A. Frazer, ed. *The Roman Villa: Villa Urbana*. Philadelphia: University Museum, University of Pennsylvania.

RWP. 1997. H. Béarat, M. Fuchs, M. Maggetti, and D. Paunier, eds. *Roman Wall Painting: Materials, Techniques, Analysis and Conservation*. Fribourg: Institute of Mineralogy and Petrography.

Saalman, H. 1980. *Filippo Brunelleschi: The Cupola of Santa Maria del Fiore*. London: Zwemmer.

Sanpaolesi, P. 1971. "Strutture a cupola autoportanti." *Palladio* 21, 3–64.

Scavizzi, C. P. 1983. *Edilizia nei secoli XVII e XVIII a Roma*. Rome: Ministero per i beni culturali e ambientali, Ufficio studi.

Schwartz, G. T. 1968. "Antike Vorschriften für Fundamente und ihre Anwendung auf römische Bauten in der Schweig." In *Provincialia: Festschrift Rudolf Laur-Belart*, ed. E. Schmid, L. Berger, and P. Bürger, 446–56. Basel: Schwabe.

Scully, V. 1979. *The Earth, the Temple, and the Gods: Greek Sacred Architecture*. Rev. ed. New Haven: Yale University Press.

Sear, F. B. 1989. *Roman Architecture*. Rev. ed. London: Batsford.

Sear, F. B. 1977. *Roman Wall and Vault Mosaics*. Heidelberg: Kerle.

Shelby, L. R. 1971. "Mediaeval Masons' Templates." *JSAH* 30, 140–54.

Shirley, E. 2001. *Building a Roman Legionary Fortress*. Shroud, Gloucestershire: Tempus.

Smith, N. A. F. 1991. "Problems of Design and Analysis." In *Future Currents in Aqueduct Studies*, ed. A. T. Hodge, 113–28. Leeds: Cairns.

Sperling, G. 1999. *Das Pantheon in Rom: Abbild und Maß des Kosmos*. Neuried: Ars Una.

Steinby, E. M., ed. 1993–2000. *Lexicon Topographicum Urbis Romae*. 6 vols. Rome: Edizioni Quasar.

Strong, D. E. 1968. "The Administration of Public Building in Rome during the Late Republic and Early Principate." *BICS* 15, 97–109.

Taylor, R. 2000. *Public Needs and Private Pleasures: Water Distribution, the Tiber River, and the Urban Development of Ancient Rome*. Rome: "L'Erma" di Bretschneider.

Taylor, R. 1996. "A Literary and Structural Analysis of the First Dome on Justinian's Hagia Sophia, Constantinople." *JSAH* 55, 66–78.

Terenzio, A. 1933. "La Restauration du Panthéon de Rome." In *La Conservation des monuments d'art et d'histoire* (International Conference of 1931, Athens), 280–5. Paris: Office international des musées.

Thornton, M. K., and R. L. Thornton. 1989. *Julio-Claudian Building Programs: A Quantitative Study in Political Management*. Wauconda, Ill.: Bolchazy–Carducci.

TR. 1991. *Les Thermes romaines: Actes de la table ronde organisée par l'École française de Rome*. Rome: École française de Rome.

Tybout, R. A. 1989. "Die Perspektive bei Vitruv: Zwei Überlieferungen von *scaenographia*." In *MNI* 55–68.

Varone, A. 1995. "L'organizzazione del lavoro di una bottega di decoratori: Le evidenze dal recente scavo pompeiano lungo via dell'Abbondanza." *Meded* 54, 124–36.

Varone, A., and H. Béarat. 1997. "Pittori romani al lavoro. Materiali, strumenti, tecniche: Evidenze archeologiche e dati analitici di un recente scavo pompeiano lungo via dell'Abbondanza (reg. IX ins. 12)." In *RWP* 199–214.

Villedieu, F., ed. 2001. *Il giardino dei Cesari: Dai palazzi antichi alla Vigna Barberini, sul Monte Palatino: Scavi dell'École française de Rome, 1985–1999*. Rome: Ministero per i beni e le attività culturali; Soprintendenza archeologica di Roma.

Viollet-le-Duc, E.-E. 1875. *Dictionnaire raisonné de l'architecture française du XIᵉ au XVIᵉ siècle*. 10 vols. Paris: Morel.

Von Gerkan, A. 1925. "Das Obergeschoß des flavischen Amphitheaters." *RM* 40, 11–50.

Von Gerkan, A., and F. Krischen. 1928. *Milet 1.9: Gymnasien, Thermen und Palaestren in Milet*. Berlin: Verlag der Akademie der Wissenschaften; De Gruyter.

Waddell, J. J. 1984. *Concrete Manual*. Whittier, Calif.: International Conference of Building Officials.

Walker, S. 1979. "The Architectural Development of Roman Nymphaea in Greece." Ph.D. thesis, Institute of Archaeology, University of London.

Wallace, W. E. 1994. *Michelangelo at San Lorenzo: The Genius as Entrepreneur*. Cambridge and New York: Cambridge University Press.

Wallace-Hadrill, A. 1994. *Houses and Society in Pompeii and Herculaneum*. Princeton: Princeton University Press.

Ward-Perkins, J. B. 1993. *The Severan Buildings of Lepcis Magna: An Architectural Survey*. London: Society for Libyan Studies.

Ward-Perkins, J. B. 1992a. "Columna Divi Antonini." In *MIA* 107–14.

Ward-Perkins, J. B. 1992b. "Nicomedia and the Marble Trade." In *MIA* 61–105.

Ward-Perkins, J. B. 1992c. "The Roman System in Operation." In *MIA* 23–30.

Ward-Perkins, J. B. 1981. *Roman Imperial Architecture*. Harmondsworth, Middlesex: Penguin.

Ward-Perkins, J. B. 1951. "Tripolitania and the Marble Trade." *JRS* 41, 89–104.

Wattenbach, W. 1896. "Über die Legende von den heiligen Vier Gekrönten." *Sitzungsberichte der Königlich Preußische Akademie der Wissenschaften zu Berlin*. Berlin: Akademie–Verlag.

Wheeler, M. 1962. "Size and Baalbek." *Antiquity* 36, 6–9.

Wiegand, T., ed. 1921–5. *Baalbek: Ergebnisse der Ausgrabungen und Untersuchungen in den Jahren 1898 bis 1905.* 3 vols. Berlin and Leipzig: De Gruyter.

Wilkinson, C. 1991. "Building from Drawings at the Escorial." In *Les Chantiers de la Renaissance*, ed. Jean Guillaume, 263–78. Paris: Picard.

Will, E. 1985. "La Maquette de l'adyton du temple A de Niha (Beqa)." In *DASA* 277–81.

Wilson-Jones, M. 2000. *Principles of Roman Architecture.* New Haven: Yale University Press.

Wilson-Jones, M. 1999. "The Practicalities of Roman Entasis." In *AAE* 225–49.

Wilson-Jones, M. 1997. "Los procesos del diseño arquitectónico: Comprender a Vitruvio a partir de los dibujos y maquetas romanos." In *CDA* 119–28.

Wilson-Jones, M. 1993. "Designing Amphitheatres." *RM* 100, 391–442.

Wright, G. R. H. 2000. *Ancient Building Technology*, vol. 1: *Historical Background.* Leiden: Brill.

Yegül, F. 1992. *Baths and Bathing in Classical Antiquity.* Cambridge, Mass.: MIT Press.

Zimmer, G. 1984. "'Zollstöcke' römischer Architekten." In *BBA* 265–76.

INDEX

Notes: Particular structures are organized by locale. Illustrations are indicated by an "f" following a page number. When a subject is both discussed and illustrated on the same page, the page is not repeated for the illustration.